ENCYCLOPEDIA

THE ULTIMATE GUIDE TO THE BUFFYVERSE

NANCY HOLDER AND LISA A. CLANCY

HARPER DESIGN

An Imprint of HarperCollinsPublishers

Nancy Holder

To Joss, of course. And to Paul and Lisa, with love.

Lisa A. Clancy

To Dad, who always loved a good fight scene and a good lawyer joke; and to Mom, for everything.

— Introduction —

Twenty years ago, *Buffy the Vampire Slayer* came on the air and changed the lives of millions of devoted fans who saw themselves in the story of an unwitting (and, at first, unwilling) hero thrust into a life-and-death struggle against the forces of darkness from which there appeared to be no escape. A young, teenage girl bested terrifying demons and monsters, both without and within—not just vampires and Polgara demons, but mortality, loss, and failure. Buffy didn't always win, but she never gave up. And neither did the creative team who brought her story to television.

After a theatrical feature with a modest box office return, it was difficult to convince television executives to take a chance on Buffy. Eventually the television show was picked up as a midseason replacement with twelve episodes, which expanded over the years to seven seasons. Lisa implemented a vast Buffy publishing program supplemental to the series, and Nancy served as one of her writers. We worked on Buffy (and Angel) short stories, novellas, novels, guidebooks, a Sunnydale High School yearbook, and penned essays and articles about the Matter of Whedon over the past twenty years.

We were thrilled to reunite to work on this encyclopedia. We are happier people when we are awash in the Whedonverse together, and we hope you have as much fun thumbing through our entries as we had compiling them. We have tried to be as comprehensive as possible while acknowledging that the Buffyverse continues to expand with new seasons in comic book form even as we write this introduction.

This encyclopedia covers the *Buffy the Vampire Slayer* and *Angel* television shows and the core comic books that are generally considered canon, and had been published as of this writing. Entries include references to all of these works, citied in abbreviated form.

TELEVISION

BtVS—*Buffy the Vampire Slayer* television episodes

AtS—*Angel* television shows (*Angel*, the Series)

COMIC BOOKS

Buffy—*Buffy the Vampire Slayer* comic books set in seasons 8, 9, 10, and beyond

Angel—*Angel* comic books taking place "After the Fall" and beyond

Angel and Faith

Spike

Willow: Wonderland

Fray

Tales—Collection combining *Tales of the Slayer* and *Tales of the Vampires*

Within each entry, we have further broken down the citation to include the name of the television episode or, in the case of comics, the title of the volume of collected comics or the individual issues when we wanted to throw a spotlight on a particular event. Because there are continuing stories as well as one-offs and mini-series within the comics, our hope was to focus on the most direct means of identifying the source material.

We have had a wonderful time assembling this encyclopedia for you. Here's to twenty more years of Buffy and Angel stories!

With all our best wishes,

—Nancy Holder and Lisa A. Clancy

– A –

AARON | ALEX TOMA | Homeless teen enslaved by Ken and the Family Home demons who was bludgeoned to death for saying his own name rather than declaring that he was "nobody" (*BtVS* "Anne").

ABRAMS, JENNA | Woman whom an unnamed dying soldier at the battle against Twilight in Tibet regretted not asking to the dance before he shipped out (*Buffy* "Twilight").

ABRAMS, PARKER | ADAM KAUFMAN | Doe-eyed student at UC Sunnydale who was Buffy's rebound after Angel left town. Living in the Kresge dorm, he slept with Buffy and then dumped her, blaming her for misinterpreting the situation when she let him know that he had hurt her badly (*BtVS* "The Harsh Light of Day"). She still saved him when he almost died in a fire started by the Black Frost Beer cavemen (*BtVS* "Beer Bad").

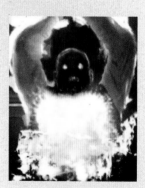

ABSALOM | BRENT JENNINGS | Member of the vampiric Order of Aurelius who oversaw the preparations for the resurrection of the Master. He attacked Buffy with a sledgehammer when she attempted to stop the ritual, but she set him on fire with a torch, destroying him (*BtVS* "When She Was Bad").

ACATHLA | Demon who planned to swallow the world, but was turned to stone by a virtuous knight who pierced his heart with a blessed sword. Acathla's stone body was unearthed in Sunnydale, leading to Angelus's attempt to revive the demon so he could suck the world into hell. The invocation to wake

Acathla required a bloodletting and the following chant: "*Acathla … Mundatus sum … pro te necavi. Sanguinem meum … pro te effundam quo me dignum … esse demonstrem.*" (Translation: Acathla … I am cleansed … here before you. My blood … flowing before you makes me worthy … as I demonstrate)(*BtVS* "Becoming, Part 1").

ACREY, HUNT | NICOLAS SUROVY | Lawyer at Wolfram & Hart who appointed Lilah and Lindsey as Joint Acting Co-Vice Presidents of special projects, and warned them that the Senior Partners were watching (*AtS* "Redefinition").

ACTING COACH | IRIS FIELDS | Cordelia's teacher who was impressed with her progress (*AtS* "Judgment").

ADAM | GEORGE HERTZBERG | Hybrid creature developed by Maggie Walsh in her secret lab at the Initiative. Adam was part demon, part human, and part robot—intended to be the perfect supersoldier. He killed Walsh with the Polgara demon skewer attached to his arm (*BtVS* "The I in Team") and then began ripping apart humans and demons to see how they were made (*BtVS* "Goodbye Iowa"). Adam regarded Riley Finn as his brother, and intended that the two of them would preside over a vampire-human-demon war resulting in an abundance of parts

from which they could construct more of their cyborg-demon kind. Buffy, Xander, Willow, and Giles defeated him by uniting in an enjoining spell (*BtVS* "Primeval"). Later, in Buffy's dream, Adam's original human face was revealed—he was once a handsome man (*BtVS* "Restless").

ADAM | **JEFFREY STEVEN SMITH** | Sunnydale High School student who enjoyed dishing with Cordelia about Buffy during computer class (*BtVS* "The Harvest"). Students possessed by hyena spirits later stole his lunch (*BtVS* "The Pack").

ADAMS, DOUGLAS | Author of *The Hitchhiker's Guide to the Galaxy*; Angel credits reading the book in the 1980s with preventing him from committing suicide. He went to Highgate Cemetery to pay his respects (*Angel and Faith* "Daddy Issues").

ADDAMS, CECILY (CECILY UNDERWOOD) | **KALI ROCHA** | Visage of the vengeance demon Halfrek. William Pratt (Spike) pined for Cecily and wrote doggerel about her. She rejected him, and their friends mocked his "bloody awful poetry," which earned him the nickname "William the Bloody" (*BtVS* "Lies My Parents Told Me").

ADVENT OF SEPTUS, THE | The Anointed One rose one thousand days after this date, as prophesied by Aurelius (*BtVS* "Never Kill a Boy on the First Date").

AIKO | New Slayer created after Willow magically activated the powers of all the Potentials in the world. Buffy sent Aiko after a

group of Japanese goth vampires who had stolen the Scythe. After defeating some Kabuki Demons, Aiko tracked down the vampires, but their leader, Toru, drained her Slayer powers with an amulet. Toru killed her and tied her corpse to a building, together with a banner that read "Welcome to Tokyo" written in Aiko's blood (*Buffy* "Wolves at the Gate").

ALESSANDRA | Vampire who sired Severin's girlfriend Clare (*Buffy* "Freefall").

ALEXIA | New Slayer who lived in Nashua, New Hampshire and faced intense anti-Slayer prejudice fostered by Harmony Kendall and others. Her best friend, Jacob, became a vampire and drained her to the point of death, inviting her to choose to become a vampire or to die (*Tales* "The Thrill").

ALFONSE | **MICHAEL NAGY** | Vampire whom Mayor Wilkins sent to kill Willow. He became the minion of the Wishverse version of Willow instead. Buffy dusted him at the Bronze (*BtVS* "Doppelgangland").

ALFONSO | **DAVID LEE** | Goran Demon with long, pointed ears in his cheeks, gray skin, a big nose, and greasy hair. He stole the *Capo* head from Angel and Spike, and when he showed up at the ransom drop, he gave them a bomb instead of the head (*AtS* "The Girl in Question").

ALGURIAN CONJURING ORB | Artifact used by Marcus Roscoe to switch bodies with younger men and then Angel, who crushed it once he was switched back (*AtS* "Carpe Noctem").

ALLISON (ALLY) | **SUNNY MABREY** | Client of Angel Investigations who was being stalked by her dead ex-boyfriend. Even though she'd poisoned him, in the end, she was attracted to his devotion, and they were reunited (*AtS* "Provider").

ALL SOULS' DAY | Christian feast day that honors the departed. It is celebrated on November second (*AtS* "The Cautionary Tale of Numero Cinco").

ALPHA DELTA | Fraternity at UC Sunnydale that hosted a cursed Halloween party at its frat house, resulting in several deaths (*BtVS* "The Freshman," "Fear Itself").

ALTHENEA | Head of the Devon witch coven that rehabilitated Willow after she went dark and flayed Warren Mears (*BtVS* "Lessons"). Althenea later called Willow to inform her that a seer in the coven located a Potential who was already living in Sunnydale (*BtVS* "Potential").

ALUWYN (SAGA VASUKI) | Beautiful demonic sorceress who thrives on chaos. Blue-green with white hair, she is human in appearance from the waist up, with a long serpentine tail. She served as Willow's mentor on her magical walkabout. Her sidekicks included Muffitt (who appeared as a young kid in a wheelchair) and Gnog, the black knight (*Buffy* "Goddesses and Monsters"). After the destruction of magic, she repaired the Scythe and created Wonderland, a magical oasis, in hopes that Willow would stay with her (*Willow: Wonderland*).

AMANDA | JAIME BERGMAN | Pregnant woman willing to turn her unborn baby over to the Fell Brethren to save her husband, because she knew the child would have a good life (*AtS* "Time Bomb").

AMANDA | SARAH HAGAN | Potential who first landed in Buffy's office at Sunnydale High School for fighting. Sarah was revealed to be the Sunnydale Potential detected by the Devon Coven (*BtVS* "Potential"). She and Dawn fought off vampires together in the high school, but she died at the Battle of the Hellmouth (*BtVS* "Chosen").

AMANDA | SASCHA SHAPIRO | Niece of the werewolf Nina Ash (*AtS* "Unleashed").

AMETHYST VIBRATORY STONE | Talisman used for charm bags, money spells, and cleansing one's aura (*BtVS* "Helpless").

AMIRAH, PRINCESS | Vampire Slayer from the southern Asia region during the 1870s (*Fray* "Ready, Steady...").

AMMA | Radie Haddyn tavern keeper and the mother of Loo (*Fray* "Ready, Steady..."). She joined Melaka Fray's forces in the battle against Harth and his Lurk army (*Fray* "All Hell").

AMPATA | ARA CELI | Inca Mummy Princess who chose to retain her victim's name after she drained the life out of him. Sacrificed at sixteen, she was entombed for centuries yet conscious of everything that went on around her. When the pottery disk that magically restrained her was broken, she masqueraded as a contemporary teen girl and fell in love with Xander. Unable to absorb Xander's life force in time, she reverted to the withered mummy she had become, and broke apart (*BtVS* "Inca Mummy Girl").

AMULET, THE | Mystical gem worn by Buffy's champion, Spike, at the Battle of the Hellmouth. The gem blazed with brilliant light, turning the invading army of Turok-Han to dust and destroying the town of Sunnydale along with its Hellmouth (*BtVS* "Chosen"). The ghost of Wolfram & Hart attorney Lilah Morgan had given the amulet to Angel, who took it to Sunnydale and passed it to Buffy. The amulet was mysteriously returned to Angel after the battle, and Spike emerged from it in ghostly form (*AtS* "Just Rewards").

AMULET OF BALTHAZAR | Source of the demon Balthazar's power. A Sunnydale landowner named Gleaves once defeated the demon and hid the amulet in his crypt. Over a century later, Balthazar sent his minions to retrieve the amulet so he could exact revenge on Mayor Wilkins. Buffy intercepted the amulet and eventually gave it to Angel to dispose of it (*BtVS* "Bad Girls").

AMULET OF CALDYS | Item for sale when Giles owned the Magic Box (*BtVS* "Checkpoint").

AMULET OF REVELATION | Artifact with the power to identify the location of portals for Dawn as she and Xander attempted to return to Earth after being trapped in a hell dimension (*Buffy* "Own It").

ANAHEED | One of Buffy's roommates in San Francisco (*Buffy* "Freefall"), she was also secretly a Slayer from Rona's Chicago squad. Anaheed was sent to protect Buffy from the mundane threats of everyday life, such as not being able to pay her share of the rent. While viewing a recorded zompire attack, she realized that Tessa was the zompire sire, and theorized that Simone was creating Slayer-Zompire hybrids (*Buffy* "Welcome to the Team").

ANDERSON, CALLIE MEGAN | JORDANA SPIRO | Student at Kent Preparatory School who went missing for over a week. She'd been kidnapped by the Delta Zeta Kappa fraternity and was intended to be a victim for Machida, the demon they worshipped. Buffy rescued her (*BtVS* "Reptile Boy").

ANDERSON FAMILY | Family that was preyed upon by the Sunnydale High School "hyena pack." Family members include: Joey (Justin Jon Ross), Mr. Anderson (David Brisbin), and Mrs. Anderson (Barbara K. Whinnery) (*BtVS* "The Pack").

ANDERSON, PAIGE | KATY BOYER | Mother of Ryan, the boy possessed by an Ethros Demon. She believed in angels, but wouldn't accept that her son was bad until he lured her into a trap and tried to choke her (*AtS* "I've Got You under My Skin").

ANDERSON, RICHARD | GREG VAUGHAN | Delta Zeta Kappa frat guy at Crestwood College and member of a wealthy family that owned Anderson Farms, Anderson Aeronautics, and Anderson Cosmetics (*BtVS* "Reptile Boy").

ANDERSON, RYAN | JESSE JAMES | Young boy with a void where his soul should have been. He was temporarily possessed by an Ethros Demon. For a time, it was suspected that the possession was the cause for his violent behavior, but it was not. The demon was just as fearful of Ryan's inherent cruelty. After the demon was exorcised, Ryan locked his parents in their bedroom and set his sister Stephanie's room on fire. He was placed in the custody of social services (*AtS* "I've Got You under My Skin").

ANDERSON, SETH | WILL KEMPE | Investment advisor who moved his family from Baton Rouge to Miami and then Akron, Ohio in the last three years to avoid the trouble that he believed his son Ryan caused (*AtS* "I've Got You under My Skin").

ANDERSON, STEPHANIE | ASHLEY EDNER | Her brother Ryan set her room on fire in one of his final acts of cruelty before the police turned him over to social services (*AtS* "I've Got You under My Skin").

ANDREW'S KNIFE | Ritual blade that Andrew used to kill Jonathan Levinson on top of the Seal of Danzalthar (*BtVS* "Conversations with Dead People"). Guided by the First, who appeared to him as Warren, Andrew obtained the knife in Mexico from demons. It was engraved with words in proto-Tuwarik that translated to "The blood which I spill I consecrate to the oldest evil." After the murder, Andrew washed it and stored it in Buffy's cutlery drawer (*BtVS* "Storyteller").

ANDY | Resident of Magic Town who was warned by Nadira to stay away from Angel. He brought Corky Smallwood a jar that probably contained magic, but because he had spoken to Angel, Smallwood killed him and strung him up from a sewer ceiling as a warning (*Angel and Faith* "Where the River Meets the Sea").

ANGEL/ANGELUS | See following pages.

ANGEL INVESTIGATIONS | See following pages.

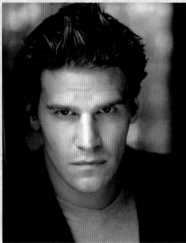

Angel/Angelus

LIAM, THE DEMON WITH THE ANGELIC FACE, THE ONE WITH THE ANGELIC FACE, THE SCOURGE OF EUROPE, TWILIGHT
| DAVID BOREANAZ |

Originally named Liam while human, Angelus was sired by Darla in Galway in the eighteenth century and immediately killed his human family. With Darla, Angelus developed a reputation as the most brutal vampire who had ever lived. He met Spike in London in 1880, confessing that he longed for another male companion to run around with, but he tested Spike's will first (*AtS* "Destiny"). Angelus left a trail of bodies across Europe. In 1898, after he murdered a Kalderash girl, her clan cursed him by returning his soul, forcing him to endure guilt for all his many atrocities.

For almost a century, the ensouled vampire was a shell of his former self. In the late twentieth century, Angelus— now calling himself Angel—was approached by the demon Whistler, who successfully rehabilitated him. Angel moved to Sunnydale, where he fell in love with Buffy and ingratiated himself into her circle of friends. He lost his soul again when they consummated their relationship and he "experienced a moment of true happiness," which triggered the Kalderash curse (*BtVS* "Surprise").

As Angelus once again, he tortured Buffy and her friends, killing Jenny Calendar before she could return his soul. Her spell was found, but not in time to save Buffy from having to push him into a demon dimension to save the world. He was changed when he returned, but he found it hard to reconnect with the Scoobies after all Angelus had done. Tortured by the First Evil with ghosts of his past, Angel attempted to commit suicide at sunrise, but other-worldy forces (possibly the Powers That Be) saved him with a freak snowstorm (*Buffy* "Amends"). Realizing he could never be together with Buffy, Angel left Sunnydale for Los Angeles (*AtS* "City Of").

After arriving in Los Angeles, Angel tried not to form any attachments, but a half demon named Doyle told him the Powers That Be had a mission for him, and together with Cordelia they formed Angel Investigations. The loss of Doyle staggered Angel, but the arrival of Wesley convinced him to keep trying (*AtS* "Parting Gifts"). The law firm Wolfram & Hart made it their mission to destroy Angel, but the Senior Partners realized he had a role in the upcoming apocalypse and forbade killing him, so the lawyers just continued to make his work harder (*AtS* "Blood Money"). There were times the fight seemed overwhelming, such as when Darla was turned back into a vampire, and he gave in to dark impulses—like locking Wolfram & Hart lawyers in the cellar with Darla and Drusilla—but a brief tour of the Home Office by a deceased Holland Manners reminded him that hell was here on Earth and he had to keep fighting. The arrival of his son, Connor, gave Angel the one thing he'd never had—hope—and he threw himself into fatherhood with joy, anxiety, and optimism (*AtS* "Dad"). The loss of Connor into

stop the pain was to hurt someone else; then he drank from her (*AtS* "Release"). Unconscious due to the Orpheus drug in Faith's system, Angelus revisited Angel's good deeds as his version of hell. He fought Faith and his inner Angel, but was merged back into Angel thanks to Willow's spell (*AtS* "Orpheus").

After Jasmine turned the world upside down, Angel made a deal with Wolfram & Hart to work for them in exchange for Connor getting a normal family life. He had to live with the memory of his son, while his friends' memories of Connor were wiped (*AtS* "Home"). The return of Spike rattled Angel, and he wondered if he was really the champion for the Powers That Be, or if Spike would fulfill the Shanshu Prophecy that the vampire with a soul, once he fulfilled his destiny, would become human as his reward (*AtS* "Destiny"). Angel began a relationship with Nina the werewolf, but struggled in his role at Wolfram & Hart, trying to fight the good fight from behind the scenes. His willingness to sacrifice a companion—namely Fred—brought him to the notice of the Circle of the Black Thorn, who issued him an invitation to join their small, elite group of evil demons. He accepted, even killing his old friend Drogyn to seal his entrance, and was forced to sign away any claim to the Shanshu Prophecy to prove his loyalty to them. Once inside the Circle, he told his gang that while they could never defeat the Senior Partners, he wanted to hurt them. He and his surviving team members took on a demon army of thousands (*AtS* "Not Fade Away") as the Senior Partners sent Los Angeles to hell.

Angel continued to protect the inhabitants of the city and was about to die when the Senior Partners reversed time so that he would live to fulfill the Shanshu Prophecy (*Angel* "After the Fall"). When magic ended, Angel assumed the persona of Twilight, at first believing that he was doing so to minimize the losses on Buffy's side of the war against Slayers; however, he and Buffy ascended, made love, and birthed a new dimension that was called Twilight (*Buffy* "Twilight"). Under its more direct influence, Angel killed Giles.

Distraught, he left; Faith took care of him in London, and he was able to resurrect Giles. After Whistler exploded a magic ball over a section of London, the area became saturated with magic and caused mutations among the citizenry (*Angel and Faith* "What You Want, Not What You Need"). Angel assumed the role of "unofficial sheriff of Magic Town" and continues to protect the inhabitants to this day.

a hell dimension caused Angel to turn on Wesley. Connor's return as a teenager caught him off guard, and he had to reconcile his former eagerness to watch Connor grow up with this angry teen who hated him. Angel forgave Connor for leaving him on the bottom of the ocean, where his hunger led him to have dreams of a fictional family. Once rescued, Angel threw Connor out (*AtS* "Deep Down"), but continued to keep track of his son as the vampire tried to reintroduce the descended Cordelia to this world.

Angelus reasserted himself when the Beast came to Los Angeles and it was determined that the evil vampire's presence was required to vanquish it. He escaped the hotel pretending to be Angel before it was revealed that Cordelia was the one who had freed him and murdered Lilah while under Jasmine's influence (*AtS* "Calvary"). Angelus killed the Beast while fighting against and alongside Faith (*AtS* "Salvage"). He told Faith he knew what it was like to be forced to be something one was not, and that the only way to

Angel's Pre-Sunnydale Timeline

1727: Born with the name Liam in Galway, Ireland.

1753: Sired by Darla. When he rose as a vampire, he went to his family's home, where his little sister, Kathy thought he was an angel and let him in. He killed her, his father, and his mother before adopting the name Angelus.

1760: Darla introduced him to the Master in London.

1764: Killed the wife and son of Daniel Holtz before fleeing across Europe with Darla.

1767: Holtz cornered him in Marseilles, France, but wanted Darla instead.

1771: Captured and tortured by Holtz in Rome until Darla rescued him.

Late 1700s: Angelus adopted the custom of "signing" his victims by carving a Christian cross into their left cheek.

1786: Sired Penn, a Puritan who adopted some of Angelus's habits.

1789: Encountered the Beast in Prussia.

1838: Killed a man named Daniel in Dublin, Ireland on Christmas Day.

1860: Angel sires Drusilla after receiving her as a "gift" from Darla.

1880: Welcomed William (Spike) into his "family" with Darla and Drusilla.

1883: Killed a serving woman and her son.

1890: First saw the Blinnikov Ballet's production of *Giselle*. He was so moved by the production that he cried like a baby.

1894: Captured by followers of the Immortal while the vampire was otherwise engaged with Darla and Drusilla.

1898: In Borsa, Romania, Darla gave him a Kalderash girl as a birthday present. He drank from her, leading to her clan cursing him with a soul.

1900: Reunited with Darla in China, but she rejected him because he was only feeding on vermin.

1902: Arrived at Ellis Island, NY.

1920s: Spent part of the Depression in Missoula, Montana. Also saved a puppy in Chicago, but blew off the grateful young owner to avoid feeding on her.

1928: Lived in room 217 at the Hyperion Hotel in LA.

1940: Spent time in Las Vegas with Bugsy Siegel.

1943: US military conscripted him to rescue the crew of a captured German submarine.

1960s: Hung out with Sammy Davis Jr., Frank Sinatra, and Dean Martin at the Sands Casino.

1967: Attended the wedding of Elvis and Priscilla Presley.

1970: Failed to save a donut shop clerk from being shot, and in a moment of weakness drank from the dead man.

1996: Arrived in Sunnydale.

ANGELMAN, DR. FRANCIS | JACK STEHLIN | Medical doctor who worked with Maggie Walsh on the 314 Project in the creation of the hybrid, Adam (*BtVS* "The I in Team"). He took over the project after Walsh's death (*BTVS* "Goodbye Iowa"). Adam killed him as well and turned him into a semisentient laboratory worker (*BtVS* "Primeval").

ANGEL'S MANSION | One of Angel's Sunnydale residences, located on Crawford Street (*BtVS* "Becoming, Part 2").

ANHARRANS DEMON | Species from Anharra, a hell dimension under the rule of the god-king Kerberon. Dawn and Xander taught them to be peace-loving and to build stone houses (*Buffy* "In Pieces on the Ground").

ANNA | STEPHI LINEBURG | Young woman whom Connor kidnapped because Cordelia needed the blood of a virgin to bring their baby forth. Connor hesitated in killing Anna after seeing his mother Darla warn him from this path. Cordelia killed her instead and used her blood to bring forth their baby/Jasmine (*AtS* "Inside Out").

ANNABELLE | COURTNEE DRAPER | Vegetarian British Potential brought to Sunnydale by Giles. She cracked under the pressure of her new situation and fled before being killed by the Turok-Han. Buffy buried her body in the woods. She was the first Potential to die while in Buffy's care (*BtVS* "Bring on the Night").

ANNALS OF HISTORY | Textbook used at Dawn's middle school. The fact that the mean girl Kirstie could not properly pronounce "Annals" was a source of amusement for Dawn (*BtVS* "The Body").

ANNAPOLIS OLIVE OIL IMPORT/EXPORT | Corporate client of Wolfram & Hart (*AtS* "Darla").

ANNE | British nurse and the mother of Hannah, a young girl whose body served as host to a Plagiarus Demon (*Angel and Faith* "Live through This").

ANO-MOVIC DEMON | Once a nomadic tribe with violent leanings, they gave up those orthodox teachings around the turn of the twentieth century. Now they are a peaceful clan, totally

assimilated into society, except when one marries a previously married woman, in which case they have to ingest the first husband's brains to bless the marriage. Characterized by red skin, facial ridges, and horns, they are polite, and they generally prefer wives whose knees bend in more than one way (*AtS* "The Bachelor Party").

ANTHONY, JEAN | Counselor at the Mission Women's Center who contacted Detective Dowling about a male succubus who was psychically harassing her (*Buffy* "Old Demons").

APHRODESIA | AMY CHANCE | Sunnydale High School student who mocked Buffy's unusual name (*BtVS* "Welcome to the Hellmouth").

APOLLO'S BRAZIER | Artifact required for the attempted resurrection of Rupert Giles (*Angel and Faith* "What You Want, Not What You Need").

APRIL | SHONDA FARR | Robot girlfriend that Warren Mears built for himself. She almost killed his human girlfriend, Katrina, before running out of energy and deactivating (*BtVS* "I Was Made to Love You").

APRIL FOOLS | Store where Cordelia worked part-time after her father lost all their money (*BtVS* "The Prom").

ARACHNOPHOBIA | Buffy's nickname for Simone Doffler's captive Ragna Demon (*Buffy* "Predators and Prey").

ARADIA | Goddess of the lost, called upon when performing guiding spells (*BtVS* "Fear Itself," "Bargaining, Part 2").

ARASHMAHARR | Hell dimension that is home to the Vengeance Demons (*Buffy* "Own It").

ARATUSCAN | Language spoken by Ano-movic Demons. The language was once thought to be dead (*AtS* "The Bachelor Party").

Angel Investigations

Supernatural detective agency whose motto is (usually) "We help the hopeless." They were founded when Cordelia put Angel's mission together with a staff initially consisting of her and Doyle (*AtS* "City of"). They had business cards, but the Angel logo was frequently mistaken for a paperclip or lobster. After their office was blown up (*AtS* "To Shanshu in LA"), the agency—now including Wesley (who replaced Doyle)—operated out of Cordelia's apartment in Silverlake until the quarters proved too tight (*AtS* "Judgment"). They moved to the Hyperion Hotel (*AtS* "Are You Now or Have You Ever Been") and Gunn began working with them on a recurring basis before joining the team (*AtS* "War Zone"). After a brief disbanding, the group reunited, adding Fred after rescuing her from Pylea (*AtS* "Through the Looking Glass"). Fred explained the organizational structure to her parents as, "Angel's the champion, and Wesley's the brains of the operation; Gunn's the muscle and Cordy's the heart" (*AtS* "Fredless"). Lorne also joined the team after serving as a consultant for some time. Lilah offered the gang the opportunity to run Wolfram & Hart, pointing out that they actually aligned themselves with evil when they banished Jasmine. The gang resisted at first, but their curiosity was piqued and after personalized tours of the law firm, they agreed to move into the Wolfram & Hart offices (*AtS* "Home").

ANGEL
INVESTIGATIONS

ARCHAEUS | Ancient Demon Lord who sired the Master, and thus part of his essence was transferred to Darla, Angel, Drusilla, and Spike, as the Master's progeny. He plagued Spike and Angel with murderous dreams and attempted to open a demonic portal in San Francisco (*Buffy* "Love Dares You"). Thwarted by the Scoobies and Angel, he relocated to Magic Town, where Drusilla joined forces with him. He kidnapped Nadira and acquired a mystical golem for the magical force of Magic Town to inhabit. Instead, the magical force trapped Archaeus inside the golem, where he would be entombed for a thousand years (*Angel and Faith* "A Tale of Two Families").

ARCHFIEND.ORG | Not an intraspecies dating site. Yet (*AtS* "The Ring").

ARLENE | Buffy's aunt who lives in Illinois. Joyce called Arlene to tell her that Buffy had been accepted to Northwestern University (*BtVS* "Choices").

ARNI | **ANGELO SURMELIS** | Demon electrician who helped Lorne rebuild Caritas (*AtS* "Offspring"). When Lorne fired him for ripping him off, Arnie provided information about Darla and her baby to Sahjhan and Holtz for money. He can replicate conversations and voices, while his eyes light up (*AtS* "Lullaby").

ARTODE | **MICHAEL MAIZE** | Henchman for Archduke Sebassis. He wore the skin of a Pylean to the Wolfram & Hart Halloween party and was ripped apart by Lorne's alter ego (*AtS* "Life of the Party").

ASCENSION, THE | Event in which a human becomes pure demon (*BtVS* "Bad Girls"). Mayor Wilkins was planning to ascend on Graduation Day. He was impervious to harm for one hundred days before he changed, but as a demon, he could be killed (*BtVS* "Graduation Day, Part 1").

ASCLEPIAN VIAL | Potion that revealed Andrew's sexual orientation and made him invincible (*Buffy* "Love Dares You").

ASH, NINA | **JENNY MOLLEN** | Angel's werewolf ex-girlfriend. She was bitten by a werewolf while jogging in East Hollywood. Angel caught her and explained that she would need to be locked up a few nights every month, but Jacob Crane's team kidnapped her and took her to his home, where she was prepped to be the main course at a dinner party. Nina was about to be eaten alive when Angel rescued her (*AtS* "Unleashed"). She became involved with Angel, but Angel sent her and her family away before the big fight with the Senior Partners because of his feelings for her (*AtS* "Smile Time," "Power Play"). Nina was still in Los Angeles when Wolfram & Hart sent the city to hell. Because the sun and moon shone at the same time, she could not transform. She, Connor, and Gwen Raiden offered sanctuary to humans and good demons. She eventually got married, and she and Angel have lost touch (*Angel* "After the Fall").

ASHET | **MICHAEL CHINYAMURINDI** | Second Totem of the Sun God Ra that hired Gwen Raiden to steal some amulets to protect him from the Beast. He was ultimately killed by the Beast, who removed a pair of metal wings from his chest (*AtS* "Long Day's Journey")

ASHIKAGA BUILDING | Location where Toru took the Scythe in preparation for reversing its power to take away the abilities of all the Slayers (*Buffy* "Wolves at the Gate").

ASMODEA | Entity Dark Willow called upon when battling Giles in the Magic Box (*BtVS* "Grave").

ASPHYX DEMON (CAVE DEMON) | STEVEN W. BAILEY | Demon with fissured skin, spines on its shoulders, and glowing eyes. The demon forced Spike to undergo a series of tortures and trials, and then, once satisfied with Spike's worthiness, gave Spike back his soul (*BtVS* "Grave").

ASSASSINATION AND INFILTRATION | Subject heading listed on page 54, chapter 11, of Marcie Ross's textbook in her FBI-organized invisible students class (*BtVS* "Out of Mind, Out of Sight").

ATKINS, JANE | Member of the Fondren High pep squad who died in a car crash. Sunnydale High student Chris Epps harvested parts of her body to create a mate for his revivified brother, Daryl (*BtVS* "Some Assembly Required").

ATKINSON, CAPTAIN | STEVEN BARR | LAPD officer who worshipped Granath so he could bring good cops back to life. Angel beat him with Granath's idol (*AtS* "The Thin Dead Line").

AUGMENTATION SPELL | Jonathan performed this spell to make himself the coolest celebrity in the world; the proof was the symbol on his arm, which matched that of the monster that resulted. Because he had created a new force of good, the spell had to produce an equally strong force of evil (*BtVS* "Superstar").

AUGUSTINE'S CURSE REVERSE INCANTATION | Performed while holding Dracula's sword, this incantation drained special powers that Japanese vampires won in a poker game from Dracula (*Buffy* "Wolves at the Gate").

AURA | Willow's girlfriend for a time in San Francisco (*Buffy* "Freefall").

AURA | PERSIA WHITE | Cordelia's friend who stayed in touch after Cordy moved to Los Angeles. (*Buffy* "Welcome to the Hellmouth").

AURELIUS AND HIS ORDER | Twelfth-century vampire who founded the Order and foretold the coming of the Anointed One. After his death, the Master became the head of the Order (*BtVS* "Never Kill a Boy on the First Date").

AVERY, HOLLIS | Man suffering from schizophrenia who posed as God to convince the Ratcatcher to immolate in the sunshine (*Tales* "Taking Care of Business").

AVILAS | TROY BRENNA | Tall, horned demon summoned by a group of male students at the new Sunnydale High School. Avilas promised riches in return for "a sacrifice of flesh." Buffy set his abdomen on fire and he quickly burned to death (*BtVS* "Help").

AXE OF DEKERON | Mystical weapon lost since the Children's Crusade. Reputed to have been forged in hell, it was used to kill children (*BtVS* "End of Days").

AXIS OF PYTHIA | Ancient power bridging all dimensions. Forged from the tripod of the Delphic oracle, the Axis—a metal arch set into a marble base—stands approximately two feet high and weighs eighteen pounds. Imbued with many mystical qualities, one of which is finding souls or entities across dimensions. Gwen Raiden stole the Axis from Chandler's Auction House, and later, Angel used it to learn that Cordelia was a higher being (*AtS* "Ground State").

AYALA | Female entity invoked by Willow and Tara to access the nether realm (*BtVS* "Who Are You?").

AZTEC SLAYER | Fourteenth-century Slayer and warrior princess who slew the Soul Glutton's family with an enchanted sword (*Buffy* "I Wish").

B

BACKER, DR. STANLEY | RICHARD HERD | Doctor at Sunnydale Memorial Hospital whose history of reprimands and censures led Buffy to suspect he was murdering the children he was supposedly attempting to cure. But when his unorthodox procedure began to work, the real culprit, Der Kindestod, viciously killed him (*BtVS* "Killed by Death").

BAIRD, CHARLENE | Woman who was attacked and killed by her husband of thirty years while he was under the influence of half-demon Billy Blim (*AtS* "Billy").

BAKER | Demon inadvertently stabbed by Angel (*AtS* "The Ring").

BAKER'S BOY, THE (UNNAMED GILES) | Son of the owner of the Giles Bakery in London. He married Watcher Edna Fairweather, and his son and grandson (Rupert Giles) also became Watchers (*Tales* "Tales of the Vampires, Part 6").

BALTHAZAR | CHRISTIAN CLEMENSON | Obese demon that once unsuccessfully challenged the Mayor for control of Sunnydale. The source of Balthazar's power, an amulet, was taken by a landowner named Gleaves. Learning of the Mayor's impending Ascension, the demon kidnapped Rupert Giles and Wesley Wyndam-Pryce to make them disclose its location. He was electrocuted by Buffy (*BtVS* "Bad Girls").

BALTIC STONES | Objects used as a catalyst for transferring magical energy (*BtVS* "Get It Done").

BAND OF BLACKNIL | A plain ring that was really the source of power to move between dimensions. Angel used the ring to take a ride to the Home Office (*AtS* "Reprise").

BANKS, REGGIE | Englishman who used the money with which he was supposed to pay back the Russian mob to buy Mohra blood to heal a gut wound. The Mohra blood mutated him into a hideous creature in constant pain (*Angel and Faith* "Live through This").

BANSHEE | Species of Irish fairy regarded as omens of death and messengers of the unknown. They steal leprechauns' gold (*Buffy* "I Wish").

BAPHON | Demon with a head resembling a skeletal ram and a space in the middle of his chest that would freeze anything inserted into it. A foot soldier of Mal Fraser who sold Mohra Demon blood to Kurth (*Angel and Faith* "Live through This").

BARABBAS | Evil being Willow called upon when casting her curse on Oz and Veruca (*BtVS* "Wild at Heart").

BARNEY | MAURY STERLING | Empath Demon with the ability to read people's emotions. Barney used his gift to gamble, but also made a living hunting for rare demon parts and selling them to the highest bidder. After learning Cordelia received Doyle's gift of visions, he kidnapped her and put her on auction. Cordy stabbed him with a Tak horn and he was incinerated (*AtS* "Parting Gifts").

BARSHON | ANDREW PARKS | Pylean priest and member of the Covenant of Trombi. He hated that their princess, Cordelia, was a "cow" (*AtS* "Through the Looking Glass").

BARTENDER | JOSH RANDALL | Employee at La Brea Lounge (*AtS* "Expecting").

BARTENDER | OBI NDEFO | Murder suspect who worked at D'Oblique when he was infected with the Burrower. Angel threw him into a burning barrel, and Kate shot him dead, ending the Burrower's life as well (*AtS* "Lonely Heart").

BARTON, MS. | PEG STUART | Sunnydale High School faculty member who reverted to teenage behavior after eating the band candy (*BtVS* "Band Candy").

BARVAIN, DEMON PRINCE | Rises on the third new moon after the nine-hundredth feast of Delthrox (*BtVS* "A New Man").

BAYARMAA (BAY) | Tibetan werewolf romantically linked to Oz, and the mother of his child. She encouraged the Slayers to seek peace through hard work and meditation, yet fought to defend them in the battle against Twilight. Bay showed Buffy and Amy how to raise the three Tibetan goddesses who had been absorbing their power (*Buffy* "Retreat").

BEACH, MR. | **ROBERT ARCE** | Teacher at the original Sunnydale High School. During the time when Buffy was a telepath she heard him think *"If we could just get rid of all the students,"* making him a suspect in a plot to kill everyone at school (*BtVS* "Earshot").

BEAKMAN, MISS | **LORNA SCOTT** | Tough American literature teacher at the original Sunnydale High School who failed students for missing homework. Amy Madison's magic spell made her believe that Amy had turned in an assignment when she had not (*BtVS* "Bewitched, Bothered, and Bewildered").

BEAST OF AMALFI | Razor-toothed, six-eyed harbinger of death. The demon was due to rise in 2003 in Reseda, according to the *Prophecies of Aberjian* (*AtS* "To Shanshu in LA").

BEAST, THE | **VLADIMIR KULICH** | Massive, horned creature with rocky skin and hooves for feet, and a deep voice; he appeared in Cordelia's vision when her memory was returned. The Beast clawed through the ground in the alley where Connor was born (*AtS* "Spin the Bottle"). He killed everyone in Wolfram & Hart, stabbed Lilah, and hurt Connor (*AtS* "Habeas Corpses"). The Beast also killed the Ra-Tet to get their pieces for a ritual that blocked the sun (*AtS* "Long Day's Journey"). In 1789 the Svea priestesses hunted him to banish him. He sought out Angelus for help but was banished by them until now (as confirmed by Freyan runes) (*AtS* "Soulless"). Angelus killed him with the knife from his own bones, and the energy released from it freed the sun (*AtS* "Salvage").

BECK | Half-human, half-demon inmate at the Mosaic Wellness Center. Beck accompanied Spike to Las Vegas to take on Wolfram & Hart. She counseled Spike to take his soul back from Drusilla after John magically stole it from him, and took a direct hit from one of the Senior Partners when they attempted to commandeer the Bug ship (*Spike* "After the Fall").

BEETS, CAROL | Vampire who sired Brandon from the sewer gang and told Harmony that a Lei-ach Demon was recruiting his brethren to kill Buffy (*BtVS* "Family").

BEHAVIOR MODIFIER | Classification of chip Dr. Walsh implanted in Riley. The Chip was directly tied into his nervous system. Adam activated it to begin Riley's transformation into a hybrid, but Riley dug it out with a glass shard (*BtVS* "Primeval").

BEHEMOTH | Name of a Vahrall Demon Giles spotted while researching the source of a recent earthquake (*BtVS* "Doomed").

BELFLEUR, AGNES (AGGIE) | **PERSIA WHITE** | Psychic friend of Lorne's who worked at a psychic hotline. She told him he had to go back to Pylea one last time to get over it all (*AtS* "Over the Rainbow").

BELJOXA'S EYE | Creature that lives in another dimension and is composed of varying sizes of eyes that can see the truth of the present and the past. It explained to Giles and Anya that the First Evil was able to mount an offense due to an imbalance in good and evil caused by Buffy's resurrection (*BtVS* "Showtime").

BELLOWS, TRACY | KRISTIN RICHARDSON | News reporter for the KTLA network in Los Angeles (*AtS* "Peace Out").

BEN | RYAN TASZREAK | Student at the original Sunnydale High School who had Algebra II with Buffy. He invited her to ask him to the Sadie Hawkins dance and she turned him down (*BtVS* "I Only Have Eyes for You").

BENNY | SAUL STEIN | Thug for Magnus Bryce who kidnapped Wesley, thinking he was Angel (*AtS* "Guise Will Be Guise").

BENNY | STEVE SCHIRRIPA | Employee of Tony Papazian who was going to water his plants after Tony left the city for Yerevan (*AtS* "Sense and Sensitivity").

BENSON, MR. | The best cheerleading coach money can buy (*BtVS* "Witch").

BERMAN, KEVIN | J. EVAN BONIFANT | Cute boy in Dawn's art class who commiserated with her on the difficulties of life, alluding to what he assumed was her suicide attempt (*BtVS* "The Body").

BETH | AMY ADAMS | Tara Maclay's cousin who sided with Tara's brother and father against Tara's staying in Sunnydale (*BtVS* "Family").

BETTA GEORGE | Splenden Beast transported along with Los Angeles into the hell dimension. This large, floating, telepathic fish creature was first enslaved by Kr'ph, Demon Lord of Westwood, and later by Gunn when he was a vampire. Betta George warned Spike and Angel that Illyria planned to destroy time itself. At Angel's request, he filled Illyria's mind with memories of Fred and Wesley to weaken her resolve (*Angel* "After the Fall"). Later he traveled to Las Vegas with Spike (*Spike* "Stranger Things").

BETTY | CARRIE SOUTHWORTH | One of Caleb's earliest victims. The First appeared to Caleb as her so that Caleb could reexperience the pleasure of killing her (*BtVS* "Dirty Girls").

BETTY LOUISE PLOTNICK OF EAST CUPCAKE, ILLINOIS | Buffy's self-deprecating nickname for herself when she started college (*BtVS* "The Freshman").

BEZOAR | Pre-historic parasite. The mother hibernates underground laying eggs, and then her offspring attach themselves to a host, taking control of their motor functions through neural clamping. The mother Bezoar killed Tector Gorch and Buffy killed the Bezoar (*BtVS* "Bad Eggs").

BIANCHI, ILONA COSTA | CAROLE RAPHAELLE DAVIS | CEO of Wolfram & Hart's Rome office. An expert on ransoms and conducting business in Italy, she assured Angel and Spike that the Immortal did not use magic (*AtS* "The Girl in Question").

BIG BAD | Colloquial term for the most challenging of the enemies of the Slayer(s) thus far. Spike has adopted it as a nickname for himself. See following page.

BIG BOB | MICHAEL CUDLITZ | Sunnydale High School student who was raised from the dead by Jack O'Toole after being shot while trying to rob a liquor store. Xander crushed Bob's revenant form with a vending machine (*BtVS* "The Zeppo").

BIG UGLY | GREGORY SCOTT CUMMINS | Large vampire, and a member of Spike's gang. He claimed to have been present at the Crucifixion. Buffy staked him outside the Bronze after he attacked a young woman (*BtVS* "School Hard").

BILLENGER, MIKE | Young man whose life was saved by a Slayer who would become Buffy's underground decoy. He was involved with Holly Braeburn (*Buffy* "The Long Way Home").

BILLINGS, MAJOR | Military officer who briefed Deepscan on the operation to extract Walt Zane (*Angel and Faith* "Lost and Found").

BLACK CHRONICLES, THE | Book Giles assigned to Xander for researching the source of Angel's torment by visions of his past victims (*BtVS* "Amends").

Buffy's Big Bads

THE MASTER/THE ORDER OF AURELIUS

THE ORDER OF AURELIUS/ANGELUS

MAYOR RICHARD WILKINS

ADAM

GLORIFICUS (GLORY)

THE TRIO

DARK WILLOW

THE FIRST EVIL

TWILIGHT

SIMONE DOFFLER

D'HOFFRYN

BLACK FROST BEER | Brand name of the cursed beer that turned college students into Neanderthal primitives. It was brewed by Jack, a local college bar owner with a warlock for a brother-in-law (*BtVS* "Beer Bad").

BLACK KNIGHT'S HATCHET | Mystical weapon Willow read about on a website while searching for information on the Scythe (*BtVS* "End of Days").

BLACK TOMORROW, THE | Cult specializing in the creation of quick-fire chemical and biological weapons (*AtS* "Conviction").

BLAIR | DOMINIC KEATING | Watcher turned vampire when Watchers Council prisoner Zachary Kralik sired him during the preparation for Buffy's Cruciamentum. Blair helped Kralik escape to attack Buffy, but the newly sired vampire was incapacitated by the Slayer and ultimately killed by Giles (*BtVS* "Helpless").

BLAISDELL, LARRY | LARRY BAGBY III | Originally a Sunnydale High School bully, Larry attempted to attack Buffy when he was magically transformed into a pirate on Halloween (*BtVS* "Halloween"). Later, believing that Larry was a werewolf responsible for a number of deaths, Xander pressured him to confess; misunderstanding, Larry came out to Xander as gay (*BtVS* "Phases"). Relieved of his secret, Larry stopped harassing the girls at school and became a caring, warm person who died a hero's death on Graduation Day (*BtVS* "Graduation Day, Part 2"). He was also a brave vampire fighter in the Wishverse (*BtVS* "The Wish").

BLAKE | Watcher who perished along with the rest of the council when Caleb blew up the Watchers headquarters in London (*BtVS* "Never Leave Me").

BLAKE, MICHELLE | TORI MCPETRIE | Sunnydale student who ran against Buffy and Cordelia for homecoming queen. Of her, Cordelia said, "Open to all mankind, especially those with a letterman's jacket and a car. She could give me a run." She tied with Holly Charleston for the title (*BtVS* "Homecoming").

BLANE, TIMOTHY | ANDREW REVILLE | Doublemeat Palace employee with a robotic demeanor that personified the soul-crushing work environment (*BtVS* "Doublemeat Palace").

BLIM, BILLY | JUSTIN SHILTON | Nephew of Congressman Blim. Lilah forced Angel to free Billy from a demon dimension fortress, where he was constantly on fire (*AtS* "That Vision Thing"). Billy brought out a primordial misogyny in men, but his family knew to keep him away from their girlfriends and animals, and was willing to pay him to stay away. He tried to turn Angel but failed. He was able to draw strength from the ground, but as his fight with Angel came to a standstill, Lilah shot him dead (*AtS* "Billy").

BLIM, CONGRESSMAN NATHAN | RICHARD LIVINGSTON | Wolfram & Hart client who was uncle to Billy (*AtS* "Billy").

BLIM, DYLAN | KRISTOFFER POLAHA | Billy's cousin. He gave Billy "fun money" to take the family jet and go away. Dylan was fine with telling Angel where Billy was, even though he knew Angel wanted to kill his cousin (*AtS* "Billy").

BLINNIKOV WORLD BALLET CORPS | Premiere dance company that came to LA for a one-night-only performance of its signature piece, *Giselle*. Angel saw them in 1890 and cried like a baby, even though he was Angelus at the time. He was surprised to see that the LA production was the exact same performance, right down to the same dancers (*AtS* "Waiting in the Wings").

BLIX | DREW WICKS | Boyhood chum of Lorne's on Pylea. They were the best of buds, always playing games and watching out for each other, and close as a Torto Demon and its parasite. Blix was not happy that Lorne returned for a visit (*AtS* "Over the Rainbow").

BLOOD BANK DOCTOR | **MARY-PAT GREEN** | Los Angeles doctor who singled out healthy donors for Ken, the demon who ran Family Home (*BtVS* "Anne").

BLOOD RITES AND SACRIFICES | Book confiscated from Giles's collection in the Sunnydale High School library by order of Principal Snyder (*BtVS* "Gingerbread").

BLOODSTONE VENGEANCE SPELL | Cast on Buffy by Catherine Madison, this spell hits the body hard, like drinking a quart of alcohol, then eradicates the immune system. Lead, sulfur, a frog, and some kind of diacetate are ingredients in the counterspell (*BtVS* "Witch").

BLUE MAN GROUP | Musical act with performers wearing blue makeup. According to Angel, only two of them are actually demons (*AtS* "The House Always Wins").

BLUSH BEAUTIFUL SKIN CARE AND COSMETICS | Cosmetic company whose products Order of Taraka assassin Norman Pfister offered as free cosmetic samples (*BtVS* "What's My Line? Part 1").

BLUTH, STACEY | Runaway teen victim whose death caused Wesley to take notice of the attacks and Angel's lack of response (*AtS* "Power Play").

BLYTHE | Student at St. Cuthbert's who was a New (Evolved) Vampire working for Drusilla. Faith dusted her (*Angel and Faith* "A Little More than Kin").

BOAL, CHRIS | **CARMINE GIOVINAZZO** | Student who goaded Darla into breaking into Sunnydale High with him. She bit him and dumped him into Aura's locker in the girls' gym (*BtVS* "Welcome to the Hellmouth").

BOB | Vampire member of the Order of Aurelius who participated in the attempt to raise the Master. He was dusted when Buffy attacked the group during the ritual (*BtVS* "When She Was Bad").

BOB, POLICE CHIEF | **BRIAN REDDY** | Sunnydale's chief of police who colluded with Principal Snyder (*BtVS* "School Hard"), the city council, and the Mayor (*BtVS* "I Only Have Eyes for You") to cover up the supernatural reasons for many of the murders and crimes that occurred in Sunnydale.

BOBBY | **SAM LITTLEFIELD** | College student. When vampires kidnapped him from a dorm party, they asked him to choose whether to save himself or his girlfriend. He chose himself but fled with his girlfriend when Angel attacked (*AtS* "Heartthrob").

BOBBY | **SEAN P. YOUNG** | Member of Gunn's gang who died from battle wounds (*AtS* "War Zone").

BOCA DEL INFIERNO | Spanish name for Sunnydale, translated as "The Mouth of Hell" (*BtVS* "The Harvest"). (See: Hellmouth)

BOGARTY, MR. | Previous owner of the Magic Box who was murdered by Harmony's gang of vampires (*BtVS* "Real Me").

BOHG'DAR DEMON | **BRETT WAGNER** | Three-horned demon with droopy skin (*AtS* "Salvage").

BOINTONS, THE | Wealthy family in Los Angeles whose eldest son, Derek, was murdered, leading a family friend to hire the Angel Investigations team to investigate (*AtS* "Happy Anniversary").

BOLUZ | One of two Old Ones who sent Urkonn to train Melaka Fray so that she would defeat her twin brother, thus clearing the path for their own planned apocalypse (*Fray* "All Hell").

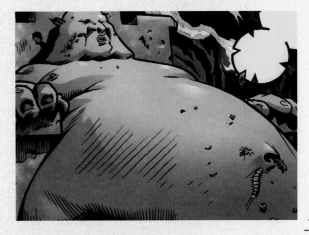

BON | Original religion of Tibet that focuses on the spiritual life in ordinary things like rocks, trees, and water. Oz learned to channel the wolf by letting the energy pass through himself and into the earth, the sky, and the living plants (*Buffy* "Retreat").

BOOK OF TARNIS | Text the Watchers Council consulted to discover Glory's origins as a Hellgod (*BtVS* "Blood Ties").

BOOKS OF ASCENSION | Essentially the "manuals" for how to conduct an Ascension (*BtVS* "Enemies"). Faith murdered the demon Skyler to get them for the Mayor (*BtVS* "Choices").

BOONE | MARK ROLSTON | Gray-skinned, red-eyed former enemy of Angel who claimed they had a falling out over a woman in Juárez in the 1920s. Boone projected metal cords to reinforce his fists. Angel used him to expose Wolfram & Hart's fundraising scheme at the East Hills Teen Center (*AtS* "Blood Money").

BOONE | RICK STEAR | Follower of Adam who entered the church Riley attended in Sunnydale and took the congregation hostage. Buffy staked him from behind as he prepared to attack Faith (*BtVS* "Who Are You?").

BOOST BARS | Brand of energy bar sold by Xander that came in three flavors: cherry-berry, maple walnut, and almond licorice (*BtVS* "The I in Team").

BORBA, ANDREW | GEOFF MEED | As a human, Borba was wanted for questioning in a double murder. He was sired when members of the Order of Aurelius attacked the bus he was a passenger on. Taken to a local funeral home, his bizarre religious spouting led Buffy and Giles to assume that he was the prophesied Anointed One. After he attacked Owen Thurman, Buffy tossed him into the crematorium and he was destroyed (*BtVS* "Never Kill a Boy on the First Date").

BORETZ DEMONS | Foul-smelling demons with a poisonous bite that dressed as transients to attack homeless people (*AtS* "Power Play").

BOSH M'AD | Opposers of the awakening, they fought the Beast's acolytes in the third century. They created the Tooth of Light to defeat the Beast (*AtS* "Awakening").

BOX OF GAVROK | A deceptively small wooden box containing hundreds of large magical spiders that the Mayor had to eat as part of the process of Ascension (*BtVS* "Choices").

BOYER, ROBERT | Reporter for the *Sunnydale Press* (*BtVS* "Smashed").

BRACHEN DEMONS | Rumored to have a good sense of direction, they are capable of twisting their necks far enough to look broken (*AtS* "Hero").

BRAEBURN, HOLLY (TRAMPO) | Classmate of the Slayer who became the underground decoy Buffy. She was involved with Mike Billenger (*Buffy* "The Long Way Home").

BRAHMA, THE | Zen demon who joined D'Hoffryn's Magic Council after the end of magic (*Buffy* "Welcome to the Team"). He first repelled, and then aided the Slayer's attempt to enter the Deeper Well and survived Severin's attack (*Buffy* "The Core"). After the restoration of magic and the parceling out of powers among the members of the Magic Council, he acquired the ability to detect a foe's greatest weakness. D'Hoffryn killed him to gain this magical talent (*Buffy* "In Pieces on the Ground").

BRANCH, MICHELLE | HERSELF | Singer who performed at the Bronze (*BtVS* "Tabula Rasa").

BRANDT, INSPECTOR | Member of the City of London Police who helped Angel when he became the unofficial sheriff of Magic Town. Brandt gave Angel information on Corky Smallwood (*Angel and Faith* "Where the River Meets the Sea"); assisted on cases involving Amy Madison and the Evolved Vampire, Parnell (*Angel and Faith* "Lost and Found"); and pretended to help Faith and

Fred investigate the vampire murders at St. Cuthbert's Private School (*Angel and Faith* "A Little More than Kin"). Faith dusted him when he was finally revealed as a vampire who served Drusilla and Archaeus (*Angel and Faith* "A Tale of Two Families").

BREATH OF THE ENTROPICS | Ritual to destroy the Box of Gavrok. Ingredients and equipment include essence of toad, twice-blessed sage, a pedestal, and an urn (*BtVS* "Choices").

BREKENKRIEG GRIMOIRE | Magical text located in the Magic Box, used by Tara to determine if Buffy came back "wrong" after being resurrected (*BtVS* "Dead Things").

BRENDA | Secretary at the museum where Niles Weatherford worked. Drusilla made her call Weatherford to learn the whereabouts of the magical golem and then murdered her (*Angel and Faith* "A Tale of Two Families").

BREWER, VANESSA | **JENNIFER BADGER** | Assassin who blinded herself at twenty-one in order to achieve higher awareness. She spent five years in Pajaur studying the Nanjin and used a cane with a hidden knife inside. Represented pro bono by Wolfram & Hart. According to her case file, she was arrested once on a misdemeanor charge and twice for felonies, but had zero convictions. She beat Angel in their first fight, but she was later stabbed and killed by her own cane when Angel turned it on her (*AtS* "Blind Date").

BRIAN | Joyce's last date before she died. He worked at a publishing company (*BtVS* "I Was Made to Love you").

BRIAN | **ERIC BRUSKOTTER** | Zombie who ultimately reunited with his murderous ex-girlfriend when even death would not end his obsession with her (*AtS* "Provider").

BRIAN | **MELIK** | Spike's minion who aided in the search for the Gem of Amarra (*BtVS* "The Harsh Light of Day").

BRIE | **MELANIE SIRMONS** | Young woman Amy Madigan enchanted into flirting with Willow at the Bronze (*BtVS* "Smashed").

BRIE'S GIRLFRIEND | **LAUREN NISSI** | She was unhappy with Brie for flirting with Willow at the Bronze (*BtVS* "Smashed").

BRIGITTA | Loose-Skinned Demon, like Clem, who had plastic surgery to pass as human. She went on a date with Clem (*Buffy* "Predators and Prey").

BRINGER OF CARNAGE, THE | Contender for the position of Demon Lord of Westwood after Charles Gunn killed Kr'ph. Connor beheaded him when he attacked Angel (*Angel* "After the Fall").

BRINGERS (HARBINGERS OF DEATH) | High priests of the First who can conjure spirit manifestations and set them on people to influence and haunt them. They summoned the spirit of the First (*BtVS* "Amends"). Faith and company captured a Bringer and he spoke to them through Andrew, hinting about a weapons cache before Giles sliced his throat (*BtVS* "Touched").

BRINGERS' DAGGER | Razor-sharp, jewel-encrusted weapon of choice for the First's Bringer lackeys (*BtVS* "Lessons").

BRISTOW'S DEMON INDEX | Book that Joyce Summers noticed in the Sunnydale High School library when she went there in search of Buffy (*BtVS* "Bad Eggs").

BRODER | Erin Fray's superior officer on the Haddyn Police Force (*Fray* "The Calling").

BRONCATO, IZZY | LA crime boss who was in competition with Tony Papazian. Broncato's crew worked out at Johnny Red's gym (*AtS* "Sense and Sensitivity").

BRONZE, THE | The only club in Sunnydale worth going to. It was in the bad part of town, which was about a half block from the good part of town (*BtVS* "Welcome to the Hellmouth"). The scene of many vampire and demon battles.

BROOKS, LANCE | BRANDON KEENER | Big man on campus at Sunnydale High when he wore his father's magic letterman's jacket, which was then passed on to his brother, R.J. Their mother was Miss Arkansas in the 1970s (*BtVS* "Him").

BROOKS, R.J. | THAD LUCKINBILL | Sunnydale High School student whose father's enchanted letterman's jacket literally cast a spell over Anya, Buffy, Dawn, and Willow. Buffy and company burned the jacket (*BtVS* "Him").

BROOMFIELD, DETECTIVE | TOM KIESCHE | LAPD investigator who threatened Wesley about a heist at the Natural History Museum (*AtS* "The Shroud of Rahmon").

BROTHERHOOD OF SEVEN | Demons that take on the appearance of young humans. Every seven years they must harvest human organs—including a brain and a heart—to maintain their human appearance. Giles suspected Sid the dummy of carrying out the murders actually committed by the demon appearing as Marc the Magician (*BtVS* "The Puppet Show").

BROWN, AGENT | ERIK BETTS | Former Initiative agent called in when Riley began to deteriorate from withdrawal (*BtVS* "Out of My Mind").

BROWNING'S SONNETS | Poetry book Angel gave Buffy on her eighteenth birthday (*BtVS* "Helpless").

BROWNLEY, DR. | Medical professional at Sunnydale Memorial Hospital (*BtVS* "Blood Ties").

BRUCKER, SENATOR | STACEY TRAVIS | Longtime client of Wolfram & Hart who worked with Holland Manners. She clawed her way up from hell and was installed in a human body, in which she planned to run for the White House in 2008 (*AtS* "Power Play"). Gunn killed her with an axe to the forehead (*AtS* "Not Fade Away").

BRYCE, MAGNUS | TODD SUSMAN | Software and cable-network mogul whose business was a front for wizardry. His great-grandfather created a simple spell for tallness in his garage. Magnus worshipped Yeska, whom he believed to be a goddess, and he was willing to sacrifice his daughter, Virginia, to reap her blessing (*AtS* "Guise Will Be Guise").

BRYCE, VIRGINIA | BRIGID BRANNAGH | Twenty-four-year-old daughter of the wizard Magnus Bryce. She felt trapped by her father and dreamed of running away and getting a little apartment and a mundane job like perfume sprayer or tire salesperson. She was slated for sacrifice by her father, but rejected by the demon Yeska for being impure. Virginia started dating Wesley after he came back to save her (*AtS* "Guise Will Be Guise"). She later broke up with him when she began to understand how dangerous his life was (*AtS* "Reprise").

BUB | Violent, temperamental Anharrans Demon with low self-esteem. Bub accompanied Xander, Dawn, and Rancidus through many dimensions as they searched for Earth. He wound up staying in Bodaceia to repopulate it after Dawn and Xander rehabilitated him (*Buffy* "Own It").

BUCHANAN, TED | **JOHN RITTER** | Originally a dying man whose wife was about to leave him, he built himself a robot body, kidnapped his wife, and held her hostage until she died. The robot then "married" three more wives, stashing their corpses in the closet of a 1950's-style basement "house." As a successful software salesman, Robot Ted courted Joyce Summers, intending to make her wife number five. Buffy fought him and it was assumed that she had killed him until he reactivated and attempted to kidnap her mother. He was destroyed . . . although Willow kept parts to study (*BtVS* "Ted").

"BUD" | **JOHN KNIGHT** | Sunnydale High School student and friend of Cordelia's boyfriend, Mitch. Bud discovered Mitch unconscious in the boys' locker room after the invisible Marcie Ross attacked him with a baseball bat (*BtVS* "Out of Mind, Out of Sight").

BUFFYBOT I | Originally programmed by Warren as a sex toy for Spike (*BtVS* "Fool for Love"). The Buffybot aided in the defeat of Glory (*BtVS* "The Gift") and acted as a guardian for Dawn (*BtVS* "Bargaining, Part 1"). The Hellions demon motorcycle gang destroyed it ("Bargaining, Part 2").

BUFFYBOT MARK II | Andrew transferred Buffy's mind and essence into a second robot body to protect her from harm. As a result, this version of Buffy decided to get an abortion after a mechanical flaw caused it to have a positive result on a pregnancy test (*Buffy* "On Your Own"). Andrew showed the Buffybot Mark II its real body, which had been living a yuppie existence in the suburbs until it was kidnapped and brainwashed by Simone Doffler, and then he successfully transferred her mind back into her actual body (*Buffy* "Apart of Me"). Later, Andrew attempted to transfer Dawn's mind into the Buffybot when Dawn began to die because magic had ended, and Dawn had been magically created (*Buffy* "Welcome to the Team").

I DON'T UNDERSTAND. I'M *ME*. I'M BUFFY. I'M NOT A ROBOT.

BUFFYBOT MARK II

BUG DEMONS | Spike's crew. They include: King KiKK RKKKK Fkkkt (deceased), Bug One (Spike's second), Bug Seven, Paolo, Elizabeth, Frisky, Bub, Lester, Jumpy, Fido, Irene (turned into a space-bug-zombie), Spotty, Rick, Colin, and Sebastian (who sacrificed himself to save the crew from Morgan's ritual) (*Spike* "Stranger Things," "A Dark Place"; *Buffy* "Last Gleaming")

BUILDING MANAGER | CATHY COHEN | Attractive rental agent who came on to "confident Xander" when he was split in two by Toth (*BtVS* "The Replacement").

BURBA WEED | Herb Spike crumbles in blood to "make it all hot and spicy" (*BtVS* "All the Way," "Dead Things").

BURDWIZER | "Duke of All Beers" (*Buffy* "Own It").

BURGE | Demon Lord of Downtown LA who brokered a temporary truce with Angel. Burge's son broke the truce, forcing Angel to kill him, which resulted in Burge's calling for his fellow Lords to unite against Angel. After time was reset, Burge and his son attempted to kill Charles Gunn in the hospital but were warned off by Illyria (*Angel* "After the Fall").

BURKE | WILLIAM OSTRANDER | Wolfram & Hart employee who was Gavin Park's battle commander. He never lost a battle before he invaded the Hyperion. Holtz and the Grapplers killed him (*AtS* "Quickening").

BURKLE, ROGER | GARY GRUBBS | Fred's father from Texas. He was impressed that his daughter knew about demons and didn't care that Angel was a vampire so long as he saved Fred (*AtS* "Fredless"). Roger came to see his daughter in LA and was worried about her life (*AtS* "The Girl in Question").

BURKLE, TRISH | JENNIFER GRIFFIN | Fred's mother, a school bus driver who killed a demon with a bus on her first visit to LA (*AtS* "Fredless"). She was happy to see her daughter in LA again when she and her husband stopped off on their way to a Hawaiian cruise (*AtS* The Girl in Question").

BURKLE, WINIFRED | AMY ACKER | See following page.

BURKLE WYNDHAM-PRYCE WING | Angel renamed a part of the Los Angeles Public Library in Fred's and Wesley's honors after the Senior Partners reset the Fall of Los Angeles (*Angel* "After the Fall").

BURNS, MELISSA | TUSHKA BERGEN | Angel Investigations' first paying customer. She was being stalked by Dr. Ronald Meltzer, a surgeon who had operated on the infected nerve behind her right eye (*AtS* "I Fall to Pieces").

BURNS, STEWART | GEORGE D. WALLACE | Former human turned demon by Anyanka in 1914 as a punishment for philandering. Stewart pretended to be Xander from the future, showing his erstwhile younger self visions of the miserable lives Xander and Anya would endure if they married. Xander dispatched him with a pillar (*BtVS* "Hell's Bells").

BU'SHUNDI RITUAL | Locater spell used to find Cordelia. It required a sacred Hutamin paw (*AtS* "Inside Out").

BUSKI GOLEM | Faith wondered aloud to Giles if this was to be her target when he asked for her help to slay Genevieve Savidge (*Buffy* "No Future for You").

BUTTERFIELD | Dracula's diminutive purple manservant, who bears more than a passing resemblance to the actor Peter Lorre (*Buffy* "Wolves at the Gate," "New Rules").

Burkle, Winifred

FRED | AMY ACKER |

UCLA physics grad student from Texas, who moved to Los Angeles against her father's wishes and worked in the public library. She disappeared through a dimensional portal and spent five years as a slave in Pylea, which deeply affected her emotional state (*AtS* "Over the Rainbow"). Still, despite seeing the true beast inside Angel, she was not afraid, and returned to LA with the gang (*AtS* "There's No Place like Plrtz Glrb"). Her behavior upon her return was odd and jumpy, and she preferred to stay in her room and write on the walls. When she finally saw her parents again, she tried to pretend they weren't real because it would make everything that happened to her real and she was avoiding it. She planned to return home with her parents, but once she was able to save the day, Fred realized she did have a place on the team, that she was not normal anymore, and stayed in LA (*AtS* "Fredless").

Unaware of Wes's feelings for her, Fred eventually began a relationship with Gunn. She tried to bond with Connor, telling him that she had once been lost too, but when she discovered Connor lied to them about Angel's whereabouts, she Tasered him (*AtS* "Deep Down"). Thrilled to have a physics article on quantum particles published in *Modern Physics Review*, Fred was invited to speak at the California Physics Institute, where she reconnected with her PhD adviser, Professor Seidel. Though her professor claimed to want to work with her again, she realized he was the one who sent her through to Pylea and that he'd done it to others. When Gunn wouldn't help her seek vengeance, she turned to Wesley for help opening a portal in Seidel's classroom. Gunn tried to stop her from sending the professor through a portal that would kill him. When she hesitated, Gunn killed the professor for her, but she couldn't look at him afterward (*AtS* "Supersymmetry").

After touching Jasmine's blood, only Fred could see the true Jasmine, and her friends hunted her. She was able to release Angel and then the others from Jasmine's thrall, though she was distressed by the violence Gunn used to keep a little boy from falling under the demon's spell, and she admitted that she didn't want to fight for a world without love and feelings. Gunn reminded her that when she wanted to kill Seidel, she had turned off her emotions and hadn't cared what anyone else said. She admitted that she'd prefer to feel that guilt than nothing at all (*AtS* "Peace Out").

Employed by their former enemy at Wolfram & Hart, Fred wondered if this gray area—helping evil people—was what their lives had become (*AtS* "Conviction"). Spike's continued disappearance and apparent unstable mental state concerned her, reminding her of the time in Pylea and her reentry to LA, so she worked tirelessly to figure out a way to make him corporeal (*AtS* "Hellbound"). Initially attracted to Knox, she eventually turned him down in favor of someone who made her smile. Wesley, long used to being ignored, missed her signals until she finally kissed him (*AtS* "Smile Time"). Intrigued by the sarcophagus Gunn cleared through customs, she touched it, releasing air that infected her. Her organs began to liquefy, and the gang believed she was being hollowed out in preparation to gestate something new. Nothing they tried could stop the transition, so she asked Wes to take her home, to her apartment, where he read to her until she died in Wesley's arms and her body was reborn as Illyria's shell (*AtS* "A Hole in the World").

During the Fall of Los Angeles, Fred appeared on the streets, but she was actually Illyria, who eventually ruled Beverly Hills with Spike (*Spike* "After the Fall"). Afterward, Illyria intermittently manifested both the appearance and personality of Fred, usually when someone was in danger (*Angel* "After the Fall"). When magic was restored, Angel found Fred wandering the streets of Magic Town (*Angel and Faith* "Lost and Found"). Illyria still inhabits her, and when Fred is stressed, Illyria reappears (*Angel and Faith* "United"). She, Faith, and Angel went on a number of adventures, and after the defeat of Drusilla and Archaeus, Fred asserted her place as a member of the family by making potato salad for their victory party (*Angel and Faith* "A Tale of Two Families").

— C —

CADRIA (BLIND CADRIA, DESOLATE QUEEN) | Deity Tara Maclay called upon to make those around her blind and deaf to the presence of demons (*BtVS* "Family").

CAFFREY, COUNTY SUPERVISOR | Victim of the hitman Tony Papazian. Caffrey was found shot in the back of the head, wrapped in plastic, and stuffed in the back of his car (*AtS* "Sense and Sensitivity").

CAGE, NICHOLAS | Actor who plays Angel Cartwright (aka Angel), in the film *Last Angel in Hell* (*Angel* "Last Angel in Hell").

CAHAIR BINSE (THE TRIBUNAL) | The "Chair of Judgment," a tribunal of mystical events that can rise up in our reality whenever it pleases. It claims that "Asylum is not ours to give. Two are chosen to meet in combat. One can save your life. One can take it. This is the ancient law" (*AtS* "Judgment").

CAIN, GIB | **JACK CONLEY** | Werewolf hunter who tracked a werewolf to Sunnydale intending to kill it for its pelt. He wore a necklace composed of eleven werewolf teeth—one for every werewolf he had killed. Cain left town on the Slayer's orders after Buffy destroyed his gun (*BtVS* "Phases).

CALAX RESEARCH AND DEVELOPMENT | Computer research lab that was once the third-largest employer in Sunnydale. It closed the year before the arrival of Moloch, who took it over to create his robot body (*BtVS* "I Robot . . . You Jane").

CALEB | **NATHAN FILLION** | Defrocked priest who began his evil career as a serial killer of women attracted to his charm and religious message. He put himself in service to the First Evil, blowing up the Watchers Council headquarters and sending the Bringers out to kill Potentials wherever they were found (*BtVS* "Dirty Girls"). He paid Debbie, one of Faith's fellow inmates at the Northern California Women's Facility, to kill the Slayer (*AtS* "Salvage"). In Gilroy, California, Spike and Andrew learned that Caleb had located a secret room in the local Catholic mission bearing an inscription on the wall that translated to "It is for her alone to wield" (*BtVS* "Touched"), a reference to the Scythe. In a fury, Caleb killed all the missionaries except for one. Periodically merging with the First, Caleb possessed superhuman strength. With that, he was able to defeat Buffy and company in battle at the Shadow Valley Vineyards, where he also gouged out Xander's left eye (*BtVS* "Dirty Girls"). Once Buffy had possession of the Scythe, she cut Caleb in two, killing him (*BtVS* "Chosen").

Calendar, Jenny

JANNA OF THE KALDERASH PEOPLE | **ROBIA LAMORTE** |

Sunnydale High School computer science teacher and a new arrival to town who came to Rupert Giles's attention when she assisted with the destruction of Moloch (*BtVS* "I Robot . . . You Jane"). Jenny continued to help the Scoobies as she flirted with the less technically-minded Giles, even taking part in the battle against the Master that saved the town from the first of several apocalypses (*BtVS* "The Prophecy"). The technopagan and the librarian eventually admitted their feelings for one another and started dating in spite of the challenges they faced living on a Hellmouth. They separated for a time after Jenny was possessed by Eyghon, a demonic influence from Giles's past (*BtVS* "The Dark Age"). The pair were beginning to rekindle their relationship when it was revealed that Jenny had been sent by her people, the Kalderash Clan, to keep an eye on Angel to make sure that his curse still held. Her refusal to warn Buffy of the pending danger led to the reawakening of Angelus (*BtVS* "Surprise").

As the vampire without a soul began inflicting countless horrors on Sunnydale, Buffy and her friends ostracized Jenny. Giles was the first to warm to her again, but forgiveness was a struggle as Angelus's attacks on the town and the teens increased. Jenny continued to work on a righting the wrong and she successfully translated the Spell of Restoration to give Angelus back his soul, but he murdered her before she could share the news and reunite with Giles (*BtVS* "Passion"). Both Drusilla and the First Evil later used her form to manipulate Angel and Giles (*BtVS* "Amends," "Becoming, Part 2").

CALENDULA | Drug derived from the marigold flower that affects Lorne's psychic ability when taken by the subject of one of his readings (*AtS* "Unleashed").

CALYNTHIA POWDER | Dark-blue substance used by Darla to keep Angel sleeping so she could enter his dreams (*AtS* "Untouched").

CAPO DI FAMIGLIA | Literally the head of the Goran Demon clan. When a Goran Demon becomes heavy with age, his head sags and drops off like a ripe fig. The new body grows out of the old head if the rituals are performed in time. The most recent *Capo* was more interested in profit than chaos but if his head wasn't returned to the family in time, there would be a dangerous power vacuum in LA (*AtS* "The Girl in Question").

CAPTAIN | LEE REHERMAN | Blue-faced demon on Pylea (*AtS* "There's No Place like Plrtz Glrb").

CARIDAD | DANIA RAMIREZ | Potential who helped capture a Bringer and survived the explosion at the armory as well as the Battle of the Hellmouth (*BtVS* "Dirty Girls," Touched," "End of Days").

CARITAS | Karaoke bar and safe haven for demons, run by Lorne (*AtS* "Judgment"). Demons are welcome, but no demon violence is allowed due to a spell placed on the club by the Three Muses. The club was destroyed when the gang returned from Pylea in Angel's car (*AtS* "There's No Place like Plrtz Glrb"). It was shot up again when Gunn's old gang came demon hunting with Gio (*AtS* "That Old Gang of Mine"). It was burned down when Holtz tried to burn out Darla, who gave birth in the alley beside the bar (*AtS* "Lullaby"). Caritas was later rebuilt, but Lorne was with Wolfram & Hart by then and only went by for drinks and the occasional performance (*AtS* "Not Fade Away"). The alley outside Caritas and the whole block is a big, fat interdimensional hotspot (*AtS* "Habeas Corpses").

CARL | Green demon with tusks; employed at Deepscan to train bodyguards (*Buffy* "Guarded").

CARL | **ADAM GORDON** | Self-described "rebel" vampire who hunted on Halloween. Spike shot him with a crossbow (*BtVS* "All the Way").

CARLO | Acolyte of the demon Moloch in Cortona, Italy, 1418. As "reward" for his devotion, Moloch broke his neck (*BtVS* "I Robot . . . You Jane").

CARLO | **NYNNO AHLI** | Wolfram & Hart employee who was head of Lilah's extraction team (*AtS* "Slouching toward Bethlehem").

CARLSON, DETECTIVE JACK | **RICH HUTCHMAN** | Fellow police officer and former friend of Kate's, who went to bat for her when she had problems (*AtS* "Dear Boy").

CARNYSS | Demon who loved muscles and mirrors. Carnyss conducted Praetorian sacrifices prior to his death (*AtS* "Judgment").

CAROL | Joyce Summers's assistant at the art gallery (*BtVS* "I Was Made to Love You").

CAROL | The Mayor's secretary (*BtVS* "Band Candy").

CAROL | **JAN HOAG** | Xander's relative who wore his wedding tux cufflinks as earrings (*BtVS* "Hell's Bells").

CAROLINA'S GRASP | Rudimentary containment spell that Dracula suggested using to find the Japanese vampires (*Buffy* "Wolves at the Gate").

CARTWRIGHT, ANGEL | Nicholas Cage's character in *Last Angel in Hell*, the movie about Angel's exploits during the Fall of Los Angeles (*Angel* "After the Fall").

CATERER GIRL | **SUSANNAH L. BROWN** | Xander's uncle Rory hit on her at Xander's wedding (*BtVS* "Hell's Bells").

CATFISH BOB | Resident of Magic Town, although it is not known if he is a mutant or a demon. He defeated Angel while attacking a mutant girl and her father, but retreated from Amy Madison's shower of flying rocks (*Angel* "Lost and Found"). He later apologized to Angel and offered to buy him a drink, but was rebuffed (*Angel* "A Tale of Two Families").

CATHERINE | Employee at the Doublemeat Palace (*BtVS* "Doublemeat Palace").

CATHERINE | Vampire in the style of Jane Austen who preyed on young aristocrats. She was unaware that her target was a Slayer disguised as a man (*Tales* "Presumption").

CEDRIAN CRYSTALS | Mineral said to contain millennia of stored mystical energy; about the size of a D battery. Priceless (*AtS* "Benediction").

CEDRIC THE SLIME MAN | One of the beings that met with Buffy in San Francisco to discuss the new rules of magic (*BtVS* "I Wish"). He currently serves on the newly re-formed Magic Council (*Buffy* "Own It").

CELIA | **DENISE JOHNSON** | Buffy's cousin, with whom Buffy had been quite close as a little girl. Celia was killed by Der Kindestod in a hospital while Buffy, who was eight years old at the time, looked on helplessly (*BtVS* "Killed by Death").

CELL PHONE | Device that was "cooked up by a bored warlock," according to Angel. They would plague the vampire for years (*AtS* "She").

CENTIPEDE DEMON | Interdimensional demon species that resembles giant flying centipedes. After the birth of the new Seed, they invaded Earth and killed three hundred people in Rome (*Buffy* "In Pieces on the Ground").

CEREBRAL DAMPENER | Spherical device created by the Trio to remove victims' free will and instill them with passion for the Dampener's user. Its creation required the musk gland of a Hombja'moleev Demon and the recitation of a spell (*BtVS* "Dead Things").

CEREMONIAL SANCTEUS DAGGER | Third-century artifact (*AtS* "Fredless").

CHAIN | MAURICE COMPTE | Lieutenant in Gunn's gang (*AtS* "War Zone").

CHALMERS, REVEREND | Nineteenth-century clergyman and guest at a Christmas party attended by Angelus (*BtVS* "Amends").

CHANDLER, RAYMOND | American author who Angel spent five years trying to convince to quit working in Hollywood and write more Philip Marlowe detective stories (*Angel and Faith* "Live through This").

CHANDLER'S AUCTION HOUSE | Establishment firmly rooted in the black market. Guarded by high-tech surveillance, laser sensors, handprint recognition, and armed guards (*AtS* "Ground State").

CHAO-AHN | KRISTY WU | Lactose-intolerant Chinese Potential who speaks only Cantonese. She survived the final battle of the Hellmouth (*BtVS* "First Date," "Chosen").

CHAOS DEMON | KENNETH FEINBERG | Demon described by Spike as "all slime and antlers"; nevertheless, Drusilla left Spike for him (*BtVS* "Fool for Love").

CHARLESTON, HOLLY | Sunnydale High School student who ran for homecoming queen against Cordelia and Buffy. Cordelia as characterized her as a "nice girl, brain-dead, doesn't have a prayer." In Buffy's opinion, her strengths included "straight As" and "always studies," and her weaknesses were "no boyfriend" and "few friends" (*BtVS* "Homecoming").

CHARLOTTE | ROBINNE LEE | Vampire that Spike sired and then killed (*BtVS Sleeper*).

CHASE, CORDELIA (CORDY) | CHARISMA CARPENTER | See following page.

CHAULK, BETHANY | DAISY MCCRACKIN | Telekinetic young woman befriended by and staying with Lilah after the lawyer spoke at her school. Bethany telekinetically shoved a two-ton dumpster against two men who were chasing her, killing them. When her abusive father was mentioned in her presence, or she dreamed of him calling her Rabbit, Bethany's reaction was immediate and violent. When she was finally in a position to punish her father, she refrained from killing him (*AtS* "Untouched").

CHAULK, MR. | GARETH WILLIAMS | Bethany's abusive father, who called her Rabbit (*AtS* "Untouched").

Chase, Cordelia

CORDY | CHARISMA CARPENTER |

The rich queen of mean of Sunnydale High School, Cordelia approached Buffy when she arrived in Sunnydale because she assumed that anyone from Los Angeles had to be cool. Once Buffy befriended Xander and Willow, and Buffy pulled a stake on Cordelia at the Bronze, Cordelia decided Buffy was a loser (*BtVS* "Welcome to the Hellmouth"). Buffy saved Cordelia numerous times, and Cordelia returned the favor when the Master opened the Hellmouth by coming to the rescue with her car (*BtVS* "Prophecy Girl").

Cordelia's place in the Scooby Gang was cemented when she and Xander faced down the Taraka assassin Norman Pfister together (*BtVS* "What's My Line? Part 1"). She and Xander fell for each other in an unlikely pairing, but when she and Oz caught Xander and Willow kissing, she broke up with him. She blamed Buffy as the source of all her troubles and made a wish that Buffy had never come to Sunnydale. The Vengeance Demon Anyanka granted that wish; in the resultant Wishverse, Cordelia was killed (*BtVS* "The Wish"). In the real world, she developed a crush on the new Watcher, Wesley Wyndam-Pryce, but they realized they had no chemistry after their first kiss (*BtVS* "Graduation Day, Part 2").

After Cordelia's family lost their fortune, she left for Los Angles and ran into Angel. Feeling that she was destined for stardom as an actress, Cordelia settled for being Angel's assistant (*AtS* "City of"). She pursued paying clients despite Angel's insistence on the mission coming first. Oblivious to Doyle's attraction until it was too late, she received his gift of visions with his last kiss (*AtS* "Hero"). These visions—at first singly, then in a torrent thanks to the Mark of Vocah—increased her awareness of the suffering around her. She realized that Wesley and Angel were her family now, and she tried to help and protect them, adding Gunn, Lorne, and Fred to her circle. The visions became a torment, as a human was never intended to bear them. When she chose to keep the visions instead of pursuing a life of stardom, the Powers That Be made her part demon so she could cope (*AtS* "Birthday").

The arrival of baby Connor coincided with her growing attraction to Angel, but Groo's arrival from Pylea distracted her. Her demon powers allowed her to heal Connor but drew her away from Groo. When she was finally ready to confess her love for Angel, the Powers interrupted and elevated her to a higher plane (*AtS* "Tomorrow"). When she returned to the gang, her memory was wiped; she befriended Connor for his honesty and eventually became pregnant by him while under the influence of Jasmine. Eventually it was revealed that the visions, powers, Ascension, return, mastering the Beast, freeing Angelus, and bearing Connor's child were all part of Jasmine's plan to gain entry to this realm, which left Cordelia in a coma. When Angel traded his soul for Connor's and Cordelia's safety, she was given excellent medical care (*AtS* "Home").

A vision of Angel in danger—and losing his way—prompted her to return to his side to guide him through the challenge of Lindsey's return and also to re-inspire Angel to stick with his mission. She reminded him that Doyle sacrificed himself to keep Angel on track. They kissed and she left just as a phone call revealed to Angel that she had actually died without ever waking up from the coma (*AtS* "You're Welcome"). After LA was sent to hell and the sired Gunn severely wounded Angel, Cordelia returned to Earth in ghostly form to escort Angel into the light; when he opted to live so that he could protect Connor, she approved of his decision and departed. However, he occasionally detects her presence as a warm breeze (*Angel* "After the Fall").

CHAVALIER, DANTE | KARIM PRINCE | Knight of Byzantium who took Orlando from the mental ward of Sunnydale Memorial Hospital and assumed command after General Gregor was captured. Dante killed Orlando to prevent him from responding to Glory and allowed Ben Wilkinson through enemy lines to treat Giles's wounds. Glory killed him when she absconded with Dawn (*BtVS* "Spiral").

CHAZ | SULO WILLIAMS | Member of the Alpha Delta fraternity who inadvertently summoned Gachnar the Fear Demon to the frat's Halloween Party (*BtVS* "Fear Itself").

CHEESE MAN, THE | DAVID WELLS | Strangely random man who appeared along with sliced cheese in all four of the dreams of Buffy, Giles, Xander, and Willow after they called upon the First Slayer to defeat Adam (*BtVS* "Restless").

CHEUNG, MIRANDA | Former marine and detective with the San Francisco Police Department who was partnered with Detective Robert Dowling. The two of them deduced that a new kind of vampire had been created after the end of magic (*Buffy* "Freefall"). Miranda was eventually changed into a zompire, and Dowling staked her when she attacked Xander (*Buffy* "On Your Own").

CHINESE SLAYER | MING QIU | Spike killed this Slayer in 1900 in China, during the Boxer Rebellion (*BtVS* "Fool for Love").

CHIP, THE | Nickname for the behavior modification circuitry invented by Dr. Walsh (*BtVS* "The Initiative"). Implanted in Spike's brain, it delivered a debilitating bolt of pain whenever he tried to hurt a human being. After three years, it began to degrade, causing intense pain at random intervals. At the request of Buffy, military doctors removed the Chip (*BtVS* "The Killer in Me").

CHIRAGO DEMON | Species with individuals that can weigh six hundred pounds (*BtVS* "Once More with Feeling").

CHLOE | LALAINE | Potential Slayer who hanged herself (*BtVS* "Showtime," "Get It Done").

CHRISTINE | AMY HATHAWAY | Woman who found out that her fiancé had slept with her sister. Christine had the desire to make a vengeance wish to Anya, but Anya was too busy complaining about Xander to realize it (*BtVS* "Seeing Red").

CHRISTOPHER, WILSON | Not the famous fashion photographer, but an ethno-archaeologist from Brandeis (*AtS* "Expecting").

CHRISTOPHER, WILSON | KEN MARINO | Fashion photographer and gun enthusiast. On his third date with Cordelia, he took her and her friends to the La Brea Lounge, which was hard to get into. He slept with Cordy and impregnated her with the offspring of a Haxil Beast (*AtS* "Expecting").

CHRISTY | DAWN WORRALL | Friend of Justin, the youthful vampire who gave Dawn her first kiss. Giles staked her when she and her friends attacked (*BtVS* "All the Way").

CHUCK | TV journalist reporting on air when interdimensional demons invaded Earth after the new Seed was created (*Buffy* "In Pieces on the Ground").

CHUMASH STONE KNIFE | Ceremonial dagger belonging to the Native American spirit Hus, and the only weapon that could kill him (*BtVS* "Pangs").

CHUMASH WARRIORS | Hus summoned these seven spirit warriors, who attacked Giles's apartment while Buffy and company were having Thanksgiving dinner (*BtVS* "Pangs").

CIRCLE OF THE BLACK THORN, THE | Secret, evil society. They were the machine that kept man's inhumanity to man rolling along. To be a Black Thorn was to be the Senior Partners' instrument on Earth. Lindsey came back to LA to beat Angel and join the Black Thorn. Their initiation chant: "*The Circle entwined. Embrace this worthy son. The thorn draws blood. The thorn is the power, and the power is absolute*" (*AtS* "Power Play"). Their convocation began: "*Of the world's woe, now convene. All is bound by the Circle and its thorns. Invisible, inviolate, we, the seeds of the storm, at the center of the world's woe, now convene.*" They believed the one thing stronger than loyalty was hope, so they required Angel to sign away, in blood, his right to the Shanshu Prophecy. Together the Circle could vaporize Angel and his team, but individually they were just demons that could be—and were—taken down (*AtS* "Not Fade Away").

CIRCLE OF KAYLESS | Protective circle of individuals formed on the internet to bind Moloch the Corruptor (*BtVS* "I Robot . . . You Jane").

CLADDAGH RING | Traditional Irish symbol of devotion that Angel gave Buffy on her seventeenth birthday. The ring consists of a crowned heart embraced by two hands. The style of jewelry originated in Galway, Angel's hometown. He also wears a Claddagh ring (*BtVS* "Surprise"). When Buffy placed it in the spot where she sent Angel to hell, he reappeared (*BtVS* "Faith, Hope & Trick").

CLAIRE | DORIE BARTON | Medium brought in by Eve to help find Spike. Claire made contact with the Reaper instead. Deceased (*AtS* "Hellbound").

CLARE | Severin's girlfriend, who was attracted to the vampire community and asked her friend Alessandra to sire her. She became a zompire, and Severin accidentally killed her when his energy-siphoning power activated (*Buffy* "Freefall").

CLARK, DETECTIVE | CHET GRISSOM | Investigating detective who interviewed the doctor and nurse who were working when Faith woke up from her coma and escaped from the hospital (*BtVS* "This Year's Girl").

CLARNER, PETE | JOHN PATRICK WHITE | Student at the original Sunnydale High School who invented a Jekyll-and-Hyde mixture to make himself more macho. Boiling over with jealousy and rage, he murdered another student, the school guidance counselor, and his girlfriend, Debbie Foley. He attacked Oz and Buffy before Angel killed him by breaking his neck (*BtVS* "Beauty and the Beasts").

CLASS PROTECTOR AWARD | Given to Buffy at the senior prom by Jonathan Levinson on behalf of the graduating class. The award was in gratitude for all the times she saved people, which resulted in the lowest student mortality rate in Sunnydale history (*BtVS* "The Prom"). The colorfully decorated umbrella was deliberately broken by UC Sunnydale student vampire leader Sunday (*BtVS* "The Freshman"). In an alternate reality created by Jonathan, it was he who received the award, given to him by Buffy (*BtVS* "Superstar").

CLAUDIA | Little mutant girl who was menaced by Catfish Bob and rescued by Amy Madison (*Angel and Faith* "A Tale of Two Families").

CLAUDINE | Slayer during the French Revolution who was tricked into killing a human aristocrat by her Watcher, Jean (*Tales* "The Innocent").

CLAW GUY | Vampire who cut off his hand in penance because he displeased the Master. Noticing his terror around the She-Mantis posing as Natalie French, Buffy used him as a tracker when searching for her before staking him (*BtVS* "Teacher's Pet").

CLAY MAN | Human who was turned to clay after the explosion of the plague ball. He attacked Dr. Leishman, demanding a cure. Faith sprayed him with water and moved him to a secure location (*Angel and Faith* "United").

CLEAN, MS. | Originally one of Non's lieutenants, she moved into the Playboy Mansion with Spike and Illyria (*Spike* "After the Fall") and defended Spike against Angel (*Angel* "After the Fall").

CLEANSING SPELL | Binding spell to hold a spirit in one place in order to vanquish them. It requires hawthorn berries, lungwort, and bile. Incantation: *"Bring the truth into the light. Let the villain be revealed so that a soul can take its rightful place for eternity. Adduce veritatum in lucem. Accipiat laura suam requiatam reposcant anima suum regnum"* (*AtS* "Rm w/a Vu").

CLEM, THE LOOSE-SKINNED DEMON (CLEMENT) | **JAMES C. LEARY** | Gentle demon with baggy skin folds, big floppy ears, and tentacle-like appendages that spring out from his face when he wants to threaten an enemy (*BtVS* "Potential"). Spike knew Clem from their regular kitten poker game. Clem became an ally of the Scooby gang after he and Spike crashed Buffy's twenty-first birthday party (*BtVS* "Older and Far Away"). He babysat Dawn when called upon and attended Xander and Anya's aborted wedding (*BtVS* "Hell's Bells"). In Los Angeles he became Harmony's personal assistant, appearing on her reality show, *Harmony Bites* (*Buffy* "Predators and Prey"). After they moved to London, Clem tried to blackmail her with a tape of her siring someone because he loved her. Besides, his kind of demon feeds on embarrassment (*Angel and Faith* "Live through This").

CLEO | **JESSA FRENCH** | Hairstylist in Sunnydale (*BtVS* "Gone").

CLIVE | Warlock and head of a coven that included Julie, who had been a demonology student of Andrew Wells. Because Clive possessed the Asclepian Vial, the Sculptor attacked the coven, and Clive and Julie worked with the Scoobies to defeat him. A passionate victory kiss from Andrew (*Buffy* "Love Dares You") suggested a new relationship, but due to a miscommunication, Andrew ghosted him. Clive attempted to assuage Andrew's hurt feelings and reestablish a relationship of some kind (*Buffy* "Own It").

CLOUDING COUNTERSPELL | A revealing spell. *"Obscurate nos non diutius."* (Translation: Do not conceal any longer) (*BtVS* "The Zeppo").

CLUB COAGULATE | Location where Buffy and Spike met with Vickie to ask for her assistance in dealing with D'Hoffryn (*Buffy* "Own It").

COAMES, ALASDAIR | Retired English Archmage and demon biology expert who is an old friend to Giles. Alasdair participated in the 1970 murder of Pearl and Nash's children in Nebraska (*Angel and Faith* "Family Reunion") and fought in the Ley Line War of 1978 (*Angel and Faith* "Live through This"). He participated in the resurrection of Rupert Giles (*Angel and Faith* "What You Want, Not What You Need") and continues to help Angel by such actions as procuring a Najakot Demon to thwart Amy Madison (*Angel and Faith* "Live through This").

COAT OF ARMS | Round bronze talisman that must be presented to the Tribunal in order to address it (*AtS* "Judgment").

COBRA-FACED DEMON | Humanoid demons with cobra faces. Amy Madison summoned them to attack Command Central in Scotland (*Buffy* "Time of Your Life").

COURTESAN DEMON | Interdimensional species of Succubus Demon, like Morgan, who use physical attraction to lure wealthy targets (*Spike* "A Dark Place").

COLIN | Boy who grew several spider legs after the plague ball explosion (*Angel and Faith* "What You Want, Not What You Need").

COLIN | CHRISTOPHER DOYLE | Vampire minion of the Master who failed to bring the Slayer to him; for this, the Master pierced his eye (*BtVS* "The Harvest").

COLLEEN | RACHEL BILSON | Potential who Xander fantasized about (*BtVS* "Dirty Girls").

COLLIN (THE ANOINTED ONE) | ANDREW J. FERCHLAND | As was prophesied by Aurelius, this great warrior of the Master appeared unrecognized by the Slayer (*BtVS* "Never Kill a Boy on the First Date") and led her to her death at the Master's hands (*BtVS* "Prophecy Girl"). Collin oversaw the attempted Revivification of the Master (*BtVS* "When She Was Bad") and was murdered by Spike (*BtVS* "School Hard").

COLLINS | ALASTAIR DUNCAN | Watchers Council Special Operative sent to apprehend Faith. When she escaped, he was given permission to assassinate her. He failed, both in Sunnydale and in Los Angeles (*BtVS* "This Year's Girl"; *AtS* "Sanctuary").

COLLINS, DR. | Doctor at Sunnydale Memorial Hospital (*BtVS* "Bargaining, Part 2").

COMMAND CENTRAL | Castle in Scotland where Buffy and Xander oversaw the new Slayer Organization (*Buffy* "The Long Way Home").

CONDUIT, THE | Disembodied voices that served a mystical means of addressing the Powers That Be. The Conduit claimed that "We are the gateway, the all the time, the ever." Angel asked them to free Cordelia from her painful visions (*AtS* "Birthday").

CONLEY, MIKE | Gulf War veteran and Bronze Star recipient who was Senator Brucker's challenger in the upcoming political race. Brucker's desire to have Conley portrayed as a pedophile caused Gunn to question Angel's actions (*AtS* "Power Play").

CONNOR (CONNOR ANGEL, CONNOR REILLY, STEVEN FRANKLIN THOMAS HOLTZ, THE DESTROYER) | VINCENT KARTHEISER | See following page.

CONSOLIDATED CURSES | Business owned by someone named Briggs (*AtS* "Guise Will Be Guise").

CONSTRIXI! DEFICIO! PRESSI! | Willow's spell to construct a container for one of the Japanese vampires so he couldn't dissolve into air (*Buffy* "Wolves at the Gate").

CONSUELA | Maid at the Hyperion in the 1950s (*AtS* "Are You Now or Have You Ever Been").

COOPER, JOE | Vampire sired by his mother in dust bowl Nebraska 1933. Joe drained all his cattle and then his friend Sal, hoping to sire her but killing her instead. He turned his farm into an inn to feed on unsuspecting humans (*Tales* "Dust Bowl").

COOPER, JUSTINE | LAUREL HOLLOMAN | Wannabe Slayer whose twin sister was killed by a vampire. Holtz recruited her, intending to use her as an instrument of vengeance (*AtS* "Dad"). She planned to move to Utah with Holtz to raise Connor, but Angel interfered and Holtz left her behind (*AtS* "Sleep Tight"). Justine lied to their followers that Holtz's leaving was part of the plan, and that she would lead them to kill Angel. When they fought, Angel left her alive, which stunned her. She began to realize that Holtz had been lying to her. She confessed to Fred and Gunn that Wesley was innocent of the kidnapping and revealed the part she played. While Sahjhan and Angel fought, she retrieved Holtz's Resikian Urn and used it to trap Sahjhan's essence (*AtS* "Forgiving"). Rescued from a vampire attack by Angel, she saw the grown Connor before running away to find Holtz at the motel and tell him how he hurt her. At his request she killed him (*AtS* "Benediction") and led Connor to believe that it was Angel's handiwork (*AtS* "Tomorrow"). Imprisoned in Wesley's closet, Justine was forced to accompany him on nightly searches of the water for Angel after Connor had dumped him at sea. After retrieving Angel's coffin, she was left cuffed at the dock with the key nearby (*AtS* "Deep Down").

Connor

CONNOR ANGEL, CONNOR REILLY, STEVEN FRANKLIN THOMAS HOLTZ, THE DESTROYER | VINCENT KARTHEISER |

Born of two vampires—Angel and Darla—baby Connor was the center of his father's world (*AtS* "Lullaby"). Wesley tried to save the child from a prophesied death, but Holtz kidnapped Connor and jumped in the Quor'toth dimension (*AtS* "Sleep Tight") where he raised Connor to be a resourceful hunter, using cruel methods to train him. Connor grew up there with the nickname the Destroyer. He forced Sluks (Quor'toth demons) to show him the way back to Earth so he could kill Angel as vengeance for the death of Holtz's family. Angel barely recognized the baby who had been kidnapped a few weeks earlier but returned as an angry teenager (*AtS* "Benediction").

Under the impression that Angel killed Holtz, Connor attacked and subdued his father, leaving the vampire in a coffin at the bottom of the ocean (*AtS* "Tomorrow"). When Angel was found, he forgave Connor for his actions, then threw him out. Connor found comfort in Cordelia and the pair slept together, resulting in her pregnancy and the birth of Jasmine (*AtS* "Rain of Fire," "Salvage"). Connor eventually saw Jasmine for a false god and killed her (*AtS* "Peace Out"). Missing Cordelia, he attempted to take his own life, but Angel made a deal with Wolfram & Hart to give up the son he loved so that Connor could have a fresh, memory-free start with a new family. As Connor Reilly, he had a mother,

Colleen (Adrienne Brett Evans); father, Laurence (Jim Abele); aunt (Stacy Solodkin); sister (Emma Hunton); and a vegan girlfriend named Tracy (*AtS* "Home").

While Connor was a student at Stanford, his new parents brought him to LA to seek Wolfram & Hart's help with some frightening incidents arranged by Cyvus Vail so that Connor could fulfill a prophecy and kill Sahjhan. When the Window of Orlon returned everyone's memories, Connor the Destroyer did kill Sahjhan (*AtS* "Origins") and possibly regained his memory of his past life as well. On the day of the big battle for Los Angeles, Connor arrived at Wolfram & Hart in time to save Angel, but his father sent him away, saying he would be fine so long as Connor was okay (*AtS* "Not Fade Away").

After the Senior Partners sent Los Angeles to hell, Connor, Nina Ash, and Gwen Raiden—with whom Connor had begun a relationship—worked with Spike and Illyria to give sanctuary to humans and good demons (*Spike* "After the Fall"). Upon discovering that Angel was human and mortally wounded, he urged his father to live, and Connor, Spike, and Angel became the only three champions Los Angeles had left. The sired Gunn killed Connor, and Connor died in Angel's arms (*Angel* "After the Fall"). When time reset, Connor was resurrected, but when magic ended, his newly revived false memories of his "normal" family were disappearing again. Connor was willing to risk his happy life to return to Quor'toth and help Willow bring magic to the world again (*Angel and Faith* "Family Reunion"). There, he discovered a cult that worshipped him and refused to leave before saving his followers from the demon who ruled the dimension. Connor returned to Los Angeles to take up his college life again, and his father promised to stay in better touch (*Angel and Faith* "Family Reunion").

COP | ADAM CLARK | Sunnydale sergeant who personally came down to Jonathan's estate when one of Jonathan's staff reported a disturbance (*BtVS* "Superstar").

COP | JASON PADGETT | Police officer who was so distraught over losing Jasmine that he tried to shoot himself, but Connor stopped him. When Connor saw a photo of his family, Connor beat him up for risking it all (*AtS* "Home").

CORDELIA (THE DRAGON) | Originally sent by Wolfram & Hart to kill Angel in the Battle of Los Angeles (*AtS* "Get It Done"), this dragon instead carried a severely wounded, now-human Angel to the Wolfram & Hart headquarters after the city was sent to hell. A pain-wracked Angel maintained his sanity by holding conversations with an imaginary Cordelia, and the dragon thought his own name was Cordelia. He became an ally of Angel's and eventually died in battle fighting Gwen and an entire army of Wolfram & Hart dragons (*Angel* "After the Fall"). When time was reset, the dragon prevented Charles Gunn from being sired and Angel asked the Groosalugg to look after him. Cordelia was also instrumental in driving Wolfram & Hart from Las Vegas (*Spike* "Stranger Things").

CORDELIA (THE HORSE) | Noble steed of the Groosalugg (*Angel* "After the Fall").

CORDY! | The show that might've been, starring Cordelia Chase. The series was a sitcom from an alternate universe Skip created for Cordelia's birthday. Actor credits include Cordelia Chase, Gregory Dunne, Elliott Sims, and Carol Wright. Created by Phlegmont and Mendoza. Theme song lyrics: *"Yes, you can hear it in her laughter. / Ooh, you can see it in her smile. / Yeah, you'll be hanging from the rafters. / Ooh, you better stay awhile. / Ooh, better stay awhile. / Yes, the whole world is full of laughter. / Ooh, you got*

Starring
Cordelia Chase

my heart a little wired. / Yeah, you'll be hanging from the rafters. / Ooh, better stay awhile. / Ooh, you better stay awhile. / Ooh, better stay awhile" (*AtS* "Birthday").

CORI | Dying Slayer whom Willow found in the marsh of the Atchafalaya Basin in Morgan City, Louisiana. She knew Willow from training in Atlanta (*Buffy* "Retreat").

CORTONA, ITALY | Town in the Tuscany region that was the family seat of the demon Moloch (*BtVS* "I Robot . . . You Jane").

COUNT FLOUNCY, THEATER VAMPIRE EXTRAORDINAIRE | Foppish vampire whom Angel was sent to interrogate regarding the deaths of several women. Angel was directed to the weak vampire because the team felt his fighting skills were off and Count Flouncy was a "safe" target. Angel staked him (*Angel* "After the Fall").

COURTNEY THE VAMPIRE SLAYER | New Slayer who took Faith and Rupert Giles to the Slayer Sanctuary in Hanselstadt. Together, they destroyed the demon who kept vampires away from the town in return for a steady supply of children and Slayers. She then joined with Faith, Giles, and the townspeople to fight the vampires (*Buffy* "Predators and Prey").

COVENANT OF TROMBLI | Order of priests that had run Pylea for millennia, effectively as the local branch of Wolfram & Hart. They believed that one with sight—a direct line to the Powers That Be—would return and restore the monarchy (*AtS* "Through the Looking Glass").

COW | Racist term on Pylea, used to refer to human slaves (*AtS* "Over the Rainbow").

CRADLE, JUDAS | Vampire who led a splinter army against the Slayer Organization headquarters in Scotland. A Slayer group led by Leah and Rowena held him off (*Buffy* "Predators and Prey").

CRANDLE, BILLY | Vegan student at the old Sunnydale High School who chained himself to the school vending machines (*BtVS* "I Only Have Eyes for You").

CRANE, JACOB | BRAEDEN MARCOTT | Host of a special dining club in his mansion that centered on eating live supernatural creatures (*AtS* "Unleashed").

CRESTWOOD COLLEGE | School in which Delta Zeta Kappa fraternity members worshipped the reptile demon Machida in their basement (*BtVS* "Reptile Boy").

CRIBB, TOM | MARKUS REDMOND | Lizard-like demon with a long, prehensile tongue who was prisoner of the demon fight club XXI. His official best fight time came during his seventh kill. It was six minutes twenty-two seconds. Lilah Morgan bet $5,000 on him (*AtS* "The Ring").

CROWLEY, BERNARD | Nikki Wood's Watcher. He objected to her being forced to undergo her Cruciamentum while pregnant with her son Robin. After Spike killed Nikki, Bernard moved Robin to Beverly Hills and raised him. He also trained Robin to fight vampires (*BtVS* "Lies My Parents Told Me"; *Buffy* "On Your Own").

CROWN OF COILS | Peruvian magical artifact that could restore dead flesh. Angel and Faith retrieved it with the intention of using it to restore Rupert Giles but were unable to because his body was missing (*Angel and Faith* "Death and Consequences").

CRUCIAMENTUM | Ritual trial conducted for a dozen centuries on the Slayer's eighteenth birthday. Without her knowledge, the Slayer was drained of her powers and forced to survive an ordeal devised by the Watchers Council. This ritual is no longer conducted (*BtVS* "Helpless").

CUP OF PERPETUAL TORMENT | Mystical artifact that was rumored to hold the power to determine which of the two ensouled vampires was the subject of the Shanshu prophecy. It was a fake (*AtS* "Destiny").

CURSE OF THE ELDER WOMAN (ANGEL'S CURSE) | The Elder Woman of the Kalderash tribe used this curse, the original version of the Spell of Restoration, to give Angelus back his soul in 1898 in response to his murder of a young girl in their clan. The spell is recited as *"Nici mort, nici de-al fiintei, Te invoc, spirit al trecerii. Reda trupului ce separa omul de animal! Asa sa fie. Utrespur aceastui."* (Translation: Neither dead, nor of the living, I invoke you, spirit of the passing. Return to the body what distinguishes Man from the beast! So it shall be. Restore this one) (*BtVS* "Becoming, Part 1"). The spell was set to last until Angel experienced a moment of pure happiness, at which point he would lose his soul again and become Angelus (*BtVS* "Innocence"). Frequently discussed, the curse was more like a hex, or a recommendation (*AtS* "Guise Will Be Guise"). It did not make him a eunuch. He could have sex without perfect happiness (*AtS* "Darla"). Wesley reminded Angel that he could pursue a relationship because 99 percent of people settle for less-than-perfect happiness (*AtS* "Smile Time").

CYBORGS | Robot ninja warriors that were previously humans before having their entire systems replaced by cybernetics. They attacked Wolfram & Hart after Angel and team took control of the LA office (*AtS* "Lineage").

CYOPIAN CONJURING SPHERES | Priceless, small red glass balls (*AtS* "Offspring").

CYRUS | TOM LENK | One of Harmony's vampire minions who decided to eat Dawn despite repeated warnings. Buffy dusted him with a crossbow (*BtVS* "Real Me").

CZAJAK, MICHAEL | BLAKE SOPER | Wiccan friend of Willow, whose father beat him for practicing witchcraft (*BtVS* "Gingerbread").

D

DAGGER OF LEX | Small ritual knife stored in the basement of the Magic Box; Buffy skewered the Mummy's Hand with it (*BtVS* "Life Serial").

DAGON SPHERE | Yellow-glowing crystal sphere used to repel and weaken Glorificus the Hellgod (*BtVS* "No Place like Home"). Although Glorificus was able to destroy it, the Sphere caused her significant damage first (*BtVS* "The Gift").

DAIKAIJU | Freighter that transported Vampy Cats to Scotland (*Buffy* "Predators and Prey").

DALTON | **ERIC SAIET** | Intellectual vampire minion of Drusilla and Spike who was instrumental in translating the *du Lac* manuscript (*BtVS* "What's My Line? Part 1"). The Judge burned him to death because of his human qualities, including a love of reading and knowledge (*BtVS* "Surprise").

DANA | **NAVI RAWAT** | New Slayer who was kidnapped and tortured at age ten after the murder of her family. She'd been in a psych ward ever since. Willow's spell to enable all Potentials gave her all the powers of the Slayer, including access to memories of past Slayers. She was taken away by Andrew and the other Slayers (*AtS* "Damage").

DANIEL | **SHANE BARACH** | Young man whom Angelus killed on Christmas in 1838 in Dublin, Ireland. Daniel owed Angelus money from gambling and the vampire took "me winnings in me own way." The First made use of this memory to torment Angel (*BtVS* "Amends").

DANIELS, CYNTHIA | One of Detective Dowling's suspected vampire victims, she was born in Oakland, California, in 1941 (*Buffy* "Freefall").

DANIELS, THEO | Human computer programmer who developed TinCan, a social network for demons trapped on Earth and in other dimensions after the end of magic. Wolfram & Hart funded his work, having him create special coding that opened dimensional portals and kept them open in spite of the destruction of the Seed of Wonder. Grasping how dangerous this was, Theo contacted Deepscan, hiring it to destroy TinCan's servers and protect him from Wolfram & Hart (*Buffy* "Love Dares You").

DANIELS TECHNOLOGIES | After Deepscan successfully shut down TinCan, Theo Daniels offered Willow a job here (*Buffy* "In Pieces on the Ground").

DANNY | **DERRICK MCMILLON** | One of Xander's construction coworkers (*BtVS* "Life Serial").

DAPHNE | Slayer in Faith's London-based Slayer squad (*Angel and Faith* "Live through This," "Death and Consequences").

DARKEST MAGICK | Magic book Giles kept in his "forbidden works" section at the Magic Box. Willow broke it open and cast some powerful spells contained in its pages (*BtVS* "Tough Love").

Darla

| JULIE BENZ |

Wealthy prostitute sired by the Master in Virginia in 1609. He gave her the Anglo-Saxon name Darla, meaning "darling one" (*BtVS* "Becoming, Part 1"; *AtS* "Darla"). She introduced Angelus to the Master in London in 1760, after having cut a bloody swath through South Wales and Northern England. Five years later the vampire hunter Holtz chased her and Angelus through France, where she abandoned Angelus to save herself (*AtS* "Darla"). Almost a century later, Darla arrived in Sunnydale with the Master and assisted him in his plans (*BtVS* "Welcome to the Hellmouth," "The Harvest"). She attempted to pit Buffy and Angel against each other, but Angel staked her.

A few years later, Wolfram & Hart used a ritual in the *Prophecies of Aberjian* to raise her (*AtS* "To Shanshu in LA"). Now human, she assumed the role of DeEtta Kramer to lure Angel into siring her, but failed (*AtS* "Dear Boy"). When it was revealed that she was dying of syphilis—which she'd contracted in her first human lifetime—Angel endured a series of trials to save her, but ultimately failed. She accepted her fate, but Lindsey brought Drusilla in to sire her before she could die (*AtS* "The Trial"). Locked in Holland Manners's wine cellar by Angel, she and Dru killed all the lawyers there except Lindsey and Lilah (*AtS* "Reunion"). Darla had sex with Angel, hoping it would turn him into Angelus. The plan was unsuccessful, but it made her realize that he didn't love her and never had (*AtS* "Epiphany").

Darla wound up pregnant and later confessed that she tried to kill the baby. An ultrasound revealed she was having a son and she was momentarily moved (*AtS* "Quickening"). Emotionally distraught, she revealed that she didn't want to give birth because she loved the baby more than she'd ever loved anything and she knew the feelings she was experiencing came from the baby. Once she delivered the child, she wouldn't remember what it felt like to love. After she learned the baby was dying because her dead body couldn't sustain it, she told Angel that the baby was the one good thing they'd done and she staked herself so Connor could be born (*AtS* "Lullaby").

DAV | SHANNON HILLARY | Member of Sunday's vamp gang who worried that a sweater they had stolen made her look fat (*BtVS* "The Freshman").

DAVE | Member of the Sunnydale public works committee who worked for the Mayor (*BtVS* "Band Candy").

DAVE | One of Xander Harris's uncles, a plumber (*BtVS* "I Was Made to Love You").

DAVE | CHAD LINDBERG | Minion of Moloch who was hung by his coconspirator Fritz for refusing to kill Buffy (*BtVS* "I Robot . . . You Jane").

DAVE | CLINT CULP | Demon bartender in Sunnydale (*BtVS* "Life Serial").

DAVID | Sunnydale High School student in 1955 who helped decorate for the Sadie Hawkins dance (*BtVS* "I Only Have Eyes for You").

DAVIS, MRS. | Neighbor who handed out toothbrushes in Sunnydale on Halloween (*BtVS* "Halloween").

DAY OF THE DEAD (*DIA DE LOS MUERTOS*) | Mexican holiday to celebrate family and friends and those who have departed (*AtS* "The Cautionary Tale of Numero Cinco").

DEBBIE | SPICE WILLIAMS | Prison inmate hired to kill Faith. Deb got her nose broken by the Slayer instead (*AtS* "Salvage").

DEBRETT'S CORRECT FORM | Book describing the etiquette regarding various British peerages and titles (*Buffy* "No Future for You").

DECKER HARDWARE | Store Jack O'Toole and his revenant buddies broke into to get the equipment they needed to build a bomb (*BtVS* "The Zeppo").

DECOY BUFFYS | Two Slayers who served as decoys to protect the actual Buffy. One partied with the Immortal (*AtS* "The Girl in Question"; *Buffy* "The Long Way Home"), and the other died at the hands of Yamanh of Hoht (*Buffy* "The Long Way Home").

DEDICATION, THE | Last step before the Mayor's Ascension. The ritual involved kneeling inside an inverted pentagram, with five candles burning at each point while chanting "*Potestatem matris nostrae in tenebris invoco. Maledictum filium tuum abomni periculo custodias nunc et in saecula!*" (Translation: Our mother of darkness, I summon thee. Curse now your dangerous accursed son and protect him into the new age!) (*BtVS* "Bad Girls").

DEEPER WELL | Burial vault for thousands of sarcophagi of the Old Ones, including Illyria. There were two entrances, one in the Cotswolds in England and one in New Zealand. Members of the Magic Council known as Guardians protected the Deeper Well, but Simone Doffler penetrated the Well, fought the Guardians, and freed Maloker, the progenitor of all vampires. Every dimension contains a Deeper Well (*AtS* "A Hole in the World"; *Buffy* "The Core"). In Willow's Wonderland, it is known as the Wellspring (*Willow: Wonderland*).

DEEPSCAN | Kennedy's bodyguard company that hires Slayers to protect wealthy clients after the end of magic (*Buffy* "Guarded"). Employed Slayers include Rowena, Leah, Mai, Nell, Holly, Tonia Marsh, and Martina. Both Buffy and Faith have worked for Deepscan, although neither has lasted long on staff (*Angel and Faith* "Lost and Found").

DEEVAK | ALAN SHAW | Demon criminal who set up camp in Gunn's territory (*AtS* "First Impressions").

DELEON, COUNT | Eighteenth-century French nobleman killed by the vampire Elisabeth in 1767 (*AtS* "Heartthrob").

DELOTHRIAN'S ARROW | Magical weapon that always strikes its target. The arrow protects good magic. Willow used it to break the Muo Ping (*AtS* "Orpheus").

DELTA ZETA KAPPA | Fraternity at Crestwood College that served Machida. Following the death of the demon, all existing members were given consecutive life sentences for the murders of their sacrificial victims, and many businesses founded and/or run by alums immediately failed, inspiring boardroom suicides (*BtVS* "Reptile Boy").

DE-LUSTING SPELL | Spell that Willow planned to use to get rid of her romantic feelings for Xander. Her ingredients included skink root, essence of rose thorn, and canary feathers, but the owner of the magic shop she went to suggested that she substitute raven feathers to increase the discontent (*BtVS* "Lovers Walk").

DEMARCO, LEE | CLAYTON ROHNER | Former second-rate lounge musician who managed Lorne's Vegas show. DeMarco used the information his client got from reading the audience to steal people's destinies. He offered them on a global black market, while the victim was left with no future and no direction. Lorne destroyed the source of DeMarco's power, returning the destinies to his victims (*AtS* "The House Always Wins").

DEMATORIN | Tranquilizer-like compound Ted Buchanan was putting in the food he served, to keep others mellow and compliant. It shares components with ecstasy (*BtVS* "Ted").

DEMON (HOSTILE SUBTERRESTRIAL) | Supernatural beings native to hell dimensions. Generally they lack souls and are considered evil. They often possess great strength and endurance, as well as powers like teleportation or psychokinesis (*BtVS* "Doomed").

DEMON BARTENDER | **ALAN HENRY BROWN** | Mocked Warren when he bragged that he had shot the Slayer (*BtVS* "Villains").

DEMON LOCATOR SPELL | Spell requiring the summoning of the goddess Thespia with the following chant: "*Thespia, goddess, ruler of all darkness, we implore you, open a window to the world of the underbeing. With your knowledge may we go in safety. With your grace may we speak of your benevolence*" (*BtVS* "Goodbye Iowa").

DEMON RESEARCH INITIATIVE, THE | US government organization that monitored demon activity. Members of the organization approached Angel for help in 1943 (*AtS* "Why We Fight"). It is believed that the organization evolved to become simply the Initiative.

DEMONS, DEMONS, DEMONS | Online database of demons. Does not include Wolfram & Hart (*AtS* "The Ring").

DEMON TEEN | **NICK KOKICH** | Young horned demon who hung out with Dawn at Xander and Anya's wedding (*BtVS* "Hell's Bells").

DEMONTOWN | Demon fight club in Magic Town; when magic ended, vampires became celebrities as fighters (*Angel and Faith* "Live through This").

DENISE | **DARBY STANCHFIELD** | Theater major who was Gene Rainey's ex-girlfriend (*AtS* "Happy Anniversary").

DENVER | **BRETT RICKABY** | Los Angeles bookshop owner from 1952 to 2001. Denver kept the special demon collection, which he used to help Angel, in the back of the store (*AtS* "Are You Now or Have You Ever Been"). Years later, he assisted Angel again when he needed information on the Review. Darla killed him to obtain a magical artifact in his possession (*AtS* "Reprise").

DEPARTMENT OF DEFENSE UNIFIED SUPERNATURAL COMBATANT COMMAND | Military organization formed to fight and neutralize demons and supernatural creatures that invaded the Earth after the Sculptor opened interdimensional portals (*Buffy* "In Pieces on the Ground").

DER KINDESTOD | **JAMES JUDE COURTNEY** | From the German meaning "child death." This humanoid, fairytale-like demon was invisible to adults. Der Kindestod would pin its victims to the ground; then its eyes would extend on stalks, which would clamp onto the victim's forehead and suck out their life force. It killed Buffy's cousin Celia as well as children at Sunnydale Memorial Hospital before Buffy destroyed it (*BtVS* "Killed by Death").

DESERT GNOME | Anya purchased the last existing Urn of Osiris from him on eBay, throwing in a Backstreet Boys lunch box that Xander owned to seal the deal (*BtVS* "Bargaining, Part 1").

DESMOND | **RAY CAMPBELL** | Car thief acquaintance of Gunn who couldn't pass up old cars (*AtS* "First Impressions").

DESTROYER, THE | Bringer of pain, torment, agony, and death. The Sluks warned that it was coming after Angel (*AtS* "The Price"). It was later revealed to be Connor's name in Quor'toth (*AtS* "A New World").

DETWEILER, LENFORD | **MICHAEL MCELROY** | Little boy who loved Jasmine because she made food taste good. He wrote a poem about her (*AtS* "Magic Bullet").

DEVANDIRE SIBYLLINE CODEX, THE | Occult book that is available in the original Sanskrit or translated into English (*AtS* "Home").

DEVIL'S ROBOT, THE (*EL DIABLO ROBOTICO*) | Los Hermanos Numeros had a great victory over it, which never made it into the history books (though Wesley had heard of it) (*AtS* "The Cautionary Tale of Numero Cinco").

DEVLIN | **JIM BLANCHETTE** | Green demon who attended the Wolfram & Hart Halloween bash as a "human bean," wearing the face of a human, along with an argyle sweater and plaid pants. Lorne's alter ego killed him (*AtS* "Life of the Party").

DEVON | Self-appointed Watcher and the boyfriend of Billy Lane. Together they battled zompires to save Billy's grandmother Sky and other civilians. They spent some time in San Francisco with Buffy, but opted to return to their hometown of Santa Rosita, where they continue the fight (*Buffy* "Guarded").

D'HOFFRYN | **ANDY UMBERGER** | Lower being and ruler of Arashmaharr. As leader of the Vengeance Demons, D'Hoffryn recruited Aud in medieval Sweden, transforming her into the feared Vengeance Demon Anyanka. He later incinerated her best friend Halfrek to punish Anyanka for repudiating a wish (*BtVS* "Selfless"). When magic was restored, he created a loophole in the rules drafted by Illyria's mystical council that allowed him to absorb the powers of the other members by murdering them (*Buffy* "Welcome to the Team"). He created a ghostlike double of Anya and forced her to incinerate Xander, then turned his wrath on the other Scoobies. Buffy decapitated him with the Scythe (*Buffy* "Own It").

D'HOFFRYN'S TALISMAN | Brooch-like object that D'Hoffryn offered to Willow as a means of getting in contact with him (*BtVS* "Something Blue," "Selfless").

DIANA | Goddess of love and the hunt. Supplicated by Amy Madison during a Love Spell (*BtVS* "Bewitched, Bothered & Bewildered").

DIANA | **NICOLE HILTZ** | Woman who flirted unsuccessfully with Xander in a bar (*BtVS* "Seeing Red").

DICK, ANDY | Comedian sired by Harmony Kendall in an alley outside Elite, a famous club. The paparazzi photographed the event, thus revealing the existence of vampires to the general public (*Buffy* "Predators and Prey").

DICKIE | **SCOTT TORRENCE** | One of Jack O'Toole's revenant friends (*BtVS* "The Zeppo").

DICKINSON, EMILY | Owen Thurman's favorite morbid poet (*BtVS* "Never Kill a Boy on the First Date").

DIEGO | **ANDRE L. ROBERSON** | Friend of Cordelia's who has a tendency to lose his pants at parties (*AtS* "She").

DIEGO (MARVIN) | **JARRAD PAUL** | Leader of the vampire wannabes who congregated at the Sunset Club. He thought the Lonely Ones (vampires) were going to sire him and his friends, but Spike and his gang planned to kill them. Buffy saved him (*BtVS* "Lie to Me").

DIETRICH, MAJOR | Assumed identity of Nazi-era Slayer Rachel O'Connor (*Tales* "Broken Bottle of Djinn").

DIMENSION | Another universe outside of our own. These different planes of existence can be heaven or hell dimensions or simply considered alternate universes.

DINGOES ATE MY BABY | Oz's band (*BtVS* "Inca Mummy Girl").

DINZA | RENA OWEN | Dark demigoddess of the lost, and one of the Eleusian mysteries. Only the dead can enter her presence, and those that do are often trapped for eternity. Dinza knows all lost things, including lost love. She wanted to keep Angel with the other dead things she collects, but she released him (*AtS* "Ground State").

DISENCHANTING CEREMONY | Ritual used to render the Band of Blacknil useless (*AtS* "Epiphany").

DIVINE INTERVENTION | It's less likely than winning the lottery six times in a row. Lilah ran the numbers (*AtS* "Calvary").

DIXON | JORDI VILASUSO | Initiative soldier who tried to keep Buffy and company under arrest, until Buffy knocked him unconscious (*BtVS* "Primeval").

DJINN | Genie in a bottle released in 1937 by OSS agent Karl Mueller. The Slayer, Rachel O'Connor, inadvertently rebottled it. It escaped again when Principal Snyder purchased the lockers that the bottle was stored inside. Willow sent it through a portal (*Tales* "Broken Bottle of Djinn").

D'KORR | One of two demon assassins sent by D'Hoffryn to kill Anya (*BtVS* "Get It Done").

DOC | JOEL GREY | Human-looking demon with a short tail and a very long tongue who advised Dawn and Spike on the proper ritual for raising Joyce Summers from the dead (*BtVS* "Forever"), then later revealed himself as an acolyte of Glory the Hellgod (*BtVS* "The Weight of the World"). Doc began Dawn's bloodletting in the ritual that opened the portal between the dimensions before Buffy pushed him off the tower (*BtVS* "The Gift").

DOCTOR | MICHAEL WARREN | Mental institution employee who worked to convince Buffy that her life in Sunnydale was a result of schizophrenia and that to get better she needed to kill those who lived there (*BtVS* "Normal Again").

DODGE DESOTO FIREFLITE | Circa-1958 car that Spike drove in Sunnydale (*BtVS* "School Hard").

DOFFLER, SIMONE | One of the New Slayers created after Buffy shared her power; she was a member of the Chicago squad until Rona shipped her off to Italy to "soften her rough edges" (*Buffy* "The Long Way Home"). Simone formed a gang of rogue Slayers and took over an Italian island, offering to trade a Ragna Demon for Andrew Wells, who had been her Watcher (*Buffy* "Predators and Prey"). She attempted to kill Buffy, unaware that Andrew had transferred Buffy's mind into a robot body to keep her safe (*Buffy* "On Your Own"). Colluding with Severin, she opened the New Zealand side of the Deeper Well and awakened Maloker, who sired her as a supervampire. In a battle to the death, Buffy staked her with the Scythe (*Buffy* "The Core").

DOLL'S EYE CRYSTAL | Powerful crystal used in spell casting. Tara found one in her attic and guessed that it had belonged to her grandmother. She offered it to Willow as a token of her affection (*BtVS* "The Initiative").

DON | **WILLIE GARSON** | Hospital security guard Cordelia distracted so Xander could retrieve Dr. Backer's file from the Sunnydale Memorial Hospital records room (*BtVS* "Killed by Death").

DONNA | New Slayer and leader of the Barcelona cell (*Buffy* "The Long Way Home")

DOWLING, ROBERT | Originally a homicide detective in the San Francisco Police Department, he began to suspect that a series of dead bodies bearing no signs of trauma were actually vampires (*Buffy* "Freefall"). He brought Buffy in for questioning and mounted a manhunt for her after she escaped. Robert found her with Spike at the mercy of Severin, who was draining them of their powers, and shot Severin dead (*Buffy* "Freefall"). Intrigued by all he had seen, Robert asked to go on ride-alongs with Spike (*Buffy* "On Your Own"). He eventually became the leader of the San Francisco Police Department Vampire Task Force to battle the new zompires (*Buffy* "Guarded"). Robert was bitten by a zompire but not turned (*Buffy* "Welcome to the Team"), and continues to assist Buffy and company whenever possible.

DOWNS, SOPHIE ("DIE EINSAME" [THE LONELY]) | Child vampire masquerading as a Watcher-in-training who was discovered by Edna Fairweather and beheaded by the Watcher Dunworthy (*Tales* "Tales of the Vampires, Part 5").

DOWNTOWNER APARTMENTS | Faith's home in Sunnydale. Her apartment was number three (*BtVS* "The Zeppo").

DOXIMALL | Powerful tranquilizer that induces bliss (*AtS* "Eternity").

DOYLE, AGENT | One of two FBI agents who took Marcie Ross away (*BtVS* "Out of Mind, Out of Sight").

DOYLE, ALLEN FRANCIS | **GLENN QUINN** | See following page.

DOYLE, HARRIET (HARRY) | **KRISTIN DATTILO** | Doyle's wife; an ethno-demonologist who has been to Kiribati, Togo, and Uzbekistan. They'd been separated for four years when she got engaged to Richard Straley, whom she met while studying clans in South America. She arrived in LA to get Doyle to sign their divorce papers. Once she discovered Richard's family was about to sacrifice Doyle due to a tradition they no longer follow, she gave Richard back his ring (*AtS* "The Bachelor Party"). She remained in Los Angeles, but she and Doyle agreed they needed some space (*AtS* "Hero").

DO YOU INK I'M SEXY | Tattoo parlor where Harmony, Clem, and Soledad met. Soledad agreed to appear as an extra at Harmony's reality show, partly in order to stake her (*Buffy* "Predators and Prey").

DRACONIAN KATRA | Magical object looped through the thumb and fingers; clasping the hand of another person while wearing it causes the two people to swap bodies. Mayor Wilkins left it for Faith after he died. After Faith swapped bodies with Buffy, she destroyed it (*BtVS* "This Year's Girl").

DRACULA | **RUDOLF MARTIN** | The Prince of Darkness, who went to Sunnydale in hopes of siring Buffy. Anya hung around with him back in the day. Although Buffy defeated him, he did not die the True Death, and still owes Spike's eleven British pounds (*BtVS* "Buffy vs. Dracula"). Xander and Renee visited Dracula to discover why the Japanese goth vampires could turn into mist, wolves, bats, night panthers, and bees, getting Dracula to confess

Half-demon, half-human on his mother's side, he had blue spikes and green skin when in demon form. Sent by the Powers That Be to make sure Angel didn't lose the human connection as he atoned for his sins. Doyle directed Angel to souls in need through the visions the Powers That Be sent him in the form of migraines with pictures, a name, or a face (*AtS* "City of"). Doyle was stronger in demon form, though he preferred not to fight that way. He married Harry when they were teens, and when he turned 21 his demon side manifested itself (*AtS* "The Bachelor Party"). After he'd left Harry due to the visions and discovery of his demon half, he was visited by a demon named Lucas, who explained that they were both half Brachen demons, and they are despised by pure-breed demons like the Scourge. Doyle wasn't brave enough to help hide Lucas and others fleeing the Scourge and they were killed. He'd regretted that lack of heroism. Doyle sacrificed himself to turn off the Scourge beacon before it killed the Lister refugees, Cordelia, and Angel (*AtS* "Hero"). His first and last kiss with Cordelia passed his gift of visions to her before his death (*AtS* "Parting Gifts").

that he lost his powers to them in a poker game (*Buffy* "Wolves at the Gate"). Dracula accompanied Buffy's team to Japan and participated in the successful battle against the vampires there. Later, in San Francisco, he placed Xander under his thrall again and they stole the *Vampyr* book. Xander wrote in the book that Dracula became the most powerful vampire who ever lived, which transformed Dracula into Maloker the Old One, from whom all vampires are descended. He begged to be killed so that he would not harm his friends, and was defeated and dusted, then re-formed (*Buffy* "New Rules"). Dracula currently serves on the re-formed Magic Council (*Buffy* "Own It").

DRACULA'S SWORD | Ancient weapon with a double blade and a thick metal hilt decorated with Chinese and European elements. It has a distinctive wing-shaped crossguard, and it is linked to a demonic spirit, much in the same way as the Slayer Scythe. It can be used to remove mystical powers (*Buffy* "Wolves at the Gate").

DRAGOMIR | Romanian warlock who sent Oz to the monks in Tibet to learn to control his wolf side (*Buffy* "Retreat").

DRAGON'S COVE MAGIC SHOPKEEPER | RICHARD ASSAD |
Store owner who affected a mysterious persona for the average
lookie-loo customer, but dropped the act when Jenny Calendar
asked for an Orb of Thessulah, recognizing her as someone "in the
trade." He knew her uncle and called her "Janna" (*BtVS* "Passion").

DRAKE, LUCIEN | Evil warlock and a cult leader with over a
thousand followers who sold most of their children down the
Hades River in return for some serious demonic mojo (*AtS*
"Soul Purpose").

**DREADHOST'S COMPENDIUM OF IMMORTAL LEECHES,
THE** | Book Wesley could summon in the Wolfram & Hart
research library (*AtS* "A Hole in the World").

DREXTALCORP RECYCLING TECHNOLOGIES | Secret military
facility where Ethan Rayne, Amy Madison, and Warren Mears
were kept (*Buffy* "The Long Way Home").

DR. DEBI | In high school, Cordelia used to read her columns on
relationship advice (*BtVS* "Reptile Boy").

DROGYN (BATTLEBRAND, DEMONBANE, TRUTHSAYER) | ALEC
NEWMAN | The Keeper of the Well who was given eternal youth
a thousand years ago. He had to tell the truth when asked a
question (*AtS* "A Hole in the World"). Drogyn could track
anyone who had ever been to the Well. He was ultimately turned
over to the Circle of the Black Thorn, where Angel drank from
him and killed him as an initiation rite (*AtS* "Power Play").

DROKKEN BEAST | Gray-skinned creature from Pylea that had
poisonous venom and was powerless against a weapon dipped in
thromite. Angel was considered a hero back on Pylea for killing
the creature (*AtS* "Belonging").

DROWNING BOY | The manifestation of a little boy Genevieve
Holt "baptized" in the bath tub of Lowell House (*BtVS* "Where
the Wild Things Are").

DRUMMOND, LAURIE | JENNIFER HIPP | Teacher's assistant
to California Physics Institute Professor Oliver Seidel
(*AtS* "Supersymmetry").

DRUSILLA (DRU, MOTHER SUPERIOR) | JULIET LANDAU |
See following page.

DU LAC CROSS | One of several beautiful crosses created by
Josephus du Lac at the turn of the twentieth century that serves
as a decoder of the *du Lac* manuscript. Sheathed inside the cross
is a blade that Spike used to pierce Angel's and Drusilla's bound
hands and thereby transfered Angel's blood into Drusilla to heal
her (*BtVS* "What's My Line? Part 2").

DU LAC MANUSCRIPT | Book containing "rituals and spells
that reap unspeakable evil," including a rite to restore a weak
and sick vampire back to full health. It was written in archaic
Latin so no one except those in du Lac's religious sect could
understand it. The manuscript was stolen from the Sunnydale
High School library on Spike's order (*BtVS* "What's My Line?
Part 2").

DUNCAN | NATHAN BURGESS | Crooked cop who participated in a
setup to kill Faith (*BtVS* "Empty Places").

DUNWORTHY | Watcher and teacher at the Watchers Academy
when Edna Fairweather was a student (*Tales* "Tales of the
Vampires, Part 2").

DUPREE, TOBIAS | BRYCE MOUER | Demon rights activist
who negotiated a truce between Vinjis and Sahrvin. He met
Harmony in a bar, told her he was an astronaut, and went
home with her. Tamika, a Wolfram & Hart employee, killed
him to frame Harmony for the murder (*AtS* "Harm's Way").

Drusilla

DRU, MOTHER SUPERIOR | JULIET LANDAU |

Once a gentle, young Catholic woman living in Victorian England, Drusilla possesses second sight, which she and her mother viewed as an evil curse. She visited a priest nearly every day to keep herself pure. In 1860 Angelus, having murdered her priest in the confessional, listened to her outpourings and targeted her with the specific objective of driving her crazy. On the night she was to take her holy vows, he murdered all the nuns and sired her (*BtVS* "Angel"). In 1880 Darla, who was her grandsire, encouraged her to sire a companion, and Drusilla chose Spike (*BtVS* "Fool for Love"). She was tortured in Prague (*Tales* "The Problem with Vampires") and Spike rescued her. They then went to Sunnydale (*BtVS* "School Hard"). Her visions often presaged schemes designed to destroy Buffy (*BtVS* "What's My Line? Part 1"). She was stunned when Spike betrayed Angelus to the Slayer, even though the bargain was made partly to save her from being sucked into hell (*BtVS* "Becoming, Part 2").

Drusilla left Spike for a Chaos demon (*BtVS* "Lovers Walk") but returned to Sunnydale after Darla was resurrected, wishing for Spike to rejoin their family (*BtVS* "Crush"). In LA, Lindsey took her to Darla's motel room, where she sired Darla in front of Angel. She now considered her grandmother Darla to be her baby (*AtS* "The Trial"). When confronted, Drusilla told Darla she turned her because she thought that was what Darla wanted. Together, they went on a killing spree, including the lawyers in Holland's wine cellar (*AtS* "Reunion"). While she helped Darla recruit demons for an army, she was plagued by visions of an angry Angel coming after them. Once burned by Angel, whom she didn't recognize anymore, she left LA (*AtS* "Redefinition").

Drusilla eventually became known as Mother Superior after a Lorophage Demon sucked out her pain and trauma, turning her sane. She offered this treatment to others, including Faith. When Angel killed the demon, she went insane again (*Angel and Faith* "Daddy Issues"). Wolfram & Hart later discovered that she had been lucid and attempted to use her against Spike, but her lover, John, stole Spike's soul. Spike diverted that soul to Drusilla, and it drove her insane again (*Spike* "After the Fall"). When last seen, she had become the lieutenant of Archaeus, the head of her vampiric line, and fought with him when he attempted to take over Magic Town. When he was defeated, she fled (*Angel and Faith* "A Tale of Two Families").

DURSLAR BEAST | Subterranean creature with a lot of sound and fury signifying nothing. Bugs laid their eggs in its head, which drove it to behave erratically and go above ground. Angel cut its head off and brought it back to the hotel where Fred released the bugs back to their hive once she realized what had occurred (*AtS* "Fredless").

DURTHOCK | Child-eating demon who sang at Caritas when he was searching for the Gorrishyn mage that stole his power. He was feeling just a little bit country (*AtS* "Judgment").

DUST | Colloquial term for killing a vampire, born from the fact that their bodies turn to dust upon death.

DWAYNE AND DELL | Two guys who tried to pick up Sheila Martini; Spike killed them (*BtVS* "School Hard").

DWYER, SEAN | **SHANE WEST** | Member of the swim team at the original Sunnydale High School who explained to Xander that the coach's special steroid mixture was in the steam. He changed into a Gill Monster (*BtVS* "Go Fish").

E

EARL | Security guard at the LA Natural History Museum (*AtS* "The Shroud of Rahmon").

"EARLY ONE MORNING" | Song Spike's mother sang to him when they were both alive; it was the trigger created by the First to make Spike kill and to sire vampires (*BtVS* "Sleeper"). Robin Wood played it after trapping Spike in a garage full of crosses, so that he would be wearing his demon face when Robin intended to beat him to death for killing his mother, the Slayer Nikki Wood (*BtVS* "Lies My Parents Told Me").

EAST END | Area of London in which Drusilla grew up (*Angel and Faith* "Daddy Issues").

EAST HILLS TEEN CENTER | Youth shelter in the Crenshaw district of Los Angeles that was a client of Wolfram & Hart. It was run by Anne Steele (*AtS* "Blood Money").

EATER DEMON | THOMAS CRAWFORD | Client of Lorne's who had a habit of snacking on humans. Connor killed him when he attacked Cordelia (*AtS* "Slouching toward Bethlehem").

ED | JEFF YAGHER | Grand Potentate of the Fell Brethren (*AtS* "Power Play").

EDDIE | PEDRO BALMACEDA | UC Sunnydale freshman Buffy chatted with as they tried to figure out the way to Dunwirth Hall, which was Eddie's dorm. He always kept *Of Human Bondage* with him. The fact that the book was still in his nightstand clued Buffy that he had not left school voluntarily when he disappeared, despite the note he left and the fact that all his other belongings were missing. She subsequently discovered that he had been sired and had to stake him (*BtVS* "The Freshman").

EDMUND | Vampire whom Buffy speed-dated at Murphy's Bar. He was attracted to her because of her history with Angel and Spike (*Buffy* "Love Dares You").

EDO | Gunther's diminutive bodyguard (*Fray* "Big City Girl"). He was killed by one of Harth Fray's lackeys (*Buffy* "Time of Your Life").

EDWARDS, LENNY | JOE BASILE | Human blackmailer with a demon bodyguard (*AtS* "War Zone").

EGGBERT | Buffy's nickname for her Bezoar egg baby (*BtVS* "Bad Eggs").

E. J. | Getaway driver who set up work for Gunn's cousin Lester (*AtS* "The Shroud of Rahmon").

EKAJATI | One of three wrathful Tibetan goddesses who wreaked havoc after being invoked by Willow during the Battle of Twilight (*Buffy* "Retreat," "Last Gleaming").

ELDER | JAMES HENRIKSEN | A Lister Demon with a high-ranking position among his people (*AtS* "Hero").

EL ELIMINATI | Fifteenth-century vampire dueling cult whose members became acolytes of the demon Balthazar (*BtVS* "Bad Girls").

ELIGOR | Being to whom Spike supplicated during the ritual to restore Drusilla back to health. Described as "bringer of war, poisoners, pariahs, grand obscenity. Great master of decay" (*BtVS* "What's My Line? Part 2").

ELISABETH (LISBETH) | KATE NORBY | Vampire who—along with her boyfriend, James—traveled with Angelus and Darla through Marseilles in 1767 until they were separated by the vampire hunter Holtz. Over two hundred years later, Angel staked her to stop a killing spree in Los Angeles, causing James to vow revenge (*AtS* "Heartthrob").

ELITE | Los Angeles night club Harmony tried to get into with her dogs (*Buffy* "Predators and Prey").

ELLIOT | CHASEN HAMPTON | Juggler in the Sunnydale High talent show (*BtVS* "The Puppet Show").

ELLIOT | TOM IRWIN | Wealthy collector who hired Gwen Raiden to steal the Axis of Pythia for his private collection (*AtS* "Ground State").

ELLIS, DR. | Employee of Zane Pharmaceuticals under Reese Zane's supervision. Ellis was charged with researching cures for the effects of the mutants created by the plague ball. He also experimented on Fred Burkle to figure out a way for her to control Illyria (*Angel and Faith* "United").

ELLIS, MAJOR | NICK CHINLUND | US Army officer who oversaw operations related to the Queller Demon (*BtVS* "Listening to Fear") and later recruited Riley Finn to rejoin the army and go on special ops stopping monsters rather than experimenting on them (*BtVS* "Into the Woods").

ELSTER, HARLAN | TONY PASQUALINI | Owner of a printing company whose identity was stolen by his former employee, Sam Ryan (*AtS* "Provider").

ELYSIUM | Password to Wesley's vault. The name is derived from an afterlife reserved for those chosen, righteous, and heroic, according to some Greek sects (*AtS* "Lineage").

EMIL | TREVA ETIENNE | Weapons dealer Wesley did business with when he was a solo act. Arranged a deal to buy weapons from Wolfram & Hart through Wesley. Robot ninjas broke his neck (*AtS* "Lineage").

EMILY | Doublemeat Palace employee who was devoured by the Wig Lady (*BtVS* "Doublemeat Palace").

EMILY | KRISSY CARLSON | Dancer in the Sunnydale High talent show whose heart was removed by a demon. Cordelia claimed that she was best friends with the girl and mourned her death, while referring to her incorrectly as Emma (*BtVS* "The Puppet Show").

EMILY | LOUISETTE GEISS | Cordelia's friend who was impregnated by the procrea-parasitic Haxil Beast (*AtS* "Expecting").

ENDER DEMONS | Creatures who resemble the Old One Cthulhu to an extent. They completely obliterate their victims by consuming their souls. Spike and Faith killed a nest of them in London to obtain the Essuary (*Angel and Faith* "Death and Consequences").

ENJOINING SPELL | Magic that joined Xander, Willow, Giles and Buffy into one being to fight Adam. It required tarot cards, candles, and a gourd. The chant: *"The power of the Slayer and all who wield it. Last to ancient First, we invoke thee. Grant us thy domain and primal strength. Accept us in the power we possess. Make us mind and heart and spirit enjoined. Let the hand encompass us. Do thy will. By the generous will of the Ancients, the almighty power of the Divine Spirits, your supplicants humbly beseech thee to behold us, and that which we possess . . . the moieties of the One, the Avatar. Spiritus, spirit. Animus, heart. Sophus, mind. And Manus, the hand. We enjoin that we may inhabit the vessel, the hand, daughter of Sineya, first of the ones. Admit us. Bring us to the vessel! Take us now! We are heart, we are mind, we are spirit. From the raging storm, we bring the power of the Primeval One"* (*BtVS* "Primeval").

ENOCHIAN PROTECTION RUNES | Derived from the Enochian alphabet, Lindsey McDonald covered his body and his apartment in these symbols to form a concealment spell. They protect the bearer from being viewed remotely from higher powers, seers, mystics, and any means of modern surveillance (*AtS* "You're Welcome").

ENSOULED VAMPIRE | Angel was the first vampire to have his soul restored in an act of vengeance visited upon him by the Kalderash Gypsy Clan (*BtVS* "Angel"). Later, Spike also regained his soul after undergoing many trials to prove his worthiness (*BtVS* "Grave").

ENYOS, UNCLE (ENYOS OF THE KALDERASH) | **VINCENT SCHIAVELLI** | Jenny Calendar's uncle. He came to Sunnydale to make sure that the curse their Gypsy clan had placed on Angel in 1898 was still in effect after the Elder Woman reported that Angel was not suffering as much as usual. Angered that Angel and Buffy had fallen in love, Enyos ordered "Janna" to separate them (*BtVS* "Surprise"). When the curse was broken, Angelus tortured and killed him (*BtVS* "Innocence").

EPPS, CHRIS | **ANGELO SPIZZIRRI** | Scientific-genius-level Sunnydale High School student who robbed graves and planned to murder Cordelia in his attempt to create a Frankenstein-style mate for his reanimated brother, Daryl (*BtVS* "Some Assembly Required").

EPPS, DARYL | **INGO NEUHAUS** | Sunnydale High School football All-State star who died in a climbing accident; his brother, Chris, brought him back to life and promised him a mate (*BtVS* "Some Assembly Required").

EPPS, MRS. | **MELANIE MACQUEEN** | Mother of Chris and Daryl Epps who filled her days watching videos of Daryl's football career (*BtVS* "Some Assembly Required").

ERNESTO | **ELIMU NELSON** | Senator Brucker's assistant; a vampire who prefers to drink the blood of virgins (*AtS* "Power Play").

ERYISHON THE ENDLESS ONE | Deity invoked by Anya and Willow to find Anyanka's power pendant in a temporal fold (*BtVS* "Doppelgangland").

ESME | Irish witch who owned the motel in Galway where Angel and Fred Burkle stayed on holiday. She and her coven sisters Gytha and Marget used a Gachnar Demon to absorb the fear of tourists they led on walking tours of Angelus's murderous rampage in 1753. When the trio attempted to steal Fred's power, the threat caused Illyria to manifest and she tore them apart (*Angel and Faith* "United").

ESPRESSO PUMP | Coffee house located on Maple Court in Sunnydale (*BtVS* "Dead Man's Party").

ESSUARY, THE | Receptacle that held the pieces of Giles's soul after they were removed from Angel's body. It had not been seen since 1978, but Alasdair Coames correctly believed that a coven of Enders possessed it (*Angel and Faith* "Death and Consequences").

ETHAN'S COSTUME SHOP | Opened by Ethan Rayne for the Halloween season. The outfits in stock were enchanted so that the wearer became whatever the costume signified: Buffy became a noblewoman; Xander, a soldier; and Willow, a ghost (*BtVS* "Halloween").

ETHROS BOX | Made from six hundred species of virgin woods and handcrafted by blind Tibetan monks, this container was used to capture and hold the Ethros Demon (*AtS* "I've Got You under My Skin").

ETHROS DEMON | ANTHONY CISTARO | Demonic race that possesses the bodies of humans. According to one such demon, they have been "corrupt[ing] the spirits of men before they had speech to name me." An adolescent Ethros Demon possessed Lizzie Borden. They are considered highly intelligent and more dangerous than a vampire. A little *psylis eucalipsis* powder ingested by the host will force the demon to reveal itself and a binding powder will hold the demon in place. When cast out of one victim, it will look for another host to inhabit; the force of that change can often kill the

new host. The demon who possessed Ryan Anderson claimed this host was the only human who ever frightened him. The demon was dispatched via Angel's axe, and he welcomed his death (*AtS* "I've Got You under My Skin").

ETHROS DEMON EXCORCISM RITE | *"Omnis spiritus in munde. In nomine dei! In odorem suavitatis. Tu autem effugare, diabole. Appropinquabit enim judicium dei. Tu autem. Effugare, diabole. Abrenuntias satanae? Et omnibus operibus eus? Omnibus pompis eus? Exorcie te. Omnis spiritus immunde. Adaperiae!"* (*AtS* "I've Got You Under My Skin").

EVANS, DR. | SUSAN SAVAGE | Physician in the neuropsychiatric unit in St. Matthew's Hospital who treated Cordelia when she was suffering from issues related to the Mark of Vocah (*AtS* "To Shanshu in LA").

EVE | AMANDA FULLER | Potential killed by the Bringers; the First impersonated her in Buffy's house (*BtVS* "Showtime").

EVE | SARAH THOMPSON | Immortal child of the Senior Partners, created to do their bidding and ultimately serve as the gang's connection to the Senior Partners when Angel was placed in charge of the LA branch of Wolfram & Hart (*AtS* "Underneath," "Conviction"). The graduate of UC Santa Cruz got intimate with Angel at a party while under Lorne's magical influence (*AtS* "Life of the Party"). Eve and her lover, Lindsey McDonald, later enacted a plan to set Angel and Spike against each other (*AtS* "Destiny"). She also used a gift from Lindsey—a Selminth parasite—to keep Angel dreaming. Angel accused Eve of playing her own game and threatened her with telling the Senior Partners about her treachery (*AtS* "Soul Purpose"). Harmony later threatened her into confessing about the fail-safe. Defeated, Eve was thrown out of the firm and she promised revenge (*AtS* "You're Welcome"). When confronted by Hamilton, she signed away her liaison duties and became mortal so she could be with Lindsey (*AtS* "Underneath"). When Angel told her Lindsey wasn't coming back and to run, she said she had nowhere to go (*AtS* "Not Fade Away").

EVERYDAY WOMAN | Dress shop in the Sunnydale mall where Joyce Summers shopped (*BtVS* "Bad Eggs").

EVIL BITCH MONSTER OF DEATH, THE | Maggie Walsh's TAs used this nickname for her (*BtVS* "The Freshman").

EVOLVED VAMPIRES (NEW VAMPIRES) | Vampires sired after the new Seed restored magic to Earth. These vampires can walk in daylight, shape-shift into bats, panthers, and wolves; they are fully sentient (as opposed to zompires). Their eyes glow red instead of yellow, but otherwise they are indistinguishable from "regular" vampires (*Buffy* "The Core").

EXECUTIVE DEMON | DANNY WOODBURN | Short, green-skinned demon with sharp pointed fingers, two antennae, small pointed teeth, and no nose. He had an office with an assistant and a beautiful porcelain cup for his tea. Fred fell into his hiding place when she was being chased while the city was under Jasmine's spell. He claimed to be a vegetarian and not under the enchantment, but he later attacked Fred when his stash of human hands was revealed. She killed him with an axe to the head (*AtS* "Magic Bullet").

EXORCISM RITE | Incantation Giles performed while attempting to exorcise the child Hannah: "*Exorcizamus te, omnis immunde spiritus!*" (*Angel and Faith* "Live through This").

EXPLORING DEMON DIMENSIONS | One of the library books Buffy consulted when Angel returned from hell (*BtVS* "Beauty and the Beasts").

EYE OF FIRE | Ancient alchemical symbol for fire and destruction (*AtS* "Rain of Fire").

EYE OF RAMRAS, THE | Device that amplifies power, allowing Kr'ph to become a Demon Lord (*Angel* "After the Fall").

EYGHON THE SLEEPWALKER | Ancient Etruscan demon whose acolytes tattooed his mark on their bodies in order to summon him. In the 1970s, Rupert Giles, Ethan Rayne, and their occult circle allowed him to possess them. Their attempted exorcism went awry when Eyghon would not leave Randall's body, and Randall died. Eyghon hunted the rest of the circle down, killing each one in turn. He inhabited the body of Jenny Calendar and then Angel, who, it was thought, defeated him permanently (*BtVS* "The Dark Age"). However, during his time as Twilight, Angel learned that Eyghon escaped inside the body of a dead rat. Eyghon used the dead body of Ethan Rayne to attend Giles's funeral, then moved into Giles's body and teamed up with Whistler, Pearl, and Nash to acquire artifacts that still contained magic to serve as batteries to create a magical plague. He then possessed the body of the dead Slayer Marianne and created zombies from the Slayers that attacked him during a major battle led by Angel, Spike Faith, and the soul of Giles. Using Angel's body, Giles decapitated Eyghon with the vorpal sword (*Angel and Faith* "Death and Consequences").

FABULOUS "LADIES NIGHT" CLUB, THE | Xander's name for his place of employment on his post-high school road trip. Located in Oxnard, California (*BtVS* "The Freshman").

FAE | Tall fairylike beings with golden horns, antennae, and wings who dwell in a dimension dedicated to peace, beauty, and revelry. Fae can't lie. They judge others based on their character, not their appearance (*Buffy* "In Pieces on the Ground").

FAIRFIELD CLINIC | Primary health-care provider for the Wolfram & Hart Los Angeles office employees, offering a wide range of typical health services and providing first-class care for their people. Fairfield's research department is at the forefront of the development of advanced treatments involving the sophisticated use of demons in the therapeutic setting, allowing employees benefits that would be impossible with pure traditional means. Fairfield Clinic's state-of-the art facility was financed by Wolfram & Hart as part of an ongoing health-care partnership (*AtS* "Dead End").

FAIRWEATHER, SOPHRONIA AND LAVINIA (VIN) | The sisters of Edna (Fairweather) Giles, and therefore Rupert Giles's great-aunts. They used their magic to retain their youth and beauty rather than becoming Watchers. As a result, they racked up debts to many demons and asked Angel and Faith for help when some of those demons attacked them (*Angel and Faith* "Daddy Issues"). They assisted in Rupert's resurrection by providing the Shard of Stronnos, and it was their influence that resulted in his return as a twelve-year-old boy (*Angel and Faith* "Death and Consequences"). They welcomed the resurrected Winifred Burkle as their roommate and helped Angel, Faith, Fred, and Eldre Koh rescue Nadira when Drusilla and Archaeus kidnapped her (*Angel and Faith* "A Tale of Two Families").

FAIRY | Tiny humanoid beings with wings that lay their eggs in the ear canals of other species. The Slayer Organization effected an alliance with a group of fairies who lived in the Under-Community (*Buffy* "The Long Way Home").

FAMILY HOME | Ostensibly a shelter for runaway teens in Los Angeles, Family Home was actually a front for a demon dimension where the prisoners were enslaved (*BtVS* "Anne").

FARGO, MITCH | **RYAN JAMES BITTLE** | Sunnydale High School student whom the invisible girl Marcie Ross beat with a baseball bat because he dated Cordelia. Mitch recovered and returned to school, asking Cordelia why she was hanging out with losers like Buffy, Willow, and Xander (*BtVS* "Out of Mind, Out of Sight").

FARRELL | One of the two San Francisco police officers who stayed and danced at Buffy's housewarming party rather than write her up for disturbing the peace (*Buffy* "Freefall").

FASSAUD | Author of a Sumerian guide that Wesley once translated (*AtS* "Carpe Noctem").

FATHER | Magical dollmaker who lived in the forest near the Scottish headquarters of the Slayer Organization. After Dawn Summers was changed into a porcelain doll, he repaired her and kept her a virtual prisoner, intending to keep her safe. His dolls—who referred to him as Father—protected him when Buffy, Kenny, and Xander attempted a rescue (*Buffy* "Predators and Prey").

FEIGENBAUM | Fred Burkle's stuffed rabbit; she wanted him with her when she died (*AtS* "A Hole in the World").

FELL BRETHREN, THE | Robed demons who worshipped the Holy Vessel, which was in the form of a baby. Spike killed them and reclaimed the child (*AtS* "Not Fade Away").

FERRIS, DR. CARLYLE | Former classmate of Giles's from his days at Oxford University who holds advanced degrees in entomology and mythology. After spending years translating a pre-Germanic language, Ferris discovered the existence of a She-Mantis in the Cotswolds. He went insane while hunting it and believed that his mother had been reincarnated as a Pekinese (*BtVS* "Teacher's Pet").

FERULA GEMINI | Magical staff created by the demon Toth for the purpose of dividing Buffy into two separate individuals, one containing the Slayer's essence while the other would possess normal human attributes. Toth would then kill the "normal" Buffy, which would magically cause the death of the Slayer. Toth misfired and the Ferula Gemini split Xander instead (*BtVS* "The Replacement").

FETVANOVICH, DR. | **JOHN DURBIN** | World's foremost specialist in paranormal obstetrics who worked out of the Wolfram & Hart satellite office in the Balkans. Wore a black robe and had little chicken-like feet. Dr. Fetvanovich was preparing to dissect Darla and her baby when Holtz killed him (*AtS* "Quickening").

FEZ-WEARING CONDUIT | **KAL PENN** | Magical conduit hired by Lilah to manifest Cordelia's visions with the power of his brain. He wore a fez to cover his enormous, exposed brain. Angel killed him (*AtS* "That Vision Thing").

FILLWORTHE, DUNCAN | One of the last surviving members of the Watchers Council. He moved to the remote European village of Hanselstadt, where a demon fed on the local children, attracted by their fears and regrets. The demon's presence kept vampires at bay, but once there were no more children to feed off, Fillworthe announced the creation of a Slayer Sanctuary for girls turned Slayers who didn't want to fight. In reality, he fed those to the demons as well. He was the demon's last meal (*Buffy* "Predators and Prey").

FINCH, ALLAN | **JACK PLOTNICK** | Deputy Mayor who was quite anxious around Mayor Wilkins. It is unclear if he was on his way to warn Buffy and Faith of the Mayor's plans to ascend when Faith accidentally stabbed him (*BtVS* "Homecoming," "Bad Girls").

FINKLE, MRS. | **BONITA FRIEDERICY** | Cordelia's boss at April Fools who had it in for her newest employee (*BtVS* "Choices," "The Prom").

Finn, Riley

| MARC BLUCAS |

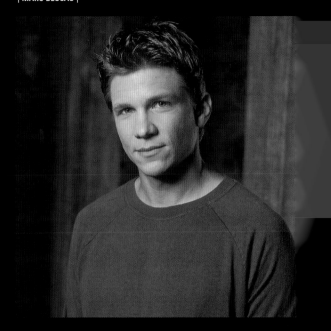

Covert ops soldier posing as a psychology grad student at UC Sunnydale. As part of his cover, he served as Maggie Walsh's teaching assistant in the psych class Buffy and Willow attended (*BtVS* "The Freshman"). Riley and Buffy began a relationship, each unaware of the other's secret identity until they met up during the attack on Sunnydale by the Gentlemen (*BtVS* "Hush"). Riley confessed that he was a member of the Initiative, covert operation tasked with killing and/or capturing demons for study. After discovering that Dr. Walsh was creating Adam—and that she had tried to kill Buffy as well—Riley left the Initiative. At the time, he had been ingesting strong chemicals he had been told were vitamins, and he went into withdrawal (*BtVS* "Goodbye Iowa"). He ultimately realized that Buffy didn't love him and frequented a vampire "bite den" to try to understand her attraction to Angel. Riley broke up with Buffy and left Sunnydale with the military (*BtVS* "Into the Woods") only to return briefly while on a demon-hunting mission with his new wife, Samantha (*BtVS* "As You Were"). Later, he served as a double agent, pretending to work for Twilight but spying for Buffy's side (*Buffy* "Time of Your Life"). In Suriname, South America, Faith and other Slayers rescued Riley and his wife while on a Deepscan mission (*Angel and Faith* "Lost and Found"). Riley later joined the newly re-formed Magic Council, on which he still serves (*Buffy* "Own It").

FINN, SAMANTHA (SAM) | IVANA MILICEVIC | Sam originally worked for the Peace Corps but joined Riley's military team after her infirmary was wiped out by a demon. The pair eventually fell in love and married once he was over his feelings for Buffy (*BtVS* "As You Were"). Samantha and Riley discussed the offer to join Twilight and spy for Buffy during a mission involving a malfunctioning missile silo, which turned out to be a setup (*BtVS* "Last Gleaming"). She teamed up with Faith and Deepscan to save Riley in South America (*Angel and Faith* "Lost and Found").

FINNEY, SUSAN | Farmer who lived in Oklahoma when it became part of the dust bowl (1935). She summoned a demon, became pregnant by it, and gave birth to Pearl and Nash (*Angel and Faith* "Family Reunion").

FIRE DEMON | Creature that lived in a cave by the beach in Sunnydale. Buffy and Angel killed it (*BtVS* "Choices").

FIREWATER | Used to loosen the tongue of Lorne's Gar-wawk snitch (*AtS* "Provider").

First Evil, the

In its own words: "I am something that you can't even conceive. The First Evil. Beyond sin, beyond death. I am the thing the darkness fears. You'll never see me, but I am everywhere. Every being, every thought, every drop of hate." (*BtVS* "Amends") The First is the incorporeal manifestation of evil. It has existed since before humans and demons (although it may be younger than the Seed of Wonder). It can take the form of any dead person, including vampires. In its natural form, it appears as a robed devil-like demon. It attempted to persuade Angel to kill himself to destroy the balance of good and evil (*BtVS* "Amends"). When that failed, it took advantage of an imbalance in the forces of good and evil—created when Willow resurrected Buffy—to attempt to take over the Earth dimension (*BtVS* "Showtime"). Using the disgraced priest Caleb as its lieutenant (*BtVS* "Dirty Girls"), the First Evil planned to open the Sunnydale Hellmouth

and unleash an army of Turok-Han on the world (*BtVS* "Get It Done"). Buffy thwarted the First Evil when she shared her power with the Potentials and Spike used an amulet to draw down the power of the sun to dust all the Turok-Han, but it was not defeated, and continues to exist (*BtVS* "Chosen").

THE FIRST EVIL APPEARED IN SUNNYDALE AS THE FOLLOWING PEOPLE:

Adam

Betty

Caleb

Calendar, Jenny

Chloe

Daniel

Drusilla

Eve

Glorificus the Hellgod

Levinson, Jonathan

Margaret

Master, the

Mears, Warren

Newton, Cassie

Spike

Summers, Joyce

Summers, Buffy

Wood, Nikki

Wilkins, Mayor Richard

FISH BOYS (GILL MONSTERS) | Members of the Sunnydale High School swim team who were turned into fish monsters (*BtVS* "Go Fish").

FISH TANK | Sunnydale dive bar frequented by Sheila Martini (*BtVS* "School Hard").

FIVE BASIC TORTURE GROUPS | Blunt, sharp, hot, cold, and loud, according to Faith (*AtS* "Five by Five").

FIVE BY FIVE | Radio communications term meaning "loud and clear." Faith uses the phrase to denote that all is well (*BtVS* "Faith, Hope & Trick").

FIVE DISCIPLES OF MORGALA | Followers of Morgala who appeared in Buffy's animated dream. They worshipped a giant dragon and believed that Morgala's impending ritual would tilt the balance of evil beyond all hope and reckoning (*Buffy* "Time of Your Life").

FLAME-FISTS WARRIOR | TANOAI REED | Adversary the Asphyx Demon set loose on Spike in Africa (*BtVS* "Two to Go").

FLAMING SWORD, THE | Weapon that the sired Charles Gunn used to kill Angel during the Fall of Los Angeles, causing the Senior Partners to reset time so that Angel remained alive (*Angel* "After the Fall").

FLOATING THE ROSE | Romantic spell Willow and Tara attempted when they started dating—floating a rose and removing the petals (*BtVS* "A New Man").

FLUFFY | Satsu's nickname for the Vampy Cat plushy that possessed her (*Buffy* "Predators and Prey").

FLUTIE, ROBERT (BOB) | KEN LERNER | Kindly principal of the original Sunnydale High School who was eaten by possessed students (*BtVS* "Welcome to the Hellmouth," "The Pack").

FLYING MONKEY | Creatures that Andrew Wells sent to attack the Sunnydale High School production of *Romeo and Juliet* (*BtVS* "Flooded").

FOLEY, DEBBIE | DANIELLE WEEKS | Student at the original Sunnydale High School and the girlfriend of Pete Clarner, an insecure teen who became violent and eventually killed her while under the influence of magic (*BtVS* "Beauty and the Beasts").

FONDREN | Location of a nearby rival school of Sunnydale High (*BtVS* "Some Assembly Required").

FONTAINE, JOHNNY | ROB BOLTIN | Acting student in Cordelia's class (*AtS* "Judgment").

FOOTMEN, THE | Demons who worked for the Gentlemen. Human in appearance, their heads were swathed in bandages and they wore straitjackets (*BtVS* "Hush").

FORDHAM, BILLY (FORD) | JASON BEHR | Former Hemery High schoolmate and crush of Buffy's in Los Angeles. Billy figured out that Buffy was the Slayer and followed her to Sunnydale when he realized he had terminal brain cancer. He led a cult of teenage vampire worshippers who believed that vampires were exalted, romantic beings whose "blessing" would lead them to "die young and stay pretty." In reality, Billy had made a deal to give Spike the Slayer in return for being sired. Spike kept up his end of the bargain but when Billy came back as a vampire, Buffy staked him (*BtVS* "Lie to Me").

FOREMAN | DAVID REIVERS | Construction worker who offered Xander a new, better position at the construction company when their current project began to wind up (*BtVS* "The Replacement").

FORK GUY (CLAW) | Vicious vampire Buffy used to locate the She-Mantis Miss French because of his fear of her. Assumed to be the vampire who was said to have displeased the Master and cut off his hand for penance (*BtVS* "Teacher's Pet").

FORMATIA TRANS SICERE EDUCATORUM | Latin inscription on the sign in front of the original Sunnydale High School. Translated, it means "Enter, all ye who seek knowledge." Vampires regarded it as an invitation to enter the school, although the campus was a public space anyway (*BtVS* "Passion").

FORSYTHE, WALTER | Reporter for the *Sunnydale Press* who wrote the story about a fifteen-year-old girl whose heart was removed during the Gentlemen's invasion of Sunnydale (*BtVS* "Hush").

FRAKES, MS. | Angel Investigations client interested in having the team investigate "hotblonde37159," the witch she believed was stealing her fiancé of eight years, Jerry (*AtS* "Couplet").

FRAMKIN, GREGOR | DAVID FURY | Creator of the *Smile Time* TV show. He came up with the idea in his garage with a couch and glue gun. When the show ratings were tanking, he made a deal with some devils but didn't read the fine print, which allowed the demons to take over, turning him into a living puppet (*AtS* "Smile Time").

FRANCES | JOSHUA GRENROCK | Ugly, fat, and fleshy demon with five conical horns of various sizes sticking out of his skull (*AtS* "Salvage"). Faith beat him up while she was looking for Angelus (*AtS* "Release").

FRANCESCA | Hank Summers's former secretary and mistress, with whom he had moved to Spain. They broke up (*Buffy* "Old Demons").

FRANK | DANIEL HAGEN | Doris Kroeger's supervisor at Social Services. Unaware that an invisible Buffy was tormenting Doris, Frank suggested the distraught social worker take the rest of the day off (*BtVS* "Gone").

FRANK (FRANKIE)| GARRETT BRAWITH | Frank used to bully Warren Mears in high school. Years later, Warren provoked him into a bar fight by flirting with his girlfriend and nearly killed him. Frank was saved only because Xander intervened (*BtVS* "Seeing Red").

FRANK, MS. | MIRIAM FLYNN | Teacher at the original Sunnydale High School. George the janitor murdered her while she was possessed by the ghost of Grace Newman (*BtVS* "I Only Have Eyes for You").

FRANKIE TRIPOD | Not a three-legged monster (*AtS* "In the Dark").

FRANKLIN, CAPTAIN | JOEL POLIS | US naval officer in World War II who was killed by Spike shortly after taking command of a German prototype vessel (*AtS* "Why We Fight").

FRASER, MAL | Half-demon gangster and supplier of Mohra blood for customers who needed regenerative aid. After the destruction of the Magic Seed, Mal continued to sell Mohra blood, even though it turned its consumers into hideous creatures who suffered great agony (*Angel and Faith* "Live through This").

FRATT, DR. | Doctor at Sunnydale Memorial Hospital (*BtVS* "Into the Woods").

FRAWLEY | BILLY MADDOX | SlayerFest '98 hunter who wore a pelt and a necklace of werewolf teeth. He used high-powered rifles and traps, and was himself caught in a spring trap. He declined fellow hunter Kulak's offer to cut off his leg in order to free him (*BtVS* "Homecoming").

FRAY, ERIN | Twenty-third-century police officer and sister of the Slayer Melaka. Erin blamed Melaka for their brother Harth's death because he and Melaka had been stealing something when he was killed. She eventually came to believe Melaka's story that their brother had become a vampire working to destroy their dimension. Under Erin's direction, a police hovercar was dropped on the Old One Neauth, which ended Harth's mission. She was severely injured but survived (*Fray* "Big City Girl").

FRAY, HARTH (THE ONE WHO WILL LEAD) | Twin brother of Slayer Melaka Fray who inherited the dreams and Slayer precognitive faculties intended for her. When Icarus attacked him, Harth knew to feed off him to become a vampire. Then he gathered some talismans to perform a ritual to raise the Old One Neauth, whose womb would serve as a portal between Earth and a demon dimension. Two other Old Ones were determined to thwart him and sent the demon Urkonn to train Melaka as a Slayer. Harth's first bid at ending the world thus came to an end (*Fray* "Out of the Past"). Later, he allied himself with a version of Dark Willow, but Buffy arrived from the twenty-first century and killed her. Harth, however, lives to fight another day (*Buffy* "Time of Your Life").

FRAY, MELAKA | Slayer in a dystopian future who was unaware of her heritage because no Slayers had been called for centuries, and the dreams that usually come to Potentials were experienced instead by her twin brother, Harth. Rather than providing her

guidance, her Watcher turned out to be insane and immolated himself (*Fray* "Big City Girl"). The demon Urkonn presented himself as Fray's mentor, though she eventually figured out he was a betrayer—even though he was also, to some degree, a friend. Melaka gathered the denizens of Haddyn into an army, and repelled Harth's vampire minions, and destroyed Neauth (*Fray* "All Hell"). Later, Buffy arrived from the twenty-first century and together they battled Dark Willow, who had lived for centuries (*Buffy* "The Time of Your Life").

FREDRICKS, FATHER | Priest who died while trying to exorcise an Ethros Demon from the body of Ryan Anderson (*AtS* "I've Got You under My Skin").

FREER, TESSA | New Slayer who was a member of Rona's squadron in Chicago with Anaheed and Simone Doffler. She left the Slayer Organization to follow Simone. After the end of magic, she was sired and transformed into a Slaypire. Tessa bit Detective Dowling and was dusted by a San Francisco police officer (*Buffy* "Welcome to the Team").

FREEZE RAY GUN | Weapon that freezes the target with a stream of ice. It was invented by the Trio (Warren, Jonathan, and Andrew) (*BtVS* "Smashed").

FRENCH, MISS | **JEAN SPEEGLE HOWARD** | Former Sunnydale schoolteacher, born in 1907 and retired in 1972. Her identity was stolen by the She-Mantis (*BtVS* "Teacher's Pet").

FRENCH, NATALIE (SHE-MANTIS) | **MUSETTA VANDER** | Human guise of the intelligent praying-mantis creature that assumed the identity of a retired schoolteacher. She killed Dr. Gregory, the Sunnydale High biology teacher, so that she could act as a substitute. She targeted Xander and Blayne Moll as two virgin boys who could fertilize her eggs, after which she would rip off their heads. The sound of bat vocalization disoriented her long enough for Buffy to hack her to death with a machete (*BtVS* "Teacher's Pet").

FRIES, CORBIN | **ROD ROWLAND** | Wolfram & Hart client on trial for smuggling Asian women into the United States for cheap labor and prostitution. He'd been charged with drugs and gun running, but nothing stuck. Fries infected his son with a virus on a time delay that could destroy LA to force Angel and team to honor their commitment to defend him (*AtS* "Conviction").

FRIES, MATT | **JORDAN GARRETT** | School-age son of Corbin Fries who was saved by Angel (*AtS* "Conviction").

FRITZ | **JAMISON RYAN** | Sunnydale High School student who became a devoted follower of Moloch the Corruptor. He hung his coconspirator, Dave, and delivered Willow to Moloch. As reward, Moloch broke his neck (*BtVS* "I Robot . . . You Jane").

FROVALAX DEMON | Species known for regurgitating (*BtVS* "Goodbye Iowa").

FRZYLCKA, SYD AND MONICA | **JOHN DAVID CONTI AND P.B. HUTTON** | Demon couple who had been married since 1702, worshipped Gurforg, and had a demon squatter in their lair (*AtS* "Double or Nothing").

FUMIGATION PARTY | Annual event at the Bronze celebrated by patrons getting a free drink for killing a cockroach (*BtVS* "Angel").

FUNGUS DEMON | Drusilla left Spike for one (*BtVS* "The Harsh Light of Day")

FYRAL DEMON | Humanoid demons with long, curving horns, orange skin, and bony protrusions on their shoulders. Fyrals tend to be dim-witted and very violent. They often serve other demons, including vampires. Silver is fatal to them. Rupert Giles was turned into a Fyral Demon by Ethan Rayne, who later changed him back again (*BtVS* "A New Man").

G

GABRIEL, FATHER | Catholic priest who was an expert on Sunnydale history, having family there since at least 1812. The spirit warrior Hus hung him and cut off his ear (*BtVS* "Pangs").

GACHNAR THE FEAR DEMON (THE DARK LORD OF NIGHTMARES, THE BRINGER OF TERROR) | ADAM BITTERMAN | Diminutive yet powerful demon who fed on the fears of Halloween partygoers. Gachnar was summoned when a drop of Oz's blood fell onto the drawing of the Mark of Gachnar on the floor of the Goat Room of the Alpha Delta frat house. The demon was small enough for Buffy to squish under her heel (*BtVS* "Fear Itself"). A few years later, a coven of Irish witches used a Gachnar Demon to gain power by generating fears during their tours of the sites of Angelus's murderous rampage in 1753 (*Angel and Faith* "United").

GANDERFLEB | Creature resembling a giant beetle that didn't make it for Willow's choice of guide on her magical walkabout because he was fighting the Great Ronok (*Buffy* "Retreat").

GARCIA, JORGE | Actor who played Gunn in the movie *Last Angel in Hell* (*Angel* "Last Angel in Hell").

GARRON | High school bully who mocked Billy Lane for being gay. During a confrontation with Billy, Garron was murdered by Post, who had turned into a zompire (*Buffy* "Guarded").

GASHUNDI | A lost language (*AtS* "Offspring").

GATBAR DEMON | Red creature with spikes; it grows to full size in the womb (*AtS* "Players").

GATES | Twenty-third-century spider-monkey demon named after the last great Watcher, who died at the Battle of Starbucks (*Buffy* "Time of Your Life"). Gunther ordered Melaka Fray to steal a box and Gates jumped out of it, stole her Scythe, and led her to a room with the Scythe symbol painted on the floor. The shelves were filled with Watchers Diaries, which was how Melaka learned about her heritage (*Tales* "Tales").

GATES, FORREST | LEONARD ROBERTS | Member of the Initiative and close friend of Riley Finn (*BtVS* "The Initiative"). Although he initially encouraged Riley to pursue Buffy romantically, Forrest's opinion of the Slayer changed once he learned her secret identity and she started working for the Initiative. Adam killed Forrest and reanimated his body forcing Riley to destroy his former friend (*BtVS* "Primeval").

GAVROK SPIDER | Creatures eaten as part of the ritual associated with an Ascension. They are high in fiber (*BtVS* "Choices," "Graduation Day, Part 1").

GEM OF AMARRA (RING OF AMARRA) | Priceless ring considered a vampiric "Holy Grail," and the object of quests that petered out after the tenth century because no one could find it. Whoever wore it could walk in daylight and withstand being staked. Spike learned that it was located in "the valley of the sun"—Sunnydale—and Harmony Kendall found it in an underground treasure trove. Armed with the gem, Spike attacked Buffy, but she defeated him and gave the ring to Oz to take to Angel in Los Angeles (*BtVS* "The Harsh Light of Day"). Spike employed vampire torturer Marcus to force Angel to reveal the ring's new location. Cordelia and Doyle gave Marcus the ring in exchange for Angel's life. Angel staked Marcus and wrenched the ring off his finger, turning him to dust. Angel then decided to destroy it, fearing its power would keep him from his mission of helping the helpless (*AtS* "In the Dark").

GENTLEMEN, THE | DOUG JONES, CAMDEN TOY, DON W. LEWIS, CHARLIE BRUMBLY | Terrifying fairytale-like men with fishbelly-white skin stretched over bald heads, silver teeth pulled back in rictus grins, and eyes set in deep, black sockets. They wore formal clothes, floated above the ground, and were attended by minions swathed in bandages and wearing straitjackets. The Gentlemen would come to a town and steal everyone's voices, storing them in a box. Then they would cut out the hearts of seven victims who were unable to call for help or scream. When the box was smashed, Buffy screamed, causing the heads of the Gentlemen to explode (*BtVS* "Hush").

GENTLEMEN NURSERY RHYME | Buffy dreamed of a little girl holding the Gentlemen's Voice Box, while she chanted this nursery rhyme: "Can't even shout / Can't even cry / The Gentlemen are coming by / looking in windows / knocking on doors / They need to take seven / and they might take yours / Can't call to Mom / can't say a word / You're gonna die screaming but you won't be heard" (*BtVS* "Hush").

GENTLEMEN'S VOICE BOX | Terracotta-colored box in which the Gentlemen placed the voices of everyone in Sunnydale. Riley smashed it, releasing the voices (*BtVS* "Hush").

GEORGE | DARRIS LOVE | Teen at the East Hills Teen Center and friend of Gunn, who chided him for leaving their streets behind. George videotaped a police attack (*AtS* "The Thin Dead Line").

GEORGE | JOHN HAWKES | Janitor at the original Sunnydale High School who shot and killed Ms. Frank while he was possessed by the spirit of James Stanley (*BtVS* "I Only Have Eyes for You").

GERHARDT, PROFESSOR | MARGARET EASLEY | Faculty member of the anthropology department at UC Sunnydale who was instrumental in developing the new UC Sunnydale Cultural Partnership Center. Hus killed her and took her ear (*BtVS* "Pangs").

GHORA DEMON | Three-headed, reptilian demons with leathery wings; they nest underground and could be found in Sunnydale by going in the sewer entrance near Tracy Street. Their lavender eggs are used in a ritual for resurrecting the dead. Dawn and Spike collected one intending to raise Joyce Summers (*BtVS* "Forever").

GHOST | Usually refers to the spirit of a dead person that is Earth-bound because it has yet to resolve an issue that will grant the being eternal peace. Some ghosts are vengeful and can wreak havoc by manifesting snakes, wasps, melting floors, and exhibiting poltergeist activities such as grabbing and pushing people. Two ways to get rid of ghosts are by solving the problem that keeps them rooted to this world, or exorcism (*BtVS* "I Only Have Eyes for You").

GIANFRANCO, ALDO | SCOTT HARLAN | Opera singer who shared Willow's nightmare duet of Puccini's *Madame Butterfly* (*BtVS* "Nightmares").

GILBERT AND SULLIVAN | Lyricist (librettist) and composer of numerous musicals whose lyrics were implanted in Gunn's head when he started work as a lawyer at Wolfram & Hart. This was standard with the legal implant to aid in elocution (*AtS* "Conviction").

GILES, EDNA (EDNA FAIRWEATHER) | Grandmother of Rupert Giles who became an esteemed member of the Watchers Council. Her son was also a Watcher (*Tales* "Tales of the Vampires"). It was she who tracked down Rupert Giles during his rebellious phase and convinced him to resume life as a Watcher (*Angel and Faith* "Death and Consequences").

Giles, Rupert

RIPPER | ANTHONY STEWART HEAD |

Although Giles's mentoring relationship with Buffy was often quite prickly, they worked well together until the time of Buffy's Cruciamentum, when he was fired from the Council for revealing the nature of the secret test to her (*BtVS* "Helpless"). At Buffy's insistence, he was later reinstated by the Council (*BtVS* "Checkpoint") and mentored Buffy for a time, but twice left Sunnydale to return to England so that she would assume her duties as an adult (*BtVS* "Bargaining, Part 1," "Tabula Rasa"). He returned to Sunnydale to battle Dark Willow (*BtVS* "Two to Go") and took the repentant witch back to England with him for rehabilitation (*BtVS* "Lessons"). When the Bringers started killing potential Slayers all over the world, Giles tracked down Potentials and delivered them to Buffy's home (*BtVS* "Bring on the Night"). He fought at the Battle of the Hellmouth and survived (*BtVS* "Chosen").

After Buffy shared her power, he assisted in running the new Slayer Organization. During this time, he sent Faith Lehane on a mission to assassinate a rogue Slayer—a secret he kept from Buffy, which caused a rift between them (*Buffy* "No Future for You"). With the looming threat of Twilight, Giles reconciled with Buffy before being murdered by Angel, who was under Twilight's influence (*BtVS* "Last Gleaming"). Angel and Faith managed to resurrect Giles in the persona of his twelve-year-old self (*Angel and Faith* "What You Want, Not What You Need") and he continues to battle against the forces of darkness. He is the vice president of the new council of magic (*Buffy* "Own It").

Born into a family of Watchers, Giles was informed by his father, at the age of ten, that he was expected to become a Watcher as well. His fate was sealed when he assisted his two great-aunts with an attacking demon. Giles attended the Watchers Academy and witnessed his cohort die at the hands of a Lorophage Demon on a mishandled "final exam" (*Angel and Faith* "Daddy Issues"). While a student at Oxford, he rebelled by dropping out and joining an occult group in London (*BtVS* "The Dark Age"). Eventually accepting his destiny, Giles left a museum post in London and moved to Sunnydale to serve as the Watcher of Buffy Summers, then the current Vampire Slayer. He worked as a high school librarian to serve as his cover while mentoring Buffy (*BtVS* "Welcome to the Hellmouth") and eventually began a relationship with the computer science teacher Jenny Calendar that ended with her tragic death (*BtVS* "Passion").

GILES, MR. | Father of Rupert Giles and son to Edna (Fairweather) Giles. He was a member of the Watchers Council and pressured his son to follow in his footsteps, informing Rupert at the age of ten that there was nothing he could do to change his destiny (*Angel and Faith* "Daddy Issues").

GILLNITZ, FRANK | J.P. MANOUX | Bellhop accused of the murders at the Hyperion Hotel in 1952. He was executed in 1954 (*AtS* "Are You Now or Have You Ever Been").

GINA | MARION CALVERT | Employee at the Doublemeat Palace (*BtVS* "Doublemeat Palace," "Dead Things").

GINGERBREAD DEMON | ROGER MORRISSEY | Hans and Greta Strauss morphed into this approximately seven-foot-tall demon. Its eyes were crimson; its skin was red and pocked, its gray hair long and tangled; and it had pointed ears and tusks extending from its lower jaw. Buffy impaled it with the stake she was tied to (*BtVS* "Gingerbread").

GIO | KHALIL KAIN | New member of Gunn's former crew. Gio originally hailed from Miami and wanted to know why Gunn was working for a vampire. Gio influenced the crew to begin hunting all demons, whether good or evil. He liked to sing "The Wind beneath My Wings," but his singing revealed a history to Lorne in which an unidentified woman trusted Gio "right up to the end, despite what he did to her in Miami." He shut Lorne up before he could say more. A demon bit Gio's head off (*AtS* "That Old Gang of Mine").

GIRL AT BAT | DEMETRA RAVEN | Little softball player Potential who felt the effects of Willow's power-sharing spell (*BtVS* "Chosen").

GITTLESON, ERIC | MICHAEL BACALL | Chris Epps's partner in his Frankenstein-like revivification of his brother, Daryl. Eric pushed to murder Cordelia for her head rather than wait for another accident to provide them with the body parts necessary to create a girlfriend for Daryl. Buffy saved him from dying in a fire that consumed their lab (*BtVS* "Some Assembly Required").

GLARGHK GUHL KASHMAS'NIK DEMON | Humanoid demon with a waxy complexion that injects hallucinogenic poison into its victims by means of retractable stingers in its arms. The only antidote is also carried in the stinger. Without the antidote, the victims' hallucinations will eventually overtake their minds, driving them into permanent insanity (*BtVS* "Normal Again").

GLASS BLOWER (THE RUTGER) | Originally a human, he was changed into a bulbous tentacled creature with a blast furnace for a mouth. He made perfect glass bottles for the pixies, who used them to bottle as much of the remaining magic in Magic Town as they could locate (*Angel and Faith* "Where the River Meets the Sea").

GLEAVES | Nineteenth-century wealthy landowner who stole Balthazar's magic amulet and had it buried with him (*BtVS* "Bad Girls").

GLENN | CHARLES DUCKWORTH | Friend of Dawn's vampire crush, Justin. Glenn was dusted by Giles on Halloween (*BtVS* "All the Way").

GLORIFICUS THE HELLGOD (GLORY, THE BEAST, THE ABOMINATION, THAT WHICH CANNOT BE NAMED) | CLARE KRAMER | Hellgod that was banished from her own dimension by two other hellgods because she was so brutal. Glorificus—better known as Glory while in her female form—was trapped inside a human being named Ben Wilkinson who had been created for just this reason (in the same way that the Key was brought into the world as Dawn Summers) (*BtVS* "No Place like Home"). She sucked the energy out of human brains as sustenance and became increasingly erratic as the division between Ben and Glory weakened to the point where she was almost both beings at once. She drained the mind of Tara Maclay before Willow

Glory's seamstress (*BtVS* "Spiral," "The Weight of the World"). She also had an unnamed High Priest Minion (Matthew Lang) (*BtVS* "The Weight of the World").

GLOVE OF MYHNEGON | Magical gauntlet stored in the Von Hauptman crypt in Sunnydale's Restfield Cemetery. A ring of spikes attached it to the forearm of the wearer and would detach only upon death. When activated by spells recited in Gaelic, it could draw down lightning and shoot it at a target. The glove was consumed by Living Flame, a type of magical fire, while worn by ex-Watcher Gwendolyn Post (*BtVS* "Revelations").

GLURGG DEMON | Species of demon that is 90 percent pus (*AtS* "Rain of Fire").

GNARL | CAMDEN TOY | Singsong demon of greenish hue with pointed ears, a long hooked nose, and rows of sharp teeth. Gnarl lived in a cave in Sunnydale. He injected a paralyzing drug into his victims, stripped off their skin, and ate it. Buffy killed him by gouging out his eyes (*BtVS* "Same Time, Same Place").

absorbed sufficient dark magic to injure her (*BtVS* "Tough Love"). Buffy used the Buffybot, the hammer of Olaf the Troll God, and the Dagon Sphere in an attempt to defeat her but ultimately, Giles destroyed her by killing Ben (*BtVS* "The Gift").

GLORY'S MINIONS | Small troll-like beings from Glory's dimension. They included Jinx (Troy T. Blendell) (*BtVS* "Checkpoint," "Tough Love"); Dreg (Kevin Weisman) (*BtVS* "Shadow," "Blood Ties"); Murk (Todd Duffey) (*BtVS* "Forever," "The Gift"); Slook (Alan Heitz) (*BtVS* "Tough Love") and Gronx (Lily Knight). Gronx was

GNOG | Demon ally of Aluwyn who challenged Willow during her magical walkabout. He was attired in armor like a medieval black knight, and while battling him, Willow learned to fly. She also released a burst of magical energy that stopped him without killing him (*Buffy* "Goddesses and Monsters").

GOAT-SHAPED DEMON | Beings that resemble Satyrs. Warren Mears and Amy Madison summoned a group of them to attack Andrew's Slayer squad in the catacombs of Rome (*Buffy* "Retreat").

GOLD, DR. | TOM BELLIN | Doctor at Sunnydale Memorial who delivered the bad news to the Mayor that Faith's head trauma was too severe for her to regain consciousness (*BtVS* "Graduation Day, Part 2").

GOLDEN, RANDALL | AVERY KIDD WADDELL | Tommy's little brother who tried to steal Gunn's ride when he was twelve. Survived in the tunnels during the time the sun went out (*AtS* "Sacrifice").

GOLDEN, TOMMY | Former member of Gunn's crew who died during Jasmine's reign over Los Angeles (*AtS* "Sacrifice").

GOLGOTHA | New (Evolved) Vampire who weighed 480 pounds. He was Buffy's opponent in Harmony's Las Vegas fighting match. Buffy dusted him with the Scythe (*Buffy* "In Pieces on the Ground").

GOODMAN, AGENT | CHRISTOPHER LEPS | Former Initiative agent. Goodman arrived in Sunnydale to help Riley Finn when he was deteriorating due to his withdrawal from the chemical cocktail he had unknowingly been given while serving (*BtVS* "Out of My Mind").

GORCH CLAN (LYLE, TECTOR, AND CANDY) | JEREMY RATCHFORD, JAMES PARKS, AND LEE EVERETT | Lyle and Tector were brothers from Abilene, Texas. They made their reputation massacring an entire Mexican village in 1886—before they became vampires. Buffy thwarted Lyle's attempt to feed off a girl at the mall. When he and Tector attacked her at Sunnydale High, the mother Bezoar devoured Tector. Lyle swore revenge on Buffy and fled (*BtVS*

"Bad Eggs"). Lyle married the vampire Candy and the two returned to Sunnydale to honeymoon at SlayerFest '98. Candy was dusted with a spatula and Lyle fled Sunnydale a second time (*BtVS* "Homecoming").

GRAMMATICUS THIRD-CENTURY GREEK COMMENTARIES, THE (THE GTCGC) | Book Wesley used to aid in his research on the Nyazian prophecy (*AtS* "Couplet").

GRANATH | Zombie god. Destroying his idol broke his hold on any zombies (*AtS* "The Thin Dead Line").

GRANOK DEMON | In the past they were all about torture and death, but when they caused too much chaos, the Senior Partners made them immaterial. Resikian Urns can trap their essence (*AtS* "Forgiving").

GRAPPLER DEMON | Gray-skinned demons with upside-down walrus tusks. They are great fighters who are not too sharp but merciless in battle (*AtS* "Quickening").

GRATHNAR DEMON | Species of demon that included Spiro Agnew, the vice president under Richard Nixon (1969-1973) (*AtS* "Fredless").

GREEN, BRIAN | California Physics Institute student considered by some to be the Sammy Sosa of physics (*AtS* "Supersymmetry").

GREENLIEGH, RUTH (RUTHIE) | CONCHATA FERRELL | School nurse at the original Sunnydale High School who assisted with Coach Marin's usage of an abandoned Soviet Union drug protocol to enhance the swim team's performance. When she realized the drug was turning the swimmers into Gill Monsters, she told the coach they had to stop the experiment. He retaliated by throwing her into the grotto under the pump room so a fully mutated Gill Monster could devour her (*BtVS* "Go Fish").

GREENWAY | Wolfram & Hart client who practiced black arts. To escape a racketeering charge, Greenway slaughtered a group of nuns as part of a ritual that allowed him to escape through a pan-dimensional doorway and disappear into any one of infinite universes (*AtS* "You're Welcome").

GREGOR, GENERAL | WADE ANDREW WILLIAMS | Leader of the Knights of Byzantium. Before Glory killed him, Gregor provided the Scoobies with information that Glory could be killed in her human form (*BtVS* "Spiral").

GREGORY, DR. STEPHEN | Sunnydale High science teacher who encouraged Buffy to do her best before he was murdered by She-Mantis Natalie French (*BtVS* "Teacher's Pet").

GREGSON, DR. | BOB MORRISEY | Slod Demon who collects rare organs, such as vampire hearts (*AtS* "Heartthrob").

GRIFF | MARKUS REDMOND | Kailiff Demon and professional hit man. His body is dark brown and he has spines sticking out of his jaw and head (*AtS* "Rm w/a Vu").

GRIFFIN, DAVE | Detective with the LAPD who called Angel when they found victims of vampires (*AtS* "Harm's Way").

GRIMES | ROBERTO SANTOS | Student at the new Sunnydale High School who vandalized school property. Principal Robin Wood faced him down and he agreed to repair the damage (*BtVS* "Never Leave Me").

GRIMSLAW DEMON | Large spiderlike demon with a green body, six legs, mandibles, and a mouth that extends from its thorax to feed on human hearts (*BtVS* "Selfless").

Groosalugg

GROO | MARK LUTZ |

Human Pylean champion not equipped to mate with other Pyleans. His smile, muscles, and chest-based heart made him a beast to the Pyleans. His life-givers abandoned him and he sought to end his life through battle. As he won every battle instead, the Covenant named him the Groosalugg and sent him to defeat evil before he was presented to Cordelia (*AtS* "Through the Looking Glass"). Cordy's vision warned him not to fight Angel, but Silas told him that Angel would kill Cordelia if Groo didn't kill him first. When he survived the battle with Angel, Groo was left in charge of the new society on Pylea (*AtS* "There's No Place like Plrtz Glrb").

Groo appeared in the Hyperion after having been overthrown in Pylea—and just as Cordelia and Angel were getting close (*AtS* "Waiting in the Wings"). He confided to Angel that he sensed sadness in Cordelia's heart, and that her heart wasn't free to give to him. With a haircut and some of Angel's clothes, he hoped he'd be more attractive to Cordy (*AtS* "Double or Nothing"). Cordelia was his first lover, but he became jealous of her attachment to Angel (*AtS* "A New World"). He eventually told Cordelia that he wasn't the one she was in love with, but he would stay if she said he was wrong. When she didn't, he left (*AtS* "Tomorrow").

When the Senior Partners sent Los Angeles to hell, Groosalugg acted as the champion of Lorne, who was Lord of Silverlake. He rode a black winged horse he named Cordelia, and joined Angel's battle against the other Demon Lords' champions. When time was reset, Angel asked Groo to take care of the dragon named Cordelia as well (*Angel* "After the Fall"). Groosalugg rode the dragon to Las Vegas, where they assisted Spike in his quest to destroy the Las Vegas branch of Wolfram & Hart, among a number of escapades (*Spike* "The Complete Series"). Groo, Cordelia the horse, and Cordelia the dragon continue to have adventures.

GROTTO, THE | Coffee house on the UC Sunnydale campus (*BtVS* "The Freshman").

GROUNDING CRYSTAL | Large blue vibratory stone used to hypnotize those who gaze into it, thus rendering them oblivious to their surroundings (*BtVS* "Helpless).

GROVE, AMBER | Sunnydale High School senior who tried out to be a cheerleader. She was magically set on fire by the witch Catherine Madison (*BtVS* "Witch"). Other girls who tried out included Buffy, Cordelia, Amy Madison, Morgan, Janice, and Lishanne.

GROX'LAR BEAST | Big, gray, horned demon who eats the heads of babies. One had an appointment with Angel to discuss a cease-eating by his clan, but was mistakenly killed by Angel before they could talk (*AtS* "Just Rewards").

GRUENSTAHLER, FREDERICK AND HANS | JERMYN DAUBE AND JOSEPH DAUBE | Human twin participants in SlayerFest '98. They were wanted in Germany for capital murder, terrorism, and the bombing of Flight 1402. Under the guidance of "the Old Man," they used technology to hunt Buffy and Cordelia, and wound up fatally shooting each other by accident (*BtVS* "Homecoming").

GUARDIAN, THE | CHRISTINE HEALY | Last of the Guardians, a group of powerful magical women who created the Scythe so that the Slayer could kill the last demon. They hid the weapon from the Shadow Men and the Watchers. Caleb killed her moments after she gave the Scythe to Buffy (*BtVS* "End of Days").

GUERRERO, MATTHEW | MARK ANKENY | Dean at UC Sunnydale who introduced Professor Gerhardt at the groundbreaking ceremony for the UC Sunnydale Cultural Partnership Center (*BtVS* "Pangs").

GUIDING SPELL | Simple incantation that guides travelers when they become lost or disoriented. According to Willow, "it conjures an emissary from the beyond that lights the way." The spell is performed by chanting "*Aradia, goddess of the lost, the path is murky, the woods are dense, darkness pervades: I beseech thee, bring the light*" (*BtVS* "Fear Itself").

GULL, DR. | Nineteenth-century physician who treated, but could not cure, William Pratt's mother of her consumption (*BtVS* "Lies My Parents Told Me").

GUNN, ALONNA | MICHELE KELLY | Charles Gunn's sister. She helped his crew, and looked after her big brother until she was kidnapped by vampires and sired. Alonna tried to sire Gunn, but he was forced to stake her instead (*AtS* "War Zone").

GUNN, CHARLES | J. AUGUST RICHARDS | See following page.

GUNTHER | Fray's watery mutant boss, a fishlike radie who originally hired her to steal artifacts for him to fence (*Fray* "Big City Girl"). He tried to warn her about the plot to make her aware of her Slayer heritage so that she could bring down her own brother, after which she would be eliminated (*Fray* "All Hell"). Later, Buffy and Fray contacted Gunther in their quest to defeat Dark Willow in Fray's timeline (*Buffy* "Time of Your Life").

GUNYARR | Four-armed monster that attempted to steal the Vampy Cat prototype. Satsu cut off his arm and Kennedy gave him a severe electric shock (*Buffy* "Predators and Prey").

GUSTAFSON PRECISION BLADES | Hunting knives made locally in Sunnydale (*BtVS* "This Year's Girl").

GUTENBERG DEMONOGRAPHY | Book that had been recently acquired by a friend of Giles. The former librarian was looking forward to seeing it (*BtVS* "Living Conditions").

GUTIERREZ, AMPATA | SAMUEL JACOBS | Male exchange student who was supposed to stay at Buffy's house before the Inca Mummy Princess killed him (*BtVS* "Inca Mummy Girl").

GWEN | KRISTEN WINNICKI | Sunnydale High School student who befriended Cordelia's foreign exchange student, Sven, at the World Culture Dance and discovered that he spoke fluent English (*BtVS* "Inca Mummy Girl"). She ridiculed Cordelia when Cordelia began dating Xander, then fell under Amy Madison's Love Spell just like all the other girls and women in Sunnydale (*BtVS* "Bewitched, Bothered, and Bewildered").

GYTHA | One of three Irish witches. Illyria tore her apart (*Angel and Faith* "United").

Gunn, Charles

| J. AUGUST RICHARDS |

A formerly homeless teenager who lost his sister to vampires, Gunn began working with Angel Investigations because he identified with Angel's mission (*AtS* "War Zone"). He didn't fully trust Angel at first and sometimes outright defied him, but whenever he had to choose between his old life and his new one, he sided with Angel's crew, even going so far as to defend a demon—Lorne—from his former gang (*AtS* "That Old Gang of Mine"). Throughout his early years working with Angel Investigations, Gunn was always conscious that he was perceived as just "the muscle" in the group, usually embracing the role, but sometimes chafing against it.

Gunn fell in love with Fred shortly after meeting her, but was surprised when his feelings were returned. Always aware of Wesley's interest in Fred, Gunn was jealous any time the pair worked together. His relationship with Fred couldn't withstand the stress of their work. Gunn resorted to violence time and again, from killing his sired sister, to snapping Professor Seidel's neck to save Fred from killing

him, to threatening a little boy in the sewers as they fled from Connor's army (*AtS* "Sacrifice"). When Wolfram & Hart extended their offer to the gang to take over the firm, he was initially suspicious that they just wanted him to work security. A meeting with the Conduit showed him the potential power of the position, and he was the first to join (*AtS* "Home").

Gunn received a brain implant so he could compete legally with their opposition and earn the respect of his teammates. But when the implanted knowledge began to degrade, he made a desperate deal that cost Fred her life (*AtS* "Smile Time"). Seeking atonement, he took on Lindsey's punishment in the Senior Partners' Holding Dimension, freeing the former lawyer to help the gang and turning down Hamilton's offer to free him in exchange for betrayal. Illyria ultimately freed him from a basement torture chamber. When he joined the fight against the Circle of the Black Thorn (*AtS* "Power Play")—and the Senior Partners—he was happy to have a chance to kill vampires again when he went after Senator Brucker. Mortally wounded and destined to die in the next ten minutes, (according to Illyria) Gunn prepared to fight the thirty thousand demons on the right side of the attacking army (*AtS* "Not Fade Away") while Angel left Gunn's side to battle the dragon later known as Cordelia.

Gunn was sired by a vampire, whom he killed, and took over the pack as Los Angeles was sent to hell. Although soulless, Gunn convinced himself that he was still doing the work of the Powers That Be. He killed Kr'ph, Demon Lord of Westwood, and kidnapped the Splenden Beast, Betta George. The ghost of Wesley Wyndam-Pryce attempted to convince him that the visions he was having were products of the Senior Partners of Wolfram & Hart, and not the Powers That Be. Gunn killed Angel's son, Connor, and decided to allow Illyria in her Old One form to unmake time itself. Succumbing to Angel's taunts, he decapitated Angel, and time was reset to before the fall because the Senior Partners needed Angel alive to fulfill their plans. With time reset, Angel rescued Gunn from the vampire who sired him when Los Angeles went to hell. He was hospitalized and recovered (*Angel* "After the Fall"). When Angel, Faith, and Willow came to Los Angeles to seek Connor's help in restoring magic, Gunn drove them, revealing that he had stayed in touch with both Connor and Angel's old girlfriend Nina (*Angel and Faith* "Family Reunion").

— H —

HABER, MARTIN | Twenty-eight-year-old victim of the Burrower (*AtS* "Lonely Heart").

HADDYN | Twenty-third-century city formerly known as Manhattan (*Buffy* "Time of Your Life").

HAGAN SHAFT | Long magical stick that caused immortal beings to explode upon contact; often used as a means for them to commit suicide. Angel colluded with Bro'os (Teeth) to provide Hagan Shafts to the Demon Lords of Los Angeles (*Angel* "After the Fall").

HAINSLEY, MAGNUS | **VICTOR RAIDER-WEXLER** | Necromancer who had power over the deceased and used it to transfer live demon spirits into dead human bodies. One of Wolfram & Hart's oldest clients who was not happy that Angel cut off his supply of bodies, Magnus tried to make a deal with Spike to put him in Angel's body, but the vampires tricked him and cut off his head (*AtS* "Just Rewards").

HAKLAR DEMON | Descended from the Klensan Order Demons, adult males of this species can weigh as much as three tons. They awake from hibernation during alternating full moons only to feed and mate—often simultaneously. Haklar Demons prefer a warm moist clime (like the one who lived on the north shore of Lake Hollywood) and they communicate with each other via a pattern of carefully timed facial tics. Some Haklar eat a whole person while others just eat parts, and they each have different feeding grounds. A Haklar appeared in Cordelia's vision and the team planned to go to its feeding ground and kill it to death (*AtS* "Belonging").

HALFREK (HALLIE) | **KALI ROCHA** | Anyanka's best friend in the Vengeance Demon community (*BtVS* "Doublemeat Palace") who was, quite possibly, the girl named Cecily who rejected Spike when he was human (*BtVS* "Fool for Love"). Halfrek specialized in reaping vengeance on behalf of neglected children and granted Dawn's wish that everyone stay with her (*BtVS* "Older and Far

Away"). D'Hoffryn destroyed Halfrek to punish Anya for asking to take back an act of vengeance (*BtVS* "Selfless").

HALL, MRS. | Sunnydale teacher in 1955 who helped students decorate the gym for the Sadie Hawkins Dance (*BtVS* "I Only Have Eyes for You").

HAMELIN DEMON | Interdimensional demons that feed on the traumas of children. They are mainly composed of eyes and tentacles, and their blood subjects humans to powerful hallucinations that force them to deal with parental issues (*Buffy* "I Wish").

HAMILTON, MARCUS | **ADAM BALDWIN** | Liaison for the Wolfram & Hart Senior Partners who replaced Eve (*AtS* "Underneath"). Hamilton tried to ingratiate himself into the team, but his advances, like offering Gunn a way out of the basement, were rebuffed (*AtS* "Origin"). He introduced Angel to Senator Brucker and delivered Drogyn to the Circle of Black Thorn (*AtS* "Power Play"). He slept with Harmony as a means of learning Angel's plans against the Senior Partners. In his final confrontation with Angel, Hamilton claimed that he couldn't be defeated because he was part of the Wolf, the Ram, and the Hart, and their ancient power flowed through his veins. Angel drank that blood, taking on some of Hamilton's power, and broke his neck (*AtS* "Not Fade Away").

HAMMER OF HAMNER | Enchanted hammer used by Trafalger the gnome against the magical barriers erected by the Irish warlock Roden. The hammer was ineffective against the barriers, and it shattered (*Buffy* "No Future for You").

HANK | LAWRENCE TURNER | Employee in the demon parts auction who was eager to remove Cordelia's eyes (*AtS* "Parting Gifts").

HANNAH | Child inhabited by a multitentacled Plagiarus Demon (*Angel and Faith* "Live through This").

HAPPY BURGER | Sunnydale fast-food restaurant where Mr. Trick ate the window attendant after purchasing a diet soda (*BtVS* "Faith Hope and Trick").

HAPPYTIME STUDIOS | Amusement park that Spike, Illyria, and Jeremy Johns lived in with their rescued humans (*Spike* "After the Fall").

HARDING, WELLING | Guest at a party hosted by wealthy software engineer David Nabbit (*AtS* "War Zone").

HARDWICKE, OFFICER | Member of the San Francisco Police Department and Anne Rice fan who developed a romanticized impression of vampires (and Spike in particular) (*Buffy* "Love Dares You").

HARKES, OFFICER PETER | DARIN COOPER | Zombie police officer, badge number 4226. In the six months after his death, Harkes's killer was caught and put up for the death penalty. Angel decapitated the undead Harkes (*AtS* "The Thin Dead Line").

HARLAN | ALEX SKUBY | Detective in Kate's precinct who was revealed to have a crush on her during sensitivity training (*AtS* "Sense and Sensitivity").

HARLEY, MARIA (SPIDER) | Originally one of Non's followers, she became one of Spike's Spikettes and fought alongside him. Maria had eight retractable spider legs on her back (*Spike* "After the Fall"). Later, after time was reset, she wrote the Twinkle series of vampire romance novels that was made into movies during the heyday of the vampire craze initiated by Harmony (*Spike* "Alone Together Now").

HARMONY BITES | Harmony's reality show on MTV. It aired at 7:00 p.m. weeknights until its cancellation (*Buffy* "Predators and Prey").

HARPY | Creature with the body of a bird and the head of a woman. The harpy who lived in Silverlake after the Fall of Los Angeles sang a song that soothed the residents (*Angel* "After the Fall").

HARRIS, ALEXANDER LAVELLE (XANDER) | NICHOLAS BRENDON | See following page.

HARRIS, ANTHONY (TONY) | CASEY SANDER | Xander's father. A bitter man, he got drunk at his son's wedding and started a brawl (*BtVS* "Hell's Bells).

HARRIS, JESSICA | LEE GARLINGTON | Xander's mother. She did not cook and often argued with her verbally abusive, alcoholic husband (*BtVS* "Hell's Bells").

HARRIS, JOSH | JOEY HIOTT AND CHRISTOPHER EMERSON | Xander and Anya's surly son in the alternate universe visions Xander saw at their wedding (*BtVS* "Hell's Bells").

HARRIS, KAREN | MEGAN VINT | Xander's second cousin (*BtVS* "Hell's Bells").

HARRIS, RORY | STEVEN GILBORN | Xander's uncle, the taxidermist. He collected DUIs and once lent Xander his powder-blue 1957 Chevrolet Bel Air convertible (*BtVS* "The Zeppo"). Rory flirted with a caterer at Xander's wedding (*BtVS* "Hell's Bells").

Harris, Alexander Lavelle

XANDER | NICHOLAS BRENDON |

Xander was the first civilian in Sunnydale to find out that Buffy was the Slayer, and he was quickly initiated into a newly forming team when he accidentally dusted his former best friend Jesse, who had been sired (*BtVS* "Welcome to the Helmouth"). He, Willow, and Giles became the Scooby Gang after helping Buffy prevent the Harvest (*BtVS* "The Harvest"). The feelings Xander felt for Buffy went beyond friendship, though they were not returned, and this often put him at odds with Angel. On more than one occasion, that jealousy endangered a mission. But Xander more than proved his value when he brought Buffy back to life with CPR after she died at the Master's hands; something Angel could not do because, as a vampire, he did not breathe (*BtVS* "Prophecy Girl").

For years, Xander suffered the abuse of Cordelia Chase; he and Willow once formed a club entitled the "We Hate Cordelia Club," in which he was the treasurer. But somehow, their intense arguing led to passion and an unlikely pairing (*BtVS* "What's My Line? Part 2"). All the while, he was largely unaware that his other best friend, Willow, had been pining for him for years. Cordelia broke up with Xander after catching him sharing a kiss with Willow (*BtVS* "Lovers Walk"). Cordelia's subsequent wish to punish Xander resulted in the demon Anyanka (Anya) becoming Sunnydale's newest resident (*BtVS* "The Wish") and Xander soon began another unlikely relationship with the former Vengeance Demon, leading to an engagement and a canceled wedding (*BtVS* "Hell's Bells").

Overall, Xander's romantic life was fraught with trouble, including romantic encounters with a human-sized praying mantis (*BtVS* "Teacher's Pet"), an Inca mummy (*BtVS* "Inca Mummy Girl"), and a demon allied with the First Evil (*BtVS* "First Date"). He also had an unfortunate incident in which the demon Toth hit him with the Ferula Gemini, a magical weapon that split Xander into a confident, suave version of himself and a nebbishy, full-hearted Xander. Willow joined them back together (*BtVS* "The Replacement"). Xander is one of the few members of the Scooby Gang to never possess magical powers, but with practice he grew more skilled in the fight against evil. This was especially true after a magical spell on Halloween gave him skills associated with the costume he wore: a soldier (*BtVS* "Halloween). Xander retained much of the knowledge he possessed during that time, which came in handy at the battle of the Hellmouth and future engagements (*BtVS* "Graduation Day, Part 2"). After losing an eye to the First's minion Caleb (*BtVS* "Dirty Girls"), Xander fought valiantly at the Battle of the Hellmouth (*BtVS* "Chosen") and afterward, when the Slayer Organization was formed, he assisted Buffy at Command Central in Scotland (*BtVS* "The Long Way Home").

After losing his new love interest Renee, a Slayer, at the hands of Japanese vampires (*Buffy* "Wolves at the Gate") Xander and Dawn got together in Tibet (*Buffy* "Retreat") and remained a couple after magic ended until she began to die (*Buffy* "The Core"). Though Dawn survived, her memories reset and she no longer felt connected to him. Despite knowing this, Xander went through the portal that the Mistress and the Soul Glutton magicked open in a hell dimension for her (*Buffy* "In Pieces on the Ground"). When they returned, Dawn's feelings for him had warmed again, and they're currently dating (*Buffy* "Own It").

HARRIS, SARA | ABIGAIL MAVITY AND ASHLEIGH ANN WOOD | Xander and Anya's sulky, demon-eared daughter in the alternate universe in which the pair were married (*BtVS* "Hell's Bells").

HARRISON | STEFAN UMSTEAD | One of the two paramedics who came to Buffy's house after she found her mother's body and called 911 (*BtVS* "The Body").

HARV | MIKE KIMMEL | Employee at the local meatpacking plant who gave Buffy information on Hellhound trainer Tucker Wells (*BtVS* "The Prom").

HARVEST, THE | Event prophesied by Aurelius in which the Master could gain power through a vampire vessel so that he could escape his magical prison. Buffy killed the vessel, Luke, before he had drained enough humans for the Master to free himself (*BtVS* "The Harvest").

HARVEY | JIM ORTLIEB | Employee at Wolfram & Hart who worked as a translator. He was excited to view the Nyazian Scrolls, but jealous of Wesley's work on them. He informed Lilah that the prophecy of the Tro-Clon wasn't about a birth, but a death (*AtS* "Lullaby").

HAUSER, AGENT | DANE NORTHCUTT | Wolfram & Hart employee who ran Angel's operations team and handled all of the wet work. Hauser didn't like the way Angel did things and didn't like working for a vampire. He tried to kill Angel and ended up with his head blown off (*AtS* "Conviction").

HAVILAND, COLONEL GEORGE | JOHN SAINT RYAN | Commanding officer of the Initiative until the facility review was complete. He oversaw the mission to capture and destroy Adam (*BtVS* "Superstar").

HAXIL BEAST | Procrea-Parasitic Demon who could only reproduce by implanting a human woman with its seed. The human mothers rarely survived labor but the ones that did wish they hadn't (*AtS* "Expecting").

HEATH | KEVIN WILL | Police officer in Kate's precinct with six brothers. While under the influence of the sensitivity training he let all the prisoners out of jail, including crime lord Tony Papazian (*AtS* "Sense and Sensitivity").

HEBRON'S ALMANAC | Book containing a spell that could be used to bind whatever would come out of the Hellmouth. The wording of the spell was "*Terra, vente, ignis et pluvia. Cuncta quattuor numina, vos obsecro. Defendete nos a recente malo resoluto.*" (Translation: Earth, wind, fire and rain. Linger four gods, we implore you. Defend us; immediately after I will release you) (*BtVS* "The Zeppo").

HECATE (GODDESS OF CREATURES GREAT AND SMALL, QUEEN AND PROTECTRESS OF WITCHES) | Greek goddess often called upon by witches—including Willow and Amy Madison—while casting spells (*BtVS* "Bewitched, Bothered, and Bewildered," "Gingerbread," "Him").

HEINRICH | Buffy's neighbor when she lived in San Francisco. He resided in apartment 2D (*Buffy* "Freefall").

HELEN'S KITCHEN | Diner where Buffy worked (as "Anne") when she ran away from home (*BtVS* "Anne").

HELGENBERG, MIKE | J BARTON | Cassie Newton's best friend. The Sunndydale High School student asked Cassie to the winter formal many times. His behavior made Buffy suspect that he might try to kill Cassie, but in reality he wanted to ask Dawn since Cassie wouldn't go (*BtVS* "Help").

HELLHOUND | Demon foot soldier bred during the Machash Wars and trained solely to kill. They feed off the brains of their foes. Tucker Wells unleashed several on the Sunnydale High prom. During their training, he showed them *Prom Night IV* and *Pump Up the Volume* (*BtVS* "The Prom").

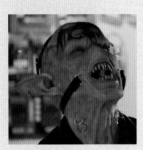

HELLIONS (RAZOR, MAG, AND KLYED) | **FRANC ROSS, GEOFF MEED, MIKE GRIEF** | Demon motorcycle gang that terrorized Sunnydale once they realized "Buffy" was just the Buffybot. They destroyed the robot (*BtVS* "Bargaining, Parts 1 and 2").

HELLMOUTH | Geographic location where the barriers between dimensions are thin, allowing for demons to cross over to Earth (*BtVS* "Welcome to the Hellmouth"). The town of Sunnydale was sucked into the Hellmouth beneath the town. There are also Hellmouths in Cleveland (*BtVS* "Chosen") and on Easter Island (*Spike* "A Dark Place"). Spanish name: *Boca del Infierno*, meaning "the mouth of hell."

HELLMOUTH, BATTLE OF THE | Name for the final battle between Buffy's forces and the First Evil's minions that destroyed Sunnydale (*BtVS* "Chosen").

HELL'S OFFSPRING | Book that Joyce Summers took note of when talking to Giles in the library about the trials of parenthood (*BtVS* "Bad Eggs").

HEMERY HIGH SCHOOL | Buffy's first high school, located in Los Angeles (*BtVS* "Welcome to the Hellmouth").

HENBANE, HELLEBORE, AND MANDRAKE ROOT | Items indicative of witchcraft confiscated from Willow's school locker (*BtVS* "Gingerbread").

HENRY | **CHRIS BABERS** | Gunn's vintage-car-stealing acquaintance (*AtS* "First Impressions").

HENRY, PHILIP | **STUART MCLEAN** | One of Giles's fellow youthful summoners of the demon Eyghon. The tattoo each adherent wore acted as a homing beacon for the demon, who reappeared and murdered Henry while he was on his way to Giles to ask for help. Eyghon then possessed his corpse (*BtVS* "The Dark Age").

HERA | Greek goddess. Willow invoked her while casting a vengeance spell against Glory (*BtVS* "Tough Love").

HERBERT | Piglet mascot of the Sunnydale High School Razorbacks, eaten by students under the influence of the Primals (*BtVS* "The Pack").

HIGH HAT MOTEL | Location where Beck, Betta George, and Jeremy Johns rested while on the run from Wolfram & Hart in Las Vegas (*Spike* "You Haven't Changed a Bit").

HIGH PRIEST (GUARDIAN OF THE WORD AND CARETAKER OF HER MOST BLESSED TEMPLE) | **ROBERT TOWERS** | This demon with little spikes all over its head and yellow-green skin was the only one who would speak the Devourer's name (*AtS* "Peace Out").

HIGHWAY ROBBERY BALL | Western-themed fundraiser for the East Hills Teen Center that was really a front for an embezzlement plot by Lilah Morgan and Lindsey McDonald. Angel thwarted the plan, ensuring that the center received all of the money raised at the event (*AtS* "Blood Money").

HISTORY OF WITCHCRAFT | Book that Willow pointed Dawn in the direction of when the younger Summers sister was looking to resurrect her mother. Topics include "Age of Levitation," "War of the Warlocks," and "Resurrection: A Controversy Born" (*BtVS* "Forever").

HOBSON | DAVID HAYDN-JONES | Tasked by the Watchers Council with guarding Zachary Kralik. After Kralik escaped, Hobson was brutally slaughtered (*BtVS* "Helpless").

HODGE | MATT GOODWIN | US Navy ensign during World War II (*AtS* "Why We Fight").

HOELICH, ANDREW | Student on the gymnastics team at the original Sunnydale High School. He was born in 1981 and died in 1998 when Cordelia and Xander staked him after he'd been turned (*BtVS* "Anne").

HOFFMAN | BOBBY BREWER | Student who vandalized the new Sunnydale High. He and his partner-in-crime, Grimes, agreed to repair the damage they had caused rather than face the cops (*BtVS* "Never Leave Me").

HOLBURN, KIT | ALEX BRECKENRIDGE | Dawn's new friend who was attacked by the angry spirits of the new Sunnydale High School (*BtVS* "Lessons").

HOLLY | Slayer who works for Deepscan. She, Kennedy, and Leah went to Santa Rosita to help Buffy and company fight a pack of Evolved Vampires led by Vicki. When Vicki retreated, Holly left with Faith (*Angel and Faith* "Where the River Meets the Sea").

HOLLY | TRISTINE SKYLER | Homeless teen who ran with Randall's crew and survived in the tunnels when the Beast put out the sun. She was in love with Randall and she used to crash in the sewers whenever the missions were full (*AtS* "Sacrifice").

HOLLY LODGE ESTATE | Public housing for the elderly in England near Highgate Cemetery. A crazed acolyte of Mother Superior killed several residents (*Angel and Faith* "Daddy Issues").

HOLT, GENEVIEVE | KATHRYN JOOSTEN | Abusive director of the orphanage formerly situated in Lowell House, where the Initiative commandos lived as college students. She punished the children for having impure thoughts (*BtVS* "Where the Wild Things Are").

HOLTZ, DANIEL | KEITH SZARABAJKA | Vampire hunter who first tracked Angelus and Darla to France in 1765 after they killed his wife and son and sired his daughter the year before (*AtS* "The Trial"). Holtz tortured Angelus in Rome but was injured when Darla rescued her beloved. In 1773 the demon Sahjhan approached Holtz and offered him a deal to let him kill Angelus. He accepted and disappeared from record, only to arrive in present-day Los Angeles as part of the Tro-Clon (*AtS* "Offspring"). Anxious to hunt Angelus and Darla, Holtz was not happy to work with Sahjhan's demon fighters (*AtS* "Quickening"). He still referred to the vampire as "Angelus," and didn't understand why Angel was trying to reason with him, something he had never done before. He allowed Angel to walk away with his newborn son after he saw Darla kill herself for Connor, but Holtz vowed to make Angel suffer more now that he was a father (*AtS* "Dad"). Holtz said that he planned to run away to Utah and live with Justine Cooper and Connor under different names, but when Angel and Lilah's men cornered him, he escaped into the Quor'toth hell dimension with the baby (*AtS* "Sleep Tight"). Holtz returned from Quor'toth a few weeks later, though it had been years in that hell dimension (*AtS* "A New World"). Holtz told Justine that he grew to love Connor after initially seeing him as a means to punish Angel. He later had Justine stab him twice in the neck to make it look like a vampire attack so Connor would blame Angel (*AtS* "Benediction").

HOLY VESSEL, THE | Human baby who carried the next spiritual leader of the Fell Brethren. The child was to be pampered, worshipped, and fed a holy diet of berries, panda meat, and (consecrated) urine before being sacrificed in the Gordobach rites in his thirteenth year (*AtS* "Not Fade Away," "Time Bomb").

HOMELESS MAN | BOB MORRISEY | Mentally unstable man who knew that Dawn was not human, calling her "curds and whey" (*BtVS* "Real Me").

HOMEOWNER | RICHARD WHARTON | Man who threatened the newly risen Buffy with a shotgun (*BtVS* "Bargaining, Part 2").

HOPE, SCOTT | FAB FILIPPO | Sunnydale High School student who dated Buffy and dumped her right before homecoming because she acted so distracted all the time (*BtVS* "Faith, Hope and Trick"). He spread a rumor that she was gay but later came out as gay himself (*BtVS* "Conversations with Dead People").

HORNED DEMON | MARK GINTHER | Played poker for kittens with Spike (*BtVS* "Life Serial").

HORNED TELEPATH DEMON | Blood from this demon with an unknown name turned Buffy into a telepath. The heart of its partner provided the antidote (*BtVS* "Earshot").

HOSTILE SUBTERRESTRIALS (HST) | The Initiative's codename for demons (*BtVS* "Doomed").

HOWLER DEMON | Bald, white, and slimy creature with clawlike hands that was drawn to the sewer under Beechwood Canyon. It made an eerie high-pitched howl when preparing to fight or mate (*AtS* "The Ring").

HUME'S PARANORMAL ENCYCLOPEDIA | Book that Giles did not have in his occult library, a fact that surprised disgraced Watcher Gwendolyn Post (*BtVS* "Revelations").

HUNDRED DAYS, THE | After devouring the spiders in the Box of Gavrok, Mayor Wilkins was invincible for these one hundred days leading to his Ascension (*BtVS* "Bad Girls," "Choices").

HUNGA MUNGA | Four-bladed, curved African tribal weapon. Part of Buffy's arsenal of weapons, it was instrumental in defeating the demon Ken (*BtVS* "Anne"),

HUNT | KAL PENN | Snobby college student turned into a Neanderthal by Black Frost Beer (*BtVS* "Beer Bad").

HUS | TODD THAWLEY | Avenging spirit of the Native American Chumash tribe who once lived where the town of Sunnydale was built. Hus was awakened when the ground above the long-buried Sunnydale Mission was disturbed. He could turn into green mist, a flock of crows, a coyote, and a bear. He called forth other spirit warriors to attack Buffy and company, who had gathered at Giles's condo for Thanksgiving. Buffy defeated him with his stone knife (*BtVS* "Pangs").

HUTAMIN PAW | Ritual artifact that Cordelia used as a backscratcher (*AtS* "Inside Out").

HYBERRAX | Enormous predator that resembles a beetle. Willow destroyed it in her wonderland dimension but it returned when she drank from the Spring of Memories (*Willow: Wonderland*).

"HYMN TO APHRODITE" | Poem by Sappho painted onto Tara's back by Willow in her dream after the destruction of Adam (*BtVS* "Restless").

HYPERION HOTEL | Former hotel that served as the headquarters for Angel Investigations prior to their move into the Wolfram & Hart offices. After the Fall of Los Angeles, Angel and his allies moved back into the Hyperion.

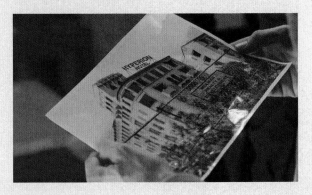

– I –

I AM WOMAN | Magazine that featured what Harmony considered to be an unflattering cover photo of her (*Angel and Faith* "Live through This").

ICARUS | Vampire who sired Harth Fray, and who served him (*Fray* "The Calling"). Erin Fray killed Icarus before the battle against Harth (*Fray* "The Gateway").

ICE DANCERS | Name of the ice show Buffy and her father used to attend together on her birthday (*BtVS* "Helpless").

IDOL OF UFTAR | Giles used a statue of this goddess of childbirth to defend himself against Toth in the Magic Box (*BtVS* "The Replacement").

ILLUMINATA, THE | Large diamond stolen by the Trio from the Sunnydale Natural History Museum. The diamond could render targets invisible, which is why the Trio incorporated it into their invisibility ray gun (*BtVS* "Smashed," "Gone").

ILLYRIA THE MERCILESS | **AMY ACKER** | See following page.

IMMORTAL, THE (THE FOULEST EVIL) | Not some common vampire. Considered an arch-enemy by Angelus, the Immortal has been described as "a giant. A titan straddling good and evil, serving no master but his own considerable desires." He was involved with both Darla and Drusilla and spent at least 300 years in Italy and 150 years in a Tibetan monastery. In Frankfurt he hatched the Rathruhn egg personally and gave nuns safe passage. He's written a life-changing book and he may have climbed Mount Everest as well. The Immortal was rumored to be dating Buffy in Rome, but it was actually a decoy for the Slayer (*AtS* "The Girl in Question," *Buffy* "The Long Way Home").

IMPOSING DEMON | **DEREK ANTHONY** | Bulbous-headed demon who thought Spike had brought the Potentials to a bar as snacks (*BtVS* "Potential").

INCAN MUMMY SEAL | Ancient pottery plate that prevented the Inca Mummy Princess from escaping her tomb (*BtVS* "Inca Mummy Girl").

INCUBUS | Male demons that feed on the human life energy during intimate contact. Their blood is blue, and when they hypnotize their victims, their eyes turn black with white flecks (*Buffy* "Old Demons").

Illyria the Merciless

| AMY ACKER |

An Old One of the demon age murdered by rivals and left adrift in the Deeper Well. When Fred touched her sarcophagus, Illyria was released into Fred's body, destroying her essence in the process. Angel tried to send Illyria back to the Deeper Well, but that action would have caused the deaths of untold innocents, so Angel was forced to let Fred die to save those lives. Illyria woke up in Fred's body, with blue hair and skin, wondrous at having a human form (*AtS* "A Hole in the World"). In a drawing of her temple, the statue of her true likeness was enormous, with four arms, a body composed of snakelike creatures coiled around a torso, and dozens of snake tails where feet should be. She only had some of Fred's memories, but she had nowhere else to go because her kingdom was dead. She told Wesley she would have to stay in this world and learn from him (*AtS* "Shells").

Desperate to stay on Earth, Illyria accused Wesley of breaking the Window of Orlon in order to restore Fred and kill the Old One. Angel later told Illyria the pain she was feeling was because she'd been trying to hold on to what she had been, just as they kept trying to hold on to Fred. Defeated, she allowed Wesley to siphon her extra energy off to another dimension (*AtS* "Time Bomb"). Depleted of her power, she didn't know how to live as a shadow of her former self. She

tried to soften up Wesley and told him she wished to explore the love he had for her body, but he told her to never do that again (*AtS* "The Girl in Question"). When Drogyn told her that her time was over and she belonged back in the Well, she admitted she wished she had never been brought out of it. With less power, she was beaten unconscious by Hamilton (*AtS* "Power Play"). She defeated Izzerial the Devil and other members of the Circle of the Black Thorn, but only arrived at Cyvus Vail's in time to hold Wesley as he died, turning into Fred to make him happy. She arrived at the alley rendezvous angry and ready to do some damage (*AtS* "Not Fade Away").

After the Fall of Los Angeles, Illyria lost her ability to control her powers and manifested as Winifred Burkle around Fred's loved ones and when she saw people in danger. Spike found her and they protected a band of humans; Spike attempted to keep her in her Illyria persona so that she could not be harmed. The Sadeki Demon Noelle revealed that there was nothing human in Illyria; she was only projecting her impressions of Fred. She and Spike became the Demon Lords of Beverly Hills; eventually, the sired Charles Gunn wounded her in her Fred manifestation, causing her to return to her alien Old One form (*Angel* "After the Fall"). After time was reset, she protected Charles Gunn in the hospital, then was stripped of her powers and "killed" by Severin in the Battle at the Deeper Well (*Buffy* "The Core").

Following the restoration of magic, Angel discovered Fred on the streets in Magic Town. This was because the old rules of magic had been reset. Fred has assisted Angel in Magic Town since their reunion. Illyria's essence still resides in Fred, and when Fred is stressed, Illyria manifests, as happened when she and Angel went to Galway and were threated by a trio of Irish witches (*Angel and Faith* "United").

INFERNO, THE | Part one of Dante's *Divine Comedy*, structured as a guided tour of the underworld, with nine levels of hell descending in concentric rings based on severity of the sin. The bottom level, the ninth circle, is reserved for the worst sinner in history—Judas Iscariot, who betrayed Jesus (*AtS* "A New World").

INGA AND ILSA | CHANIE COSTELLO AND JULIE COSTELLO | Swedish twins who lived with Jonathan in the alternate universe he created through magic (*BtVS* "Superstar").

INITIATIVE, THE | Super-secret military operation designed to capture and contain "Hostile Subterrestrials" (HSTs). Unknown to all but a handful of insiders, Dr. Maggie Walsh was attempting to build a cyborg-demon-human supersoldier named Adam. Team members included Graham Miller, Forrest Gates, Riley Finn, Jay, Kevin, Stavros, and Taggart (*BtVS* "The Initiative," "The I in Team").

INTRODUCTION TO PSYCHOLOGY | Required text for Professor Maggie Walsh's Intro to Psych class (*BtVS* "The Freshman").

ISAACS, DR. | Joyce's diagnostic physician at Sunnydale Memorial Hospital who examined her brain tumor (*BtVS* "Shadow").

ISHIHARA, KUMIKO | Daughter of Kazuo Ishihara, and a vampire witch who had studied with Saga Vasuki (Aluwyn). She provided the spell that would allow Toru to steal the power of the Slayers. It is not known if Buffy killed her, although it appears likely (*Buffy* "Wolves at the Gate").

ISHTAR | Mesopotamian goddess. Spike used her urn as an ashtray in the Magic Box (*BtVS* "Blood Ties").

ITIASHUP | Chumash word for the earth. In a chant, Hus invited the First People to walk upon *itiashup* with him again (*BtVS* "Pangs").

IVERSON, FREDDY | KERAM MELIKI-SANCHEZ | Editor of the Sunnydale High School paper. He was suspected of plotting to kill the students but his furtive behavior was a result of anxiety over a bad review he gave Oz's band (*BtVS* "Earshot").

IZZY (IZZERIAL THE DEVIL) | MARK COLSON | Wolfram & Hart client who resembled a devil, with red skin, horns, and a tail (*AtS* "You're Welcome"). He oversaw Angel's initiation into the Circle of the Black Thorn (*AtS* "Power Play") and ate dinner most nights with three members of the Circle until Illyria destroyed them (*AtS* "Not Fade Away").

— J —

JACK | STEPHEN M. PORTER | Bar owner who despised UC Sunnydale students so deeply that he served them enchanted Black Frost Beer brewed by his warlock brother-in-law (*BtVS* "Beer Bad").

JACKALS, THE | Gang that Jack O'Toole's crew wiped out in retribution after they threw Parker off the bridge (*BtVS* "The Zeppo").

JACKSON | MUSHOND LEE | Drug dealer who pushed his way into the East Hills Teen Center to get off the streets during the zombie police attacks (*AtS* "The Thin Dead Line").

JACKSON | PAUL BENJAMIN | Resident of the Monserrat Retirement Home. Friend of Marcus Roscoe who believed that his newborn granddaughter Katrina, would one day rule the world (*AtS* "Carpe Noctem").

JACOBS, ALICE | Mother to Marcie and mother-in-law of Cyrus Mitchell. Alice told her daughter that she didn't want Cyrus's father, Tom, around her grandchild. When Tom—a vampire—found out, he killed Marcie (*Tales* "Father").

JACOBI, MRS. | Harmony's elderly neighbor (*AtS* "Harm's Way").

JAMEEL | CEDRICK TERRRELL | Gunn's snitch, but really the public face of the demon Deevak (*AtS* "First Impressions").

JAMES | WILL ROTHHAAR | Little boy who was waiting for his mother in Sunnydale Park when Drusilla stalked him before Angel intervened (*BtVS* "Lie to Me").

JAMES | RON MELENDEZ | Vampire sired by Angelus and Drusilla who retained his love for Elisabeth throughout the centuries. He stole a locket for her before they were cornered in Marseilles in 1767 by Holtz, but he escaped and abandoned Angelus. Centuries later in Los Angeles, he learned that Angel had killed Elisabeth. In

response, he visited Dr. Gregson to have his heart removed, making him invincible for six hours. Angel kept him occupied until his time ran out and he turned to dust (*AtS* "Heartthrob").

JAMIE | WILLIAM VOGT | Vampire at UC Sunnydale who told Buffy that she had ruined the college experience for him and the other vampires before she dusted him (*BtVS* "Pangs").

JANE | Vampire present during the Master's Revivification Ritual. Buffy killed her (*BtVS* "When She Was Bad").

JANUS | Two-faced Roman mystical god. Janus represents the division of self into male and female, light and dark. Ethan Rayne incorporated a bust of Janus in his rituals to Chaos (*BtVS* "Halloween").

JAPE | ROB BENEDICT | One of Adam's top vampire minions (*BtVS* "New Moon Rising").

JARED | Werewolf character in the *Twinkle* novels. Jared is vampire William's rival for the heart of Maria (*Spike* "Alone Together Now").

JARED | JERRY TRAINOR | Comic-store clerk and fanboy of Team Angel (*AtS* "Supersymmetry").

JARVLEN FLESH EATER | Demon who Andrew Wells suggested the Trio conjure to devour the body of Katrina Silber (*BtVS* "Dead Things").

JASMINE (THE BLESSED DEVOURER, THE DEVOURER, THE BEASTMASTER) | GINA TORRES | A Power That Was. Forged in the inferno of creation and born fully grown as Cordelia and Connor's child, Jasmine claimed to have been around since the

beginning and fled when she could no longer fight back against the evil that covered the land. She returned when Angel earned Darla a new life, which ended up being Connor. When she was not around, her followers felt physical pain because she'd enchanted everyone and fed off their energy. Contact with her blood caused them to no longer be enchanted. Beneath her beautiful visage, her true form was hideous and disgusting (*AtS* "Shiny Happy People"). Jasmine went on TV to spread her word and her spell (*AtS* "Magic Bullet"). She was able to heal Connor and could see through the eyes of everyone around her. The governor of California dissolved his administration to turn power over to her because she wanted to free everyone from loneliness and horror (*AtS* "Sacrifice"). Jasmine ate a roomful of people and told Connor that when she fed, she wouldn't be able to see him. She swore that she would never hurt Connor or Cordelia because their love brought her here and keeps her tethered to this world. Although she had brought peace to Earth, she had done so by taking away everyone's free will. Once her spell was broken, Connor ended her life by punching her in the head so hard that his fist went through her (*AtS* "Peace Out").

JASON | STEVEN ROY | Follower of a Haxil Beast who impregnated Serena with the demon's offspring (*AtS* "Expecting").

JAY-DON | MICHAEL NAGY | Big-deal vampire from Vegas who ran with the Rat Pack. He dressed loud, wore sunglasses at night, and was dusted by Angel so he could take Jay-Don's place in the Natural History Museum heist (*AtS* "The Shroud of Rahmon").

JEAKINS, CLAIRE | CHERYL WHITE | Wife of an Angel Investigations client; she was cheating on her husband but told him she was abducted by aliens—repeatedly. Angel told her to go confess to her husband (*AtS* "Dear Boy").

JEAKINS, HAROLD | STEWART SKELTON | Angel Investigations client who believed his wife was regularly kidnapped by aliens but started to suspect she might also be cheating on him (*AtS* "Dear Boy").

Jenkins, Anya Christina Emmanuella

ANYANKA, AUD | EMMA CAULFIELD |

Vengeance Demon and Patron Saint of Women Scorned who worked to punish the unfaithful for over a thousand years. As a young woman named Aud in Sweden, she first gained the attention of D'Hoffryn when she cursed her lover, Olaf, for cheating on her. The head of the Vengeance Demons made her immortal and granted her the power to wreak vengeance on those who betrayed a lover. Anya arrived in Sunnydale to grant Cordelia the power of the wish after Xander kissed Willow. After transporting Sunnydale to a Wishverse where Buffy had never arrived in town, the Wishverse Giles destroyed Anyanka's pendant, which contained her power center. D'Hoffryn, the head of the Vengeance Demons, refused to restore her powers, dooming her to live as a mortal teenager (*BtVS* "The Wish").

Anya had a difficult time fitting in as she did not understand modern human rituals or simple everyday niceties. She often spoke bluntly and was socially awkward as she made her way through a human existence while longing to be a demon once again. Eventually Anya fell in love with Xander and the pair got engaged, but she became a Vengeance Demon once more when he left her at the altar (*BtVS* "Hell's Bells"). However, she realized her heart wasn't in the vengeance game anymore and asked to be changed back (*BtVS* "Selfless"). Following years of shifting alliances between good and evil, Anya died a hero at the Battle of the Hellmouth after using her fear of bunnies as a personal rallying cry (*BtVS* "Chosen"). She seemed to reappear in phantom form to haunt Xander, but eventually it became clear that the ghost he saw was not actually his former love. Anya has moved on and is at peace (*Buffy* "In Pieces on the Ground").

JENKINS, AUBREY | WENDY DAVIS | Woman who posed as an Angel Investigations client to set Gunn and Fred up for an attack to be filmed so Holtz could analyze their weaknesses (*AtS* "Loyalty").

JENKINS, MR. AND MRS. | Wealthy couple who donated $25,000 to the East Hills Teen Center at the Highway Robbery Ball. Their daughter from his first marriage is a fan of the TV show *Life Lessons* (*AtS* "Blood Money").

JENOFF THE SOUL SUCKER | PATRICK ST. ESPRIT | Owner of a demon casino where a young Gunn traded his soul for a truck. He wore a ring on his middle finger with a small needle to draw blood when shaking hands and he could suck people's souls out through their eyes. When Jenoff beat Angel at cutting cards, Angel cut off his head. His head grew back, but Angel encouraged his crowd of victims to take revenge on Jenoff in his weakened state and finish him off (*AtS* "Double or Nothing").

JERRY | One of Sunday's vampire minions. He was staked by Xander (*BtVS* "The Freshman").

JERRY | SCOTT DONOVAN | Fiancé of an Angel Investigations client. Jerry was lured underground by a tree demon, where his life force was nearly drained before he was rescued by Angel and Groo (*AtS* "Couplet").

JESSE | ERIC BALFOUR | Xander's best friend who was sired by one of the Master's minions. Xander accidentally dusted him at the Bronze (*BtVS* "The Harvest").

JHIERA | BAI LING | Daughter of the ruler of Oden-Tal, a demon dimension. She has been called the "Bringer of Chaos" and "a vessel of pure rage." She has two raised ridges running down her cheeks, and the ridges going down her spine are her *ko*, the center of her passions and desires. She escaped from Oden-Tal to Earth because on Earth the women have names. When she arrived on Earth, she needed cold water to control her *ko*. She guided other escaped women from her dimension to safety, hiding them in a spa outside the city, where they could cool off in ice baths. She and Angel shared a personal connection (*AtS* "She").

JILL | HEIDI DIPPOLD | Sister to the werewolf Nina Ash (*AtS* "Unleashed").

JO | JUSTINA MACHADO | Pregnant cashier at Costco who worked her way up from stock girl. Her daughter was to be a Seer, under the protection of the Tribunal until she came of age (*AtS* "Judgment").

JOHN | Serial killer that Drusilla was involved with in Las Vegas (*Spike* "Alone Together Now"). Convinced that Spike had stolen his soul, John, in turn, stole Spike's soul with a ritual (*Spike* "Something Borrowed") and was killed by Drusilla (*Spike* "Give and Take").

JOHN-LEE | NATHAN ANDERSON | Student at the original Sunnydale High School. When Cordelia pretended to come on to him, he informed her that it would hurt his social standing to be seen with Xander Harris's castoff. However in the Wishverse, he asked her to the Winter Brunch (*BtVS* "The Wish").

JOHNS, JEREMY | Human Spike befriended and worked with when Los Angeles was sent to hell. Jeremy was killed by Illyria in a preemptive strike when Non was feeding off him (*Spike* "After the Fall"). His body was possessed by a demon but ultimately he was freed of the possession and brought back to life (*Angel* "After the Fall").

JO-JO | Sunnydale High student whose enchanted dog costume turned him into a dog on Halloween. He tried to attack Cordelia, who was dressed as a cat (*BtVS* "Halloween").

JORDY | Oz's werewolf cousin, who bit him, thus turning Oz into a werewolf (*BtVS* "Phases").

JOSH | KEVIN CHRISTY | Student at the new Sunnydale High who went to see Buffy in her role as a counselor under the pretense that he needed her help to explore his sexuality (*BtVS* "Help").

JOSH | MARC ROSE | Frat boy at the Alpha Delta Halloween party who broke his neck falling down some stairs and rose as a zombie (*BtVS* "Fear Itself").

JOURNALS OF SAITAMA (THE SAITAMA CODEX) | Books that contain information about items of Eastern origin, particularly those with Dutrovic markings (*AtS* "Lineage").

JOVE | Loo's father and the husband of Amma, a radie tavern keeper in Melaka Fray's world (*Fray* "Ready Steady...." "All Hell").

JUDGE | JACQUELINE HAHN | Court official who recused herself from the Corbin Fries case due to the fact that she owned stock in Oriental Bay Exports, which was owned by Loros, Incorporated, which in turn was owned by a consortium that included the defendant (*AtS* "Conviction").

JUDGE, THE | Huge blue demon who was reassembled by Spike and Drusilla after being dismembered for six hundred years. He burned the humanity out of his victims (*BtVS* "Surprise"). Buffy destroyed him with a rocket launcher (*BtVS* "Innocence").

JULIA | JULIE MICHAELS | Vampire whom Billy Fordham told Buffy he dusted when, in reality, he let her go in return for information on Spike's location. Julia later stole the *du Lac* manuscript from the Sunnydale High library (*BtVS* "Lie To Me").

JULIE | Girl who played spin the bottle at the Lowell House party, then fled in shame and cut off all her hair in the bathroom (*BtVS* "Where the Wild Things Are").

JULIE | Member of Clive's coven. Andrew Wells was her demonology teacher. She showed Andrew the Asclepian Vial at a party (*Buffy* "Love Dares You").

JUNKIE VAMPIRE GIRL | RAINY JO STOUT | Buffy caught Riley with this vampire feeding on him. Later, Buffy dusted her (*BtVS* "Into the Woods").

JUST, SAINT | In 1398, this feared English vampire attacked a town where the Slayer (called the Maiden) and her Watcher lived. The Slayer beheaded him (*Tales* "Righteous").

JUSTIN | Vampire sired by Harmony who did not enjoy his new "life" because he was into tanning. He tried to stake her but she staked him first (*Buffy* "Predators and Prey").

JUSTIN | KAVAN REECE | Cute vampire boy Dawn ultimately had to stake during their double date. He was her first kiss (*BtVS* "All the Way").

— K —

KABUKI DEMON | Enormous reptilian demon minions of Toru who attempted to kill Aiko the Slayer. She killed them instead (*Buffy* "Wolves at the Gate").

KAKISTOS | **JEREMY ROBERTS** | Vampire so old that his hands and feet were cloven. Faith disfigured him when he killed her Watcher, and he arrived in Sunnydale to kill her. Buffy ran him through with a large wooden beam. *Kakistos* is Greek, meaning "the worst of the worst" (*BtVS* "Faith, Hope & Trick").

KALDA | Human slave in the castle of Pylea (*AtS* "There's No Place like Plrtz Glrb").

KALDERASH GIRL | **GINGER WILLIAMS** | "Most beloved daughter" of the Kalderash Gypsy Clan. Angelus killed her in 1898, and for this he was cursed with the restoration of his soul (*BtVS* "Becoming, Part 1").

KALDERASH MAN | **ZITTO KAZANN** | Taunted Angelus in 1898 as the vampire's soul was returned to his body (*BtVS* "Becoming, Part 1").

KALDERASH WOMAN | **SHANNON WELLES** | The Elder Woman who cursed Angelus by returning his soul to him in 1898 (*BtVS* "Becoming, Part 1").

KALI, HERA, KRONOS, TONIC | Willow's invocation when she confronted Glory after Glory brain-sucked Tara (*Buffy* "Tough Love").

KALISH, MRS. | Woman who lived at 1628 Revello Drive, which was next door to the Summers' house. Norman Pfister killed her so he could use her home as a base from which to initiate a plan to assassinate Buffy (*BtVS* "What's My Line? Part 1").

KALLET, DR. | Doctor at Sunnydale Memorial Hospital who treated Xander after he lost his eye (*BtVS* "Empty Places").

KALTENBACH, MR. | **JOHN O'LEARY** | Creepy old toymaker who jovially offered Halloween treats to Dawn, Janice, Zack, and Justin. Justin drained him (*BtVS* "All the Way").

KAMAL | Prio Motu Demon who—like other members of his race—didn't like being aboveground. Kamal kept a Buddhist shrine in his underground lair in Boyle Heights. Angel accidentally killed him (*AtS* "Judgment").

KANE, DESMOND | Pastor of Sharpesville. On May 26, 1723, Kane wrote in his journal about an Ascension that was supposed to take place the next day. It was the last entry in his journal . . . and the last evidence that Sharpesville ever existed (*BtVS* "Enemies").

KANE, SIR ROBERT | Author of *The Twilight Compendium*, which Gwendolyn Post expected Rupert Giles to have in his collection (*BtVS* "Revelations").

KARATHMAMANYUHG DEMON | Nocturnal breed of demon that feeds on roots or possibly human effluvia. Lorne is not a member of the species (*AtS* "Spin the Bottle").

KAREN | **ERICA LUTTRELL** | Woman who adored Jonathan and was attacked by the monster he created (*BtVS* "Superstar").

KATHERINE | Doublemeat Palace employee killed and eaten by the Wig Lady (*BtVS* "Doublemeat Palace").

KATIE | Best friend of Billy Lane (*Buffy* "Guarded").

KATIE | Name for Jack O'Toole's knife (*BtVS* "The Zeppo").

KATRIKA | Demon guest at Anya and Xander's wedding (*BtVS* "Hell's Bells").

KEANU | Palomino horse that belonged to Cordelia before the IRS confiscated her parents' belongings for tax fraud (*AtS* "The Ring").

KEEL, DESMOND | PETER BREITMAYER | Wolfram & Hart employee who served as in-house lawyer for Corbin Fries (*AtS* "Conviction").

KEEPER OF THE NAME, THE | ERIK BETTS | Large demon who knew Jasmine's true name but could not speak it because his mouth was sewn shut. Angel beheaded him and brought the head back to the hotel, where he cut open the mouth and unleashed Jasmine's true name with the beast's final breath (*AtS* "Peace Out").

KEIKO | Member of D'Hoffryn's Magic Council; a Japanese ghost who killed anyone who watched her black-and-white wedding video. D'Hoffryn murdered her for her magical ability to absorb and redirect the kinetic energy of an attack (*Buffy* "In Pieces on the Ground").

KELDEN | Oz and Bayarmaa's son (*Buffy* "Retreat").

KELKOR | Mischief demon (*BtVS* "I Robot . . . You Jane").

KEN | Oz's uncle who was the father of Jordy, Oz's werewolf cousin (*BtVS* "Phases").

KEN (KENNY) | Dawn's Thricewise Demon boyfriend at UC Berkeley; he placed a curse on her that changed her into a giant, a centaur, and a porcelain doll. Though he could appear human, in his natural state he resembled a three-eyed mollusk (*Buffy* "The Long Way Home").

KEN | CARLOS JACOTT | Bald, red-faced demon who trolled the streets of Los Angeles for homeless teenagers to lure to a fake shelter called the Family Home. It was a front for a hell dimension, where he and his fellow demons enslaved the teens until they were used up. Buffy killed him (*BtVS* "Anne").

KEN-DOLL | Willow's nickname for Kennedy (*Buffy* "Time of Your Life").

KENDALL, HARMONY | MERECEDES MCNAB | See following page.

KENDRA'S SWORD | Sword blessed by the virtuous knight who used it to slay Acathla. It was given to Kendra the Vampire Slayer by her Watcher, Mr. Zabuto. Buffy rammed the blade all the way through Angel and into Acathla, stopping the demon once more (*BtVS* "Becoming, Parts 1 and 2").

KENDRICK, DETECTIVE | ADAM VERNIER | Investigator who worked with Kate, and didn't know the difference between Scully and Mulder (*AtS* "Sanctuary").

Kendall, Harmony

| MERECEDES MCNAB |

Originally a member of Cordelia Chase's clique at Sunnydale High, Harmony usurped her friend's position as the queen of mean when Cordelia first dated and then was dumped by Xander (*BtVS* "The Wish"). Harmony fought valiantly on Graduation Day but was bitten and sired (*BtVS* "Graduation Day"). She then entered into a disastrous relationship with Spike, eventually gathering enough self-esteem to try to kill him when it became clear to her that he was in love with Buffy (*BtVS* "Crush"). For a while Harmony headed up her own gang (*Buffy* "Real Me"), but eventually she left for Los Angeles where she bonded with Cordelia again but ultimately betrayed the Angel Investigations team (*AtS* "Disharmony").

Wesley hand-picked Harmony to be Angel's assistant at Wolfram & Hart (*AtS* "Conviction"). It was not a surprise to Angel when she told Hamilton about her boss's plans. Angel fired her, but he did provide a letter of reference (*AtS* "Not Fade Away"). Harmony escaped from Los Angeles before it was sent to hell. When she bit comedian Andy Dick in an alley, paparazzi published photos, proving the existence of vampires. She used this as a stepping-stone to becoming a star of her own TV show, *Harmony Bites*. She then began a propaganda campaign to paint Slayers as evil terrorists (*Buffy* "Predators and Prey") and founded Reform Vampirism (*Buffy* "Freefall"). When magic was restored, Harmony stole the *Vampyr* book and Clem wrote in it that unicorns are real, making it so. Harmony has loved unicorns all her life and continues to love them to this day (*Buffy* "I Wish").

KENNEDY | IYARI LIMON | Wealthy Potential and Willow's girlfriend after the death of Tara (*BtVS* "Bring On the Night"). Activated as a New Slayer, Kennedy fought at the Battle of the Hellmouth (*BtVS* "Chosen"). After her breakup with Willow and the end of magic, she founded Deepscan, a security company that provides Slayers as bodyguards (*Buffy* "Guarded").

KENNY | Faith's ex-boyfriend who was a drummer (*BtVS* "Revelations").

KENNY | KYLE DAVIS | Teen who sought shelter at the East Hills Teen Center when undead police officers had control of the streets (*AtS* "The Thin Dead Line").

KENSINGTON | London district in which Harmony and Clem reside (*Angel and Faith* "Live through This").

KENT | Human pursued by mutants after the plague ball exploded over London. He sought shelter with Nadira (*Angel and Faith* "Where the River Meets the Sea," "United").

KERBERON | God-king. The Soul Glutton and the Mistress opened a portal to his hell dimension. Kerberon attacked Buffy and company with his army, but Dawn defeated him by using her Key powers (*Buffy* "In Pieces on the Ground").

KEVIN | JOHNNY MESSNER | Calvin-Klein-model-looking guy possessed by a Burrower Demon who burst through his chest to claim its next victim (*AtS* "Lonely Heart").

KEY, THE | Ball of mystical green energy that was transformed by the Monks of Dagon into the human Dawn Summers, assuming that Buffy would protect her "sister" with her life. The hellgod Glorificus needed the Key to open the portal between the dimensions and return home (*BtVS* "Real Me").

KHUL | High priest of the Temple of Sobek, an ancient Egyptian cult that worshipped the demon Sobek (*BtVS* "Shadow").

KHUL'S AMULET | Garish green stone serving as a conduit in the transmogrifying rituals of the Temple of Sobek. It has the power to change a living thing into an immense cobra creature (*BtVS* "Shadow").

KILLER OF THE UNDEAD | Poison that Faith used on Angel. The only cure is the blood of a Slayer (*BtVS* "Graduation Day, Part 1").

KIM | MARINA BENEDICT | Singer, former med student, and friend of Lorne's who was infected by a Wraither (*AtS* "Sleep Tight").

KINDEL, WALTER | STAN KLIMECKO | Serial killer who kidnapped a New Slayer named Dana. He killed her family and tortured her in the basement of a whiskey factory. Kindel was shot dead during a liquor store holdup (*AtS* "Damage").

KINGMAN'S BLUFF | Cliff above downtown Sunnydale from which the Pacific Ocean can be seen. Angel tried to commit suicide there on Christmas Eve in 1998 by waiting for the sun to rise (*BtVS* "Amends"). Four years later, Willow raised the Temple of Proserpexa at that location as it had been buried in an earthquake in 1932 (*BtVS* "Grave").

KIP | JAKE PHILLIPS | Snobby UC Sunnydale frat boy who drank Black Frost Beer and became a caveman (*BtVS* "Beer Bad").

KIPCHAK | Army that catapulted plague-infected corpses into Genoa during the black plague (*BtVS* "Welcome to the Hellmouth").

KIPPLER VOLUMES | Books in which Xander searched for references to the demon Olvikan (*BtVS* "Graduation Day, Part 2").

KIRA | Slayer who accompanied Buffy on her mission to free Xander from Dracula's employ (*Tales* "Antique").

KIRSCH, BRIAN | ALAN ABELEW | Father of a Sunnydale High School student; killed by Spike on Parent-Teacher Night (*BtVS* "School Hard").

KIRSTIE | KELLI GARNER | Mean girl at Dawn's middle school who was spreading rumors that Dawn had attempted suicide (*BtVS* "The Body").

KITH'HARN DEMON | Known henchmen of the warlock Cyvus Vail (*AtS* "Origin").

KLEIN & GABLER | Rival law firm to Wolfram & Hart (*AtS* "Blind Date").

KLEPTES-VIRGO | Class of female monsters that seduce and kill human male virgins. They include the She-Mantis, Siren, and Sea-Maiden (*BtVS* "Teacher's Pet").

KLEYNACH DEMON | Dark entities, like the Wolfram & Hart Senior Partners, use the form of a Kleynach to manifest because these demons don't have to rely on being conjured or brought forth. They can come and go as they please with a special ring. Legend says that the Kleynach rose up from their demon world, raped and pillaged the villages of man, and all who fought against them were incinerated, whether they struck with fist or sword. But one brave and worthy knight had a glove fashioned and blessed by all the powers of light. Whoever wore this Holy Glove could kill the Kleynach just by grabbing it at the throat. Angel killed one such demon with the glove in the Wolfram & Hart offices (*AtS* "Reprise").

KLU-(CLICK)-KA | Kungai word for "auction" (*AtS* "Parting Gifts").

KLUSMEYER, THERESA | **MEGAHN PERRY** | Girl whom Buffy protected in self-defense class when Larry Blaisdell tried to cop a feel. Angelus sired Theresa and just before Xander dusted her, she told Buffy, "Angel sends his love" (*BtVS* "Phases").

KNIGHTS OF BYZANTIUM, THE | Military order of knights and clerics sworn to destroy the Key so that it couldn't fall into the hands of Glorificus the Hellgod. Their motto was "the Key is the link. The link must be severed. Such is the will of God" (*BtVS* "Checkpoint"). The Knights sported tattoos on their foreheads,

wore chain mail, rode horses, and used medieval weapons. They were ultimately defeated (*BtVS* "Spiral").

KNOX | **JONATHAN WOODWARD** | Wolfram & Hart employee in research and development who was considered the McGyver of the company (*AtS* "Home"). He denied being evil, saying that he just mixed the potions and followed orders (*AtS* "Conviction"). Knox gave Fred a Valentine's Day card, even though she had already let him down because he'd worked at the company too long and didn't make her laugh (*AtS* "Smile Time"). Knox worshipped Illyria and chose Fred as her shell, knowing Angel would let her die (*AtS* "A Hole in the World"). Wesley shot Knox dead after he opened Illyria's temple (*AtS* "Shells").

KNOX | **MICK MURRAY** | Head vampire in a nest near Gunn's old neighborhood. He kidnapped and sired Gunn's sister, Alonna, before Angel dusted him (*AtS* "War Zone").

KOH, ELDRE | Nitobe warrior demon framed for murder and incarcerated in a mystical prison. When Buffy destroyed the Seed of Wonder, he escaped and went to Earth to thank her. He wound up on the island of Alcatraz, where he was subsequently discovered by Spike (*Buffy* "Freefall"). Koh initially helped Buffy fight off the Siphon and explained that he owed her his life (*Buffy* "Guarded"). However, he made a side deal with Wolfram & Hart to kill Theo Daniels in return for the identity of whoever framed him and wiped out his race (*Buffy* "Welcome to the Team"). Recanting his duplicity, Koh fought at the Deeper Well and later in Santa Rosita during the zompire crisis (*Buffy* "The Core"). In Magic Town, he discovered that Illyria was the mass murderer he had been seeking, but recognized that she now resides within Fred. He gave Fred a pass and continues to assist Angel and Buffy to this day (*Angel and Faith* "A Tale of Two Families").

KONIG, BRAD | CHANEY KLEY MINNIS | Vamp minion of Harmony's who kissed up to her by giving her unicorn statues, but didn't obey her when she gave the order to kill his cohort Mort. Buffy dusted him (*BtVS* "Real Me").

KOREAN SLAYER | Sid the demon hunter knew her back in the 30s (*BtVS* "The Puppet Show").

KOVACS, JUDY | MELISSA MARSALA, EVE SIGALL | Former teller at the City Trust Bank of Salina, Kansas in the 1950s. A light-skinned African-American woman, she had been passing as white since she was a teenager.

But when the truth came out, her employer fired her, and her fiancé, Peter, broke off their engagement. She stole money from the bank and fled a private investigator and federal authorities, who lost track of her after she checked into the Hyperion in 1952. At the time she asked Angel for help, but when a mob in the hotel was looking for a killer and had her cornered, she identified Angel instead, revealing that she saw the blood in his room. After the crowd hanged him, the guilt consumed her and she lived the rest of her life in the hotel, protected and fed on by a Thesulac Demon. When Angel found her again, she asked his forgiveness. He granted it and she died in peace (*AtS* "Are You Now or Have You Ever Been").

KOVITCH DEMON | Race of demons hailing from the Caucasus (*AtS* "She").

KRAIGLE, IRV | MICHAEL DEMPSEY | CFO of Lycor, a client of Wolfram & Hart (*AtS* "Dead End").

KRALIK, ZACHARY | JEFF KOBER | Insane vampire who was a serial killer before he was sired. He kidnapped Joyce, but then exploded when Buffy tricked him into drinking holy water to take his pain pills (*BtVS* "Helpless").

KRAMER, DEETTA | Darla's pseudonym when she was trying to drive Angel crazy in LA. She pretended Angel broke in and killed her husband to send Kate and the police after Angel (*AtS* "Dear Boy").

KRAMER, JOSEPH | **PETE GARDNER** | Victim of a botched procedure at the Fairfield Clinic that caused him to stab himself in his newly transplanted eye due to the psychic link it maintained with its previous owner. All evidence of him and his family was wiped away by Wolfram & Hart to cover up the incident (*AtS* "Dead End").

"KRAMER, STEPHEN" | **MATT NORTH** | Actor hired to portray Darla's husband, thinking he was helping to draw in her stalker. He was killed by a vampire to frame Angel. The real Stephen Kramer was assumed dead, as Angel could enter his house (*AtS* "Dear Boy").

KRIEGEL, DR. AARON | **RANDY THOMPSON** | Joyce's attending physician during the treatment of her brain tumor (*BtVS* "Listening to Fear"). He also performed her autopsy (*BtVS* "The Body").

KROEGER, DORIS | **SUSAN RUTTAN** | Social services caseworker who was probably going to recommend that Dawn be removed from Buffy's care. She had a breakdown when Buffy tormented her while invisible (*BtVS* "Gone").

KUHKRI | Knife with a long, sharp blade that Absalom planned to use in the Master's attempted Revivification Ritual (*BtVS* "When She Was Bad").

KULAK OF THE MIQUOT CLAN | **CHAD STAHELSKI** | Reptilian participant in SlayerFest '98. He was blown up in a cabin (*BtVS* "Homecoming").

KUNGAI DEMON | **HENRY KINGI** | Powerful race of demons from Asia with a Tak horn on their forehead. They are capable of consuming the life force of their opponents. Prior to joining Angel Investigations, Wesley hunted one such demon before another demon killed it (*AtS* "Parting Gifts").

KUN-SUN-DAI | Mystics who are acolytes of the Beast, and wear their recorded history all over their bodies (*AtS* "Awakening").

KURSKOV, COUNT | **MARK HARELIK** | Director of the Blinnikov World Ballet Corps and a wizard who was obsessed with one of his ballerinas. In a jealous rage, he pulled her out of time and out of any reality beyond his theater company, swearing she would dance for him forever. Centuries later he was weakened by the attacks on his illusion and could no longer hold the ballerina. Angel destroyed his power center—the red stone in the Russian cross he wore—leaving Kurskov devastated and unconscious (*AtS* "Waiting in the Wings").

KURTH | Triune Demon who worked for Fraser. His third arm, located in his back, regenerated when he purchased Mohra Demon blood from Baphon. Kurth told Angel where an auction was being held for the blood supply (*Angel and Faith* "Live through This").

KWAINI | Race of female demons who were generally peaceful, nonviolent, incredibly articulate, and gentle creatures. An addiction to a PCP-like drug made them violent and super strong. Disposal of their bodies is relatively standard, consisting of burial on virgin soil and a simple Latinate incantation (*AtS* "The Prodigal").

– L –

LABYRINTH MAPS OF MALTA | Documents that Giles had on order when Gwendolyn Post quizzed him about it (*BtVS* "Revelations").

LACH-NIE DEMON | Six-horned demon. A member of their race owed Lorne a favor, for which he was paid with a Cedrian Crystal (*AtS* "Benediction").

LAGOS | GARY KASPAR | Warrior demon with large round horns and four fangs who went in search of the Glove of Myhnegon. Buffy beheaded him (*BtVS* "Revelations").

LAMPKIN, NURSE | APRIL ADAMS | Psychiatric nurse at Sunnydale Memorial Hospital. She assumed the patients' shrieks were due to their mental condition, but in reality the Queller Demon was murdering them (*BtVS* "Listening to Fear").

LA MUSIQUE AUX TUILERIES | Painting by Manet first exhibited in 1863 that includes Manet and the French poet and critic Baudelaire, a friend of the artist. Angel is able to speak knowledgeably about the painting and the real-life models (*AtS* "She").

LANCE | JEFF MAYNARD | Sunnydale High School student who was bullied by the four students who became possessed by hyena spirits (*BtVS* "The Pack").

LANDOK (LANDOKMAR OF THE DEATHWOK CLAN) | BRODY HUTZLER | Lorne's cousin from Pylea. Through training, he could channel his mind to see one's aura, and he used this skill to hunt by tracking the hostility waves a Drokken Beast left behind. When he was bitten by the Drokken, he returned to Pylea for the antidote (*AtS* "Belonging").

LANE, BILLY (BILLY THE VAMPIRE SLAYER) | Young man who trained as a Slayer after being inspired by Devon, who became Billy's boyfriend and Watcher (*Buffy* "Billy the Vampire Slayer"). Billy fought in San Francisco with Buffy but returned to Santa Rosita, his hometown, to deal with the zompire epidemic. Sineya signaled her approval for this move by augmenting his strength and focus during a zompire attack (*Buffy* "The Core"). Giles confirmed that with the new Seed, the force behind the Chosen Ones had more agency than it once did, and that while men could still not be full Slayers, it was clear that the essence of the Slayer had agreed to regard Billy as an ally (*Buffy* "New Rules"). He continues to fight the good fight.

LANE, SKY | Billy Lane's grandmother. She took him in after his parents threw him out of the house for being gay (*Buffy* "Guarded").

LANIER, PAUL | PATRICK KILPATRICK | Head of a wish-granting company that was rival to Magnus Bryce (*AtS* "Guise Will Be Guise").

LARCH, SAMUEL | Demon bookie that lived in apartment 424 on the Miracle Mile. Prior to his death (and dismemberment) by rogue demon killers formerly associated with Gunn, the demon was fully assimilated with no history of violence, and presented no threat to anyone (*AtS* "That Old Gang of Mine").

LAS CUCHILLAS | Girl gang that Soledad the Slayer left when she was activated as a New Slayer (*Buffy* "Predators and Prey").

LASOVIC | MARK GINTHER | Demon who was forced to do battle in the demonic fight club XXI. He disintegrated when he crossed the red line to murder his captors and effectively entered a kill zone (*AtS* "The Ring").

LAURA | TRACEY COSTELLO | Sandwich-cart owner with a master's degree in fine arts. She thought Angel hated her after he failed at small talk at a party hosted by their mutual friend, Cordelia (*AtS* "She").

LAURIE | ANASTASIA HORNE | Percy West's snotty college girlfriend (*BtVS* "Doomed").

LAWNSDALE, MRS. | Software customer of robot Ted Buchanan (*BtVS* "Ted").

LAWSON, ENSIGN SAM | EYAL PODELL | Vampire who was formerly a soldier in World War II before being sired. Lawson inherited command of a stolen German submarine prototype in 1943 after vampires—including Spike—killed his captain. When Angel joined the mission under the direction of the Demon Research Initiative, Lawson accepted the existence of demons and vampires and followed Angel's orders until he was stabbed by a German officer. Needing Lawson to save the ship, Angel sired him so he could keep working, then put him off the sub. Lawson arrived at Wolfram & Hart sixty years later to punish Angel for turning him but not giving him a purpose. He took the team hostage and asked Angel for a mission. Angel staked him to end his empty life (*AtS* "Why We Fight").

LAZARUS INCANTATION | Spell that Angel intended to use to resurrect Rupert Giles (*Angel and Faith* "What You Want, Not What You Need").

LEAH | One of Buffy's most trusted New Slayers (*Buffy* "The Long Way Home"). She later joined Deepscan and assisted with the zompire crisis in Santa Rosita (*Angel and Faith* "Where the River Meets the Sea").

LEAN BOY | ANDREW PALMER | Vampire member of the Order of Aurelius who accompanied Spike on his raid of Sunnydale High School (*BtVS* "School Hard").

LE BANC | Seventies-era vampire crime boss who was beginning to take on demonic aspects like pointy ears. He killed Nikki Wood's lover, Li, and later fled to the Bahamas where he continued his smuggling operations. Nikki killed him (*Tales* "Nikki Goes Down!").

LEFCOURT, MS. | JOY DIMICHELLE MOORE | Teacher at Dawn's middle school who encouraged parental involvement (*BtVS* "Bargaining, Part 1").

LEGENDS OF VISHNU | One of the texts Giles consulted while researching Marcie Ross's invisibility (*BtVS* "Out of Mind, Out of Sight").

LEGGETT, DR. DALE | Morgan Shay's physician who worked in the cancer ward of the California Institute of Neurosurgery (*BtVS* "The Puppet Show").

LEHANE, FAITH | ELIZA DUSHKU | See following page.

LEHANE, PAT | Faith's ne'er do well father, who visted her in England to get money to pay off the Irish mob (*Angel and Faith* "Daddy Issues").

LEI-ACH DEMON | TORRY PENDERGRASS | Once-proud warrior demons turned scavengers. Glory sent a trio of them to kill Buffy at the Magic Box (*BtVS* "Family").

LEISHMAN | Scientist who worked for Zane Pharmaceuticals attempting to find a cure for the plague-ball epidemic. He experimented on Fred to access Illyria (*Buffy* "United").

LENNY | MARC BURNHAM | One of Spike's former henchvamps, sent as part of the Mayor's "welcoming committee" when the vampire returned to Sunnydale. He was dusted by Spike (*BtVS* "Lovers Walk").

Lehane, Faith

| ELIZA DUSHKU |

Faith was the last Slayer to be activated by the death of the current Slayer, who in Faith's case was Kendra. She came to Sunnydale because she was on the run from Kakistos, who was ultimately killed by Buffy (*BtVS* "Faith, Hope & Trick"). After accidentally killing Deputy Mayor Allan Finch, she believed herself to be irredeemably bad, and allied herself with Mayor Wilkins, and on his orders deliberately murdered Professor Worth (*BtVS* "Graduation Day, Part 1"). Faith fell into a coma after fighting Buffy and swapped bodies with Buffy when she woke up. Faith then fled a felony arrest warrant in Sunnydale and escaped to Los Angeles (*BtVS* "Who Are You?"), where Wolfram & Hart offered her a job killing Angel in exchange for clearing her record.

When Faith couldn't get Angel to fight her, she kidnapped Wesley and tortured him. Angel showed up to fight, but when he refused to kill her, she confessed to wanting it all to end (*AtS* "Five by Five"). Buffy's arrival in LA pushed Faith over the edge, but their argument was interrupted by three Council goons. She and Buffy worked together to defeat the goons; then she went to Kate's precinct and confessed to the murder of Finch, and was jailed (*AtS* "Sanctuary"). She broke out of prison when she heard Angelus was back, but told Wes she wouldn't kill him because Angel was the only person who ever tried to save her (*AtS* "Salvage"). Later, she injected herself with Orpheus and let Angelus drink from her so they'd both be unconscious. In a mystical plane, she accompanied an angry Angelus as he watched Angel relive good deeds in Angelus's version of hell. When Angel was coming back, she began to fade and he challenged her to fight because redemption required work. She came back in time to save Angel from Connor then left LA to accompany Willow back to Sunnydale upon learning about the threat of the First (*AtS* "Orpheus").

For a time Faith was elected leader of the Potentials, supplanting Buffy (*BtVS* "Empty Places"). After the victorious Battle of the Hellmouth with the New Slayers, she worked briefly with Robin Wood in Cleveland until Giles tapped her to assassinate an English rogue Slayer, Lady Genevieve (*Buffy* "No Future for You"). They went on other missions together as well. She was present when Angel, under the influence of Twilight, snapped Giles's neck, and she took a catatonic Angel to England where she inherited Giles's entire estate except for the *Vampyr* book (*Buffy* "Last Gleaming"). In London, she worked with a group of New Slayers that included Nadira, who sought revenge on Angel, Pearl, and Nash for the damage they did during Twilight (*Angel and Faith* "Family Reunion"). She accompanied Angel, Connor, and Willow to Quor'toth to bring magic back to Earth, and assisted Angel in resurrecting Giles as a twelve-year-old boy (*Angel and Faith* "What You Want, Not What You Need"). For a time, she worked for Kennedy's Deepscan company, assisting in the retrieval of Riley and Sam Finn (*Angel and Faith* "Lost and Found"), and returned to England to assist with the battle against Archaeus and Drusilla. She's currently in Magic Town, helping the helpless along with Angel (*Angel and Faith* "A Tale of Two Families").

LENNY | MICHAEL YAVNIELI | Abusive ex-boyfriend of a client who came to Angel Investigations for protection. Angel stopped him (*AtS* "In the Dark").

LESTER | DWAYNE L. BARNES | Gunn's cousin who engaged in illegal activity and wasn't keen on vampires (*AtS* "The Shroud of Rahmon").

LETHE'S BRAMBLE | Magical plant used in spells for memory loss (*BtVS* "All the Way," "Once More, with Feeling," "Tabula Rasa").

LEVINSON, JONATHAN | DANNY STRONG | Buffy's nebbish classmate at Sunnydale High. Jonathan became a sorcerer, ultimately changing reality for a brief time so that he was the most popular and accomplished person in the world (*BtVS* "Superstar"). Jonathan was a member of the Trio, which originally formed to bedevil the Slayer; later, their intentions grew more sinister and Jonathan helped Buffy defeat Warren, their ringleader (*BtVS* "Seeing Red"). Andrew killed him while under the influence of the First (*BtVS* "Conversations with Dead People"). After the end of magic, Andrew returned to Sunnydale to retrieve Jonathan's DNA sample and personality (that had been downloaded on a USB drive) and began to interact with his hologram (*Buffy* "I Wish"). When Andrew's efforts to provide him with either a robot or a real body stalled, Jonathan convinced him to make a deal with the Sculptor to provide him with a body in return for Buffy's Scythe. Andrew's double-cross

meant that Jonathan's new body would eventually decay (*Buffy* I Wish"). Jonathan made a deal with D'Hoffryn to serve him, but quit when D'Hoffryn proved too ruthless (*Buffy* "Own It").

LI | Nikki Wood's lover. An NYPD cop who died on a stakeout. Believed to be Robin Wood's father (*Tales* "Nikki Goes Down!").

LIBRARY OF DEMONIC CONGRESS | Every contract signed with the lower planes is filed there (*AtS* "Smile Time").

LIEUTENANT, THE | KEN GRANTHAM | Kate's boss. Her father rescued him from the emotional fight at Blue Bar (*AtS* "Sense and Sensitivity").

LIFE LESSONS | TV show with a cast that participated in the celebrity fundraiser for the East Hills Teen Center, pretending to rob the attendees for their donations (*AtS* "Blood Money").

LILLIAN, PROFESSOR | LELAND CROOKE | Poetry professor who told Buffy he was sorry to see her drop his class. She helped him with his slides (*BtVS* "Tough Love").

LINA | KIMBERLY JAMES | Demon with a tail and quills instead of hair who worked at Madame Dorion's brothel (*AtS* "War Zone").

LINDA | LISA JAY | Spike drained and killed her while under the influence of The First (*BtVS* "Sleeper").

LISA | RAE'VEN LARRYMORE KELLY | Dawn's friend who cheered her up in the bathroom at school after the kids talked about her "suicide attempt" (*BtVS* "The Body").

LISA (LOCALIZED IONIC SENSORY ACTIVATOR) | Covert device designed by Takeshi Morimoto's company and worn by black ops agents to regulate body temperature, heartbeat, and body chemistry. Gwen Raiden tricked Gunn into helping her steal it hoping to neutralize her electrical charges. It appeared to work as it allowed her to touch Gunn without killing him (*AtS* "Players").

LISHANNE | Sunnydale High student who made it onto the cheerleading squad. Catherine Madison used magic to remove her mouth (*BtVS* "Witch").

LISSA | ASHANTI | Demon who was quite beautiful in her human form, but reptilian in her true visage. She attempted to bleed Xander onto the Seal of Danzalthar. Buffy killed her (*BtVS* "First Date").

LISTER DEMON | Generally they have cryptic prophecies, but one was clear: a Promised One would save them from the Scourge. A group of these demons hid in Los Angeles, trying to buy safe passage to Briole. Doyle's visions allowed Angel to help them escape, but it was Doyle who fulfilled the prophecy by saving them all (*AtS* "Hero").

LI TOM | Herbal shop in Chinatown run by a seemingly elderly human couple (Ken Takemoto and Alice Lo) who were really demons. The demons trained in the martial arts were on the side of good, protecting a powerful coin (*AtS* "That Vision Thing").

LITTLE PRINCESS, THE | Children's book by Frances Hodgson Burnett. Fred asked Wesley to read it to her while she was dying (*AtS* "A Hole in the World").

LIVING DEAD | Scottish zombies who attacked the Slayer Organization Command Central after being summoned by Amy Madison (*Buffy* "The Long Way Home").

LIVING FLAME | Spell to create the magical fire that was able to destroy the Glove of Myhnegon. The spell chanted "*Exorere, Flamma Vitae. Prodi ex loco tuo elementorum, in hunc mundum vivorum.*" (Translation: Arise, Flame of Life. Come forth from your place of the elements, into this world of the living.) At this point, green powder was introduced, which turned the fire green as the chanting repeated. And finally red powder was introduced, to create bright-red flame (*BtVS* "Revelations").

LIZ | ANDY KREISS | Lizard demon who ate its young and liked to sing at Caritas (*AtS* "Judgment").

LIZARD MAN | Spike's nickname for a creature that sought retribution when Illyria killed Nata and others of his flock. Spike tried to choke him to death with his own long tongue, but Illyria stabbed the creature through the chest (*Spike* "After the Fall").

LLOYD, ALLEN | RON MARASCO | Sensitivity coach with the Sensitivity Awareness Institute. Wolfram & Hart went to a great deal of effort and expense to get him into Kate's precinct to lead a sensitivity seminar in order to neutralize the police so their client Little Tony could make his getaway (*AtS* "Sense and Sensitivity").

Lockley, Kate

ELISABETH ROHM |

Detective with the LAPD who met Angel when she was undercover tracking a killer (*AtS* "Lonely Heart"). When their cases started intersecting, she began sharing information with Angel. A serial-killer case brought her face-to-face with Angel's protégé, Penn, which was when she learned about vampires' existence, and about Angel's violent history (*AtS* "I've Got You under My Skin"). After her father was murdered by vampires, she needed Angel's help to destroy the demons responsible (*AtS* "The Prodigal"). Assigned to arrest Angel for breaking into Wolfram & Hart, she released him after realizing he was the only one who could stop Darla and Drusilla's killing spree (*AtS* "Reunion"). When she learned about the zombie cops, she was worried that her father was reanimated (*AtS* "The Thin Dead Line"). Relieved of duty for giving Angel access to that precinct, freeing him after his arrest, and other incidents, Kate turned in her badge and gun. After a drinking binge, she swallowed some pills, then called Angel, leaving him a message blaming him for everything (*AtS* "Reprise"). A repentant Angel broke into her apartment and saved her. She told him she was starting to have faith that they weren't alone in this fight because he had gotten into her apartment without an invitation (*AtS* "Epiphany"). Kate turned her life around and moved into the antiques business where she assisted Connor with weapons after the Fall of Los Angeles. Each was unaware of who the other was (*Angel* "After the Fall").

LOA, THE | KERRIGAN MAHAN | Oracle that manifests itself in the body of a drive-through speaker shaped like a hamburger at a fast-food restaurant. The Loa warned Wesley that Angel would devour his son after three portents: earthquake, fire, and blood (*AtS* "Loyalty").

LOCKLEY, TREVOR | JOHN MAHON | Kate's father, a former police officer who retired after thirty-five years on the force. He raised Kate as a single dad after her mother died, and he left his own retirement party early when Kate's moving speech seemed to spur other cops to emotional outbursts (*AtS* "Sense and Sensitivity"). Trevor used department connections to make money on the side, but was really moving demon drugs. When he warned his partners about Angel's investigation, they revealed themselves to be vampires and drained his blood. His grave marker reads Beloved Father (*AtS* "The Prodigal").

LOHESH | A pure demon. Eight hundred years ago in the Koskov Valley above the Urals, a sorcerer achieved Ascension and became the embodiment of the four-winged soul killer. It wiped out a local village within hours (*BtVS* "Graduation Day, Part 1").

LOLLY | Buffy Summers's aunt who made the kitchen curtains in the Revello Drive house (*BtVS* "Angel").

LOO | Melaka's little girl radie friend (*Fray* "Big City Girl") who was murdered by Urkonn to incite Melaka to get her head in the slaying game (*Fray* "The Worst of It").

LOOMIS, KATIE | Parker's post-Buffy conquest (*BtVS* "The Harsh Light of Day").

KREVLORNSWATH OF THE DEATHWOK CLAN, THE HOST, THE LORD OF SILVERLAKE
| ANDY HALLETT |

Former owner of Caritas, the demon-friendly karaoke bar where he could read the destiny of anyone who sang for him. A demon from Pylea with green skin, red eyes, and regenerating red horns, Lorne likes flashy suits, Sea Breezes, and singing (*AtS* "Judgment"). He arrived in LA through the same portal that Fred was sucked through, and he never looked missed Pylea, though he went back with Angel and gang to rescue Cordelia and say goodbye to his family (*AtS* "There's No Place like Plrtz Glrb"). He didn't think of himself as a magician; he just helped people find their path. Time and again he tried to help Angel and the others, whether bringing them help or tracking down information, and he usually received harsh treatment because of his association with the gang: Lorne was frequently beat up, knocked out, tortured, and mutilated. (And sometimes he was just hungover from the required ritual drinking.) While he occasionally sat out encounters he didn't feel he could handle—such as bringing Angelus forth (*AtS* "Calvary")—and was sometimes wrong, he was loyal to Angel until the end.

In the final battle, Lorne was willing to do the wet work Angel asked of him—killing Lindsey—but as he explained to Angel, that was it, he was done, and don't look for him (*AtS* "Not Fade Away"). After Los Angeles was sent to hell, Lorne assumed leadership of Silverlake and made it a heaven in the middle of hell. He rejoined Angel Investigations and became the chosen ruler of all Los Angeles. When time was reset, he had to reinvent himself once more, and is still figuring out what to do with his life (*Angel* "After the Fall").

LORD OF BURBANK, THE | One of the Demon Lords of Los Angeles. She was a victim of Bro'os who colluded with Angel to kill her along with the other Lords. Her death was undone when time was reset, and she went after Bro'os to exact her revenge (*Angel* "After the Fall").

LORD OF CENTURY CITY, THE | Demon Lord swathed in wrappings with red glowing eyes. He died by means of a Hagan Shaft but was revived and went after Bro'os when time was reset (*Angel* "After the Fall").

LORD OF COMPTON, THE | Demon Lord with a long neck, and a burnished orange half mask and tentacles extending from his head. Also died by Hagan Shaft; also went after Bro'os when time was reset (*Angel* "After the Fall").

LORD OF SHERMAN OAKS, THE | Short demon with yellow skin who wore an old-fashioned suit. He also died by Hagan Shaft, but after time was reset he sent his assassin Desdemona after Angel. However, she double-crossed him and Angel and she killed the Lord of Sherman Oaks instead (*Angel* "After the Fall").

LORD OF WEHO, THE | Telepathic, scarlet demon with enormous horns (*Spike* "After the Fall") who also died by Hagan Shaft. When time was reset he attempted to kill Charles Gunn. Illyria beheaded him and kept his severed head as a trophy and warning to the other Demon Lords to leave Gunn alone (*Angel* "After the Fall").

LORELAHN | Leader of the Forest Souls, humanoid tree-creatures who assisted Xander and Dawn in a battle against magical beings sent by Amy, Warren, and Twilight to attack Central Command (*Buffy* "Time of Your Life").

LORI | ANGELA SARAFYAN | R.J.'s girlfriend. A cheerleader who was jealous of Dawn (*BtVS* "Him").

LORNE'S MOTHER (LIFE-GIVER AND MOTHER OF THE VILE EXCREMENT) | TOM MCCLEISTER | A cruel parent who ripped Lorne's images into tiny pieces, fed them to the swine, then butchered the pigs and had their remains scattered for the dogs (*AtS* "Belonging"). She spit in Lorne's face when she saw him during his return to Pylea, claiming that "Each morning before I feed I go out into the hills where the ground is thorny and parched, beat my breast and curse the loins that gave birth to such a cretinous boy-child" (*AtS* "Through the Looking Glass"). She was dismayed to learn that her son helped free the slaves and now she has to do her own work (*AtS* "There's No Place like Plrtz Glrb").

LOROPHAGE DEMON | Demon who overwhelmed Rupert Giles's Watcher Academy class when they were sent to kill the Highgate Vampire in 1972. Years later, Drusilla used the Lorophage to suck out the negative emotions of her followers. Faith succumbed to the Lorophage but Angel stopped the draining, which would have made her insane (*Angel and Faith* "Daddy Issues").

LOS HERMANOS NUMEROS | Five *luchadores*, Mexican wrestlers, and demon fighters, who were also brothers. Four died fifty years ago and are mourned by their brother Cinco. They returned from the dead, and used the aerial stunts from their wrestling days to pin a demon, letting Angel stab it in the heart (*AtS* "The Cautionary Tale of Numero Cinco").

LOVELL, JEREMY | Journalist who wrote an article for the *Sunnydale Press* in 1999 entitled "Inventors Flock to Fair." (*BtVS* "Hush")

LOVE SPELL (AND COUNTERSPELL) | Conducted by Amy Madison on behalf of Xander Harris, the spell required her to sit cross-legged inside the symbol for woman drawn on the floor in red. Three vertical stripes were painted on Xander's bare chest, and he held a burning candle while Amy recited the following incantation: *Diana, goddess of love and the hunt, I pray to thee. Let my cries bind the heart of Xander's beloved.*" [Amy lowered a necklace into a bubbling brew.] "*May she neither rest nor sleep until she submits to his will only. Diana, bring about this love and bless it.*" Xander then blew out the candle. The spell resulted in every woman in Sunnydale except for Cordelia, the object of his desire, falling in love with Xander. The counterspell conducted by Giles went: "*Diana, goddess of love, be gone. Hear no more thy siren song.*"

This spell also succeeded in changing Buffy back from a rat into a human (*BtVS* "Bewitched, Bothered, and Bewildered").

LOVE SPELL BY WILLOW | Includes all the ingredients for her De-lusting Spell: essence of violet, cloves, a set of runic tables, and rat's eyes (*BtVS* "Lovers Walk").

LOWELL HOME FOR CHILDREN | Between 1949 and 1960, this orphanage housed runaways, juvenile delinquents, and emotionally disturbed teenagers from the Sunnydale area (*BtVS* "Where the Wild Things Are").

LOWELL HOUSE | Frat house Riley and the other members of the Initiative lived in while stationed at UC Sunnydale (*BtVS* "The Initiative"). Formerly known as the Lowell Home for Children.

LOWELL, REBECCA | TAMARA GORSKI | Actress best known for playing Raven in *On One's Own* for nine and a half years. She is represented by Oliver Simon, and has been famous since she was fourteen. She was stalked by a fan who turned out to be a stuntman hired by Simon to generate publicity for her because she was losing roles for looking too old in her twenties. She took Cordelia shopping and to lunch to pump her for information on Angel and how he became a vampire. When she learned about the curse, she drugged Angel with bliss-inducing Doximall in an effort to get him to turn her into a vampire so she'd be young and beautiful forever. Frightened by the real Angelus, she changed her mind (*AtS* "Eternity").

LOZANO, JENNIE | Journalist who wrote an article for the *Sunnydale Press* about the massacre on the train at the Sunnydale Station (*BtVS* "Crush").

LUBBER DEMON | Gray-skinned, pointy-eared, raccoon-eyed demon and member of a fanatical sect awaiting a messiah who would usher in the end of all human life (*AtS* "Happy Anniversary").

LUCA, BROTHER | Monk in Cortona who e-mailed Jenny Calendar about the Anointed One. He sent out one last email containing the Bible verse Isaiah 11:16: "The wolf shall live with the lamb, the leopard shall lie down with the kid, the calf, the lion and the fatling together, and the little child to lead them" (*BtVS* "Prophecy Girl").

LUCAS | SEAN GUNN | Brachen Demon—like Doyle—that hailed from Oregon. Lucas and other Brachen refugees were slaughtered by the Scourge when Doyle refused to help them, prior to his meeting Angel (*AtS* "Hero").

LUCIUS | Vampire minion of Spike and Drusilla (*BtVS* "Lie to Me").

LUCY | Casualty of the Highgate Vampire fiasco at the Watchers Academy (*Angel and Faith* "Daddy Issues").

LUKE | BRIAN THOMPSON | Vampire who served as the Master's Vessel for the Harvest (*BtVS* "Welcome to the Hellmouth"). Buffy decapitated him with a cymbal (*BtVS* "The Harvest").

LUNCH LADY | WENDY WORTHINGTON | Sunnydale High employee who attempted to poison the entire student body by putting rat poison in the cafeteria food (*BtVS* "Earshot").

LURCONIS | Enormous sewer-dwelling serpent-like demon who demanded human babies as tribute from the Mayor (*BtVS* "Band Candy").

LU-RITE | Demon worshipped by humans (*AtS* "Heartthrob").

LURK | Fray's term for vampire in the twenty-third century (*Buffy* "Time of Your Life")

LYCANTHROPUS EXTERUS | Type of werewolf. Undocumented in North America until McManus—the werewolf that bit Nina Ash—was killed and analyzed. This breed of werewolf is a biped with longer canines and arms (*AtS* "Unleashed").

LYCOR | Chocolate company sued because its product packaging caused cancer (*AtS* "Dead End").

LYDIA | CYNTHIA LAMONTAGNE | Watcher who wrote her thesis on Spike (*BtVS* "Checkpoint"). She died when Caleb blew up the Watchers Council headquarters (*BtVS* "Never Leave Me").

LYNETTE | Sunnydale High student who told Charity that Ben Straley had told her that Buffy had cut him dead (*BtVS* "I Only Have Eyes for You").

LYSETTE | Friend of Cordelia who went into the hospital to get a Gwyneth Paltrow nose and came out looking like Mr. Potato Head (*BtVS* "Killed by Death").

LYSETTE | WHITNEY DYLAN | Sunnydale High student who loved Xander's new car (*BtVS* "The Zeppo").

— M —

M? | Glyph that represents the ancient weapon known more commonly as the Scythe. (The character "?" is the sign for a glottal stop, a consonantal sound formed by the release of air after complete closure of the glottis.) The Guardians for the Slayer created the weapon, which combines a blade with a stake so that a Slayer could use it to kill the last Old One to walk the earth (*BtVS* "End of Days"). After Buffy dispatched Caleb with it, Willow used the Scythe in a spell to infuse every Potential with full Slayer power (*BtVS* "Chosen"). Buffy continued to carry the Scythe after the Battle of the Hellmouth, briefly losing it to Toru when he attempted to drain all the Slayers of their power (*Buffy* "Wolves at the Gate"). She used it to destroy the Seed of Wonder, which broke the weapon (*Buffy* "Last Gleaming"). Willow took the Scythe on her magical walkabout to repair it and learned that it is the counterpart to Excalibur (*Buffy* "Guarded"). Willow also used it as part of the process to bring magic back (*Willow: Wonderland, Buffy* "The Core"). The Scythe can open dimensional portals and travel through time. It is also wielded by the Slayer Melaka Fray in the twenty-third century (*Fray* "Alarums").

MA'AT | High and mighty white-magic shaman and a totem of the Ra-Tet. The Beast killed her by ripping her heart from her chest (*AtS* "Long Day's Journey").

MACHIDA | ROBIN ATKIN DOWNES | Giant reptilian demon who bestowed wealth and power on the members of the Delta Zeta Kappa fraternity at UC Sunnydale in return for sacrificial girls. He was covered with yellow-green scales, his arms were webbed, and he had taloned hands. Buffy killed Machida and cut off his tail with the fraternity's ritual sword (*BtVS* "Reptile Boy").

MACLAY, DONALD (DONNY) | KEVIN RANKIN | Tara's older brother who appeared to possess no magical abilities, unlike his mother and sister (*BtVS* "Family").

MACLAY, MR. | STEVE RANKIN | Tara's abusive father who convinced his wife and daughter that they were demons instead of witches (*BtVS* "Family").

MACLAY, TARA | AMBER BENSON | See following page.

MACLEISH, DEVON | JASON HALL | Cordelia's former boyfriend and lead singer of the band Dingoes Ate My Baby. He fought at the Graduation Day battle against the Mayor (*BtVS* "Graduation Day, Part 2") and sent Oz his stuff when Oz left town (*BtVS* "Something Blue").

MACNAMARA, DARIN | DOUGLAS ROBERTS | Co-owner of the fight club XXI. Darin posed as a client to hire Angel Investigations under the pretext that he needed help finding his brother, but it was a lie to get Angel into his demon fighting ring. He disintegrated when a demon put a fight bracelet on his wrist and threw him over a mystical containment barrier (*AtS* "The Ring").

MACNAMARA, JACK | SCOTT WILLIAM WINTERS | Ran the demon fight club XXI with his brother, Darin, who killed Jack to prove to Angel that even family was expendable (*AtS* "The Ring").

Maclay, Tara

| AMBER BENSON |

Witch born on October 16, 1980 to a patriarchal family that controlled their female relations by declaring that they were part demon. After losing her mother when she was seventeen, Tara left home to attend UC Sunnydale. Her abusive family eventually followed her to "celebrate" her twentieth birthday by insisting she return home (*BtVS* "Family"). Tara caught Willow's eye at the Daughters of Gaea Wiccan group on campus and the pair bonded through magic during the time the Gentlemen held Sunnydale under their magical sway (*BtVS* "Hush"). Willow declared her love for Tara after Oz returned and attacked Tara while he was in werewolf form (*BtVS* "New Moon Rising"). Tara later suffered a traumatic brain injury when the Hellgod Glory attacked her mind after she refused to reveal the location of the Key (*BtVS* "Tough Love"). Willow cared for Tara during her recovery and was able to repair the damage done to her during the team's final battle with Glory. Following Buffy's second death, Tara and Willow formed something of a family unit with Dawn, but ultimately Willow's growing addiction to magic became a source of tension for the pair. Tara broke up with Willow after a spell to remove Tara's memories went wrong (*BtVS* "Tabula Rasa"). The pair eventually reunited and were celebrating a new beginning when Warren Mears shot and killed Tara on May 7, 2002. This tragic loss sent Willow into a magical spiral bent on revenge (*BtVS* "Villains"). Years later, Andrew planned to revive Tara as he'd wanted to do with his friend, Jonathan, but Buffy and Willow convinced him to leave her to rest in peace (*Buffy* "I Wish").

MADISON, AMY | ELIZABETH ANNE ALLEN | Witch raised by an abusive mother who forced Amy to try to become a cheerleader (*BtVS* "Witch"). To escape being burned at the stake by a group of concerned parents under demon influence, Amy turned herself into a rat and was trapped in that form for a time (*BtVS* "Gingerbread"). Once Willow changed her back, Amy enabled Willow's addiction to magic (*BtVS* "Smashed," "Wrecked"). She later began a vendetta against Willow (*BtVS* "The Killer in Me") that continued into the era of Twilight, when it was revealed that Amy had saved Warren Mears after Willow flayed him. She and Warren went on the offensive many times, plaguing the New Slayers with undead Scotsmen, Cobra-faced Monsters, and others (*Buffy* "The Long Way Home," "Time of Your Life"), and she participated in the battle against Twilight in Tibet (*Buffy* "Retreat"). Eventually she wound up in Magic Town, pitting herself against Angel and Nadira, who changed Amy into a rat once again (*Angel and Faith* "Lost and Found").

MADISON, CATHERINE | ROBIN RIKER | Amy Madison's evil witch mother, who attempted to get onto the cheerleading team by possessing Amy's body and cursing her rivals with the following spell: "*Lord of Darkness / Lord of Night / accept thy supplicant's sacrifice / reap thy vengeance with keen and cruel might / send thy sudden darkness out of darkest night*" (*BtVS* "Witch"). After the founding of the Slayer Organization, Buffy briefly appeared to Amy in her mother's form in order to distract her (*Buffy* "The Long Way Home").

MAGDALENE GRIMOIRE, NECRONOMICON DES MORTES, AND *HOCHSTADTER'S TREATISE ON FRACTAL GEOMETRY IN 12-DIMENSIONAL SPACE* | Necessary texts for Fred's work to make Spike corporeal again. Considered to be antiquities of the rarest order (*AtS* "Hellbound").

MAGIC | An exotic form of energy (*Buffy* "Own It").

MAGIC BONE | Artifact owned by Jonathan Levinson that was decorated with runes and sigils. It was used to create time loops (*BtVS* "Life Serial") and served as a talisman in the casting of disguise spells (*BtVS* "Dead Things").

MAGIC BOX | Magic supply store that Giles purchased and operated after the death of the previous owner, Mr. Bogarty (*BtVS* "Real Me"). The store was located on Maple Street and used to be called Uncle Bob's Magic Cabinet. After the Scoobies graduated from high school and the library was destroyed, it became the *de facto* headquarters for the team, with a Slayer training room in the back. Anya took the shop over when Giles moved back to England. Dark Willow destroyed it (*BtVS* "Grave").

MAGIC SHOP CLERK | SUZANNE KRULL | Salesperson who sold Willow the ingredients for her De-Lusting Spell. Spike killed her (*BtVS* "Lovers Walk").

MAGIC TOWN | Section of northeast London (Hackney) saturated with magic that mutated the inhabitants after the explosion of the plague ball (*Angel and Faith* "What You Want, Not What You Need").

MAI | New Slayer employed at Deepscan (*Angel and Faith* "Where the River Meets the Sea," "Lost and Found").

MAIDEN WITH URN | Sculpture by Van Gieson on display at the Hotel Ramsey in LA (*AtS* "Parting Gifts").

MALITA | New Slayer and a member of the Slayer Tokyo squad (*Buffy* "Predators and Prey").

MALOKER | Old One with a batlike head, fangs, and a fur-covered body who was the father of all vampires. The Slayer Simone Doffler freed Maloker from the Deeper Well in hopes of being sired by him, but this plan failed when the new Seed of Wonder came into being. His surviving essence merged with Dracula when Xander wrote in the *Vampyr* book that Dracula was the most powerful of all the vampires. Dawn—while in giant form—staked Maloker with the spire on the Redwood Insurance Building and Dracula reasserted dominion over his original body (*Buffy* "The Core," "New Rules").

MANDEL | DANIEL DEHRING | Evil follower of Avilas (*BtVS* "Help").

MANDRAZ | FLEMING BROOKS | Demon whom Willow hallucinated about while under the influence of pure magic from the warlock dealer Rack. Mandraz subsequently manifested and went after her and Dawn. He nearly bested Buffy but Willow set him on fire with magic (*BtVS* "Wrecked").

MANETTI, AGENT | SKIP STELLRECHT | One of two FBI agents who took the invisible girl, Marcie Ross, away (*BtVS* "Out of Mind, Out of Sight").

MANGUS TRIPOD | Magic triangle formed by three chanting participants during an exorcism (*BtVS* "I Only Have Eyes for You").

MANJET (MANNY) | JACK KEHLER | Totem of the Ra-Tet, sacred guardian of the Shen, keeper of the Orb of Ma'at, and devotee of light. The midday totem signifies man, a neutral totem representing the potential of every human soul. Manjet was immortal unless ritually murdered. Angel and Gwen found him in Semkhet's cave and took him away for safekeeping. The Beast pulled an orb from Manny's head after Cordelia killed him in Gwen's safe room (*AtS* "Long Day's Journey").

MANN, AIMEE | HERSELF | Singer who performed at the Bronze even though she hates vampire towns (*BtVS* "Sleeper").

MANNERS, CATHERINE | KATHERINE ANN MCGREGOR | Wife of Holland. She invited Darla and Drusilla into his wine tasting, where the vampires attacked her and their guests (*AtS* "Reunion").

MANNERS, HOLLAND | SAM ANDERSON | Former Division Head of Special Projects at Wolfram & Hart (*AtS* "Blind Date"). Manners didn't like to be early to rituals, due to all the chanting (*AtS* "To Shanshu in LA"). He wanted Darla to corrupt Angel but was ready to sacrifice her to save the reputation of the law firm. In turn, Darla killed Manners during a wine tasting in his cellar (*AtS* "Reunion"). Holland's contract with Wolfram & Hart extended beyond his death, so he took Angel on an elevator ride to the Home Office and explained Wolfram & Hart's role in the upcoming apocalypse (*AtS* "Reprise").

MANNY THE PIG | TOM ROSALES | Former acquaintance of Doyle who hung out at a joint down on Third Street called the Orbit Room (*AtS* "In the Dark").

MARCIE | TRACEY STONE | Woman from Barstow who hit on Angel after witnessing him break up a fight (*AtS* "Lonely Heart").

MARCO | ENRIQUE ALMEIDA | Construction worker on Xander's team at his job site (*BtVS* "Life Serial").

MARC THE MAGICIAN | BURKE ROBERTS | Name assumed by a reptilian humanoid demon with pointed teeth and talons who was the last member of the Brotherhood of Seven. He masqueraded as a Sunnydale High student performing a magic act in the talent show and attempted to harvest Rupert Giles's brain with a guillotine. He survived a beheading by Xander but died when Sid—the demon hunter trapped in the body of a dummy—stabbed him through the heart (*BtVS* "The Puppet Show").

MARCUS | KEVIN WEST | Vampire torturer Spike hired to work Angel over. Marcus stole the Gem of Amarra and headed toward a pier full of children. Because Marcus could not be killed while he wore the ring, Angel impaled him on a piece of wood and then removed it, which dusted Marcus (*AtS* "In the Dark").

MARELDA | WHITNEY DYLAN | Slave girl in the Pylean castle (*AtS* "There's No Place like Plrtz Glrb").

MARGARET | CORNELIA HAYES O'HERLIHY | London maidservant whom Angelus killed in the Victorian era; the First reappeared as her in order to get the vampire to commit suicide (*BtVS* "Amends").

MARGET | Third in the trio of Irish witches who attempted to steal fear energy from tourists. Illyria killed her (*Angel and Faith* "United").

MARGO | RENEE RIDGELEY | Wealthy woman with substance abuse issues. She threw fabulous parties and filmed them so the vampire Russell Winters could find his next victim, such as Cordelia Chase (*AtS* "City of").

MARGOT (THE FREAK) | Sunnydale High student dismissed by Dawn as an unlikely candidate for the local Potential because she fainted in the middle of a fetal pig dissection in lab (*BtVS* "Potential").

MARIA | EMILY KAY | Vampire who helped her friend Justin ambush Buffy. Giles dusted her (*BtVS* "All the Way").

MARIANNE | Slayer who was a member of Faith's London squad until Drusilla killed her (*Angel and Faith* "Family Reunion"). When Nadira attempted to have Marianne resurrected, Eyghon the Sleepwalker was already possessing Marianne's body (*Angel and Faith* "Death and Consequences").

MARIN, CARL | CHARLES CYPHERS | Swim-team coach at the original Sunnydale High School, who dosed the swimmers with an experimental steroid mixture that included the DNA of tarpon and mako shark. He threw Nurse Greenliegh and Buffy to the Gill Monsters, then fell in himself while battling with Xander (*BtVS* "Go Fish").

MARISSA | INGRID SONRAY | Vampire who fed near the bluffs around the time of Angel's disappearance. She told Fred and Gunn that she saw Angel there before he went missing, but Connor staked her before she could admit to seeing him as well (*AtS* "Deep Down").

MARKALLA | ALEX NESIC | Human slave in the castle of Pylea. Silas killed Markalla by triggering his collar as punishment for giving the rebels the plans to the controls of the device all slaves wore (*AtS* "There's No Place like Plrtz Glrb").

MARK OF KEKFADLOREM, THE | A knife bearing this symbol is the only thing that will kill a Kek Demon (*AtS* "I've Got You under My Skin").

MARNOX ROOT | Ingredient in magical spells (*BtVS* "Faith, Hope & Trick").

MARQUEZ | RAINBOW BORDEN | Gang member who tried to flee instead of testifying against a drug-dealing, murderous Wolfram & Hart client. Cordelia's vision sent Angel to rescue him from demons. Angel convinced him to do the right thing and testify, which put Angel back in the law firm's crosshairs (*AtS* "Five by Five").

MARSH, TONIA | New Slayer employed by Deepscan who was killed by Evolved Vampires while on the mission to save Reese Zane (*Angel and Faith* "Lost and Found").

MARTINA | New Slayer in Tonia Marsh's unit who went to South America to find Walter Zane, as well as Samantha and Riley Finn (*Angel and Faith* "Lost and Found").

MARTINI, SHEILA | ALEXANDRA JOHNES | Tied with Buffy as Sunnydale High student most likely to be expelled. She was turned into a vampire (*BtVS* "School Hard").

MARTY | SAL RENDINO | Repairman that Claire Jeakins hit on in the Franklin Hotel bar (*AtS* "Dear Boy").

MARY | Student at St. Cuthbert's Private School who was menaced by girls that turned out to be vampires working for Drusilla. Her father found the golem statue in which Archaeus was eventually entombed (*Angel and Faith* "A Little More than Kin").

MASON | NEIL DALY | Initiative commando who was burned when the Lowell House fireplace responded to Buffy and Riley's passionate lovemaking (*BtVS* "The I in Team," "Where the Wild Things Are").

MASTER, THE (HEINRICH JOSEPH NEST, THE KING OF VAMPIRES) | MARK METCALF | Leader of the Order of Aurelius who was the oldest living vampire at the time of his destruction. Due to his great age—a result of his cunning—the Master had grown past the curse of human features, appearing more demonic than human at all times (*BtVS* "The Harvest"; *AtS* "Darla"). He sired Darla in Virginia in 1609 when he moved to the New World, and he met Angelus in London in 1760 (*AtS* "Darla"). In 1937, he was imprisoned inside a buried church in Sunnydale and initiated the Harvest to escape decades later (*BtVS* "The Harvest"). The Master successfully killed Buffy but was dusted by her after she was revived (*BtVS* "Prophecy Girl"). Buffy later thwarted an attempt by the Anointed One to resurrect him (*BtVS* "When She Was Bad"). The Master was enslaved by the Seed of Wonder in the twelfth century, and he was later resurrected to serve as its protector. Angel dusted him (*Buffy* "Last Gleaming").

MATANGO | Highly toxic mushroom-being who was a member of D'Hoffryn's Magic Council. His designated power was invulnerability to magic attacks. D'Hoffryn burned him to death with a flamethrower (*Buffy* "In Pieces on the Ground").

MATTHEW | ANTHONY HARRELL | Employee at the new Sunnydale High School who was in charge of lockers and logistics (*BtVS* "Help").

MATTHEW | MICAH HENSON | Teen whose family was killed by vampires who set a trap on the highway during the time the Beast made the sun disappear. Gunn knocked him unconscious to get him safely back indoors before he could fall under Jasmine's influence (*AtS* "Sacrifice").

MAUREEN | Oz's aunt; married Uncle Ken (*BtVS* "Phases").

MAY | Vampire who sired video gamer Jacob in Nashua, New Hampshire. Jacob's best friend, Alexia the Slayer, dusted her (*Tales* "The Thrill").

MAYHEW, JACK | DAMIEN ECKHART | Voted class clown in Buffy's high school senior class in spite of the fact that he relied on props for his humor (*BtVS* "The Prom").

MCALVY, DODD | JAKE PATELLIS | One of the two best swimmers on the swim team at the original Sunnydale High School. Dodd was once seen as a freak with jicama breath who waxed his back, but he became cool when the swim team began to win meets. He was turned into a Gill Monster (*BtVS* "Go Fish").

MCCARTHY, DR. | PAT SKIPPER | Ben Wilkinson's supervisor at Sunnydale Memorial Hospital, who reluctantly fired Ben for his many absences (*BtVS* "Tough Love").

MCCARTHY, MR. | Head recruiter for the world's leading software concern. He wanted to meet with Willow and Oz during the Sunnydale High School career fair (*BtVS* "What's My Line? Part 1").

MCCRACKEN V. THE STATE OF MAINE, 1954 | Case that determined that "any financial dealings shall be deemed the responsibility of the interested party, regardless of number or function of employees unless said party has been judged mentally incapable." Gunn cited the finding in an attempt to have a mistrial declared in the Corbin Fries case (*AtS* "Conviction").

McDonald, Lindsey

| CHRISTIAN KANE |

Ambitious lawyer at Wolfram & Hart who first met Angel when the vampire killed his client (*AtS* "City of"). Lindsey continually moved against Angel, even when it went counter to the law firm's plans. When he did have a crisis of faith in the firm, Lindsey turned to Angel for help saving some innocent children, but managed to find a way to return to the firm with a promotion (*AtS* "Blind Date"). He participated in raising Darla only to fall in love with her (*AtS* "To Shanshu in LA"). Angel cut Lindsey's hand off in a battle and the lawyer received a replacement hand from a former coworker. When he learned Darla was dying, he asked Angel for help again, and then brought Drusilla in to sire Darla when Angel couldn't save her (*AtS* "The Trial"). When Lindsey learned that Angel and Darla slept together, he tried to kill Angel again, but was soundly beaten, and left town (*AtS* "Epiphany").

Lindsey returned to LA years later, covered in glyph tattoos to keep him off the Senior Partners' radar, and he fell in love with their liaison Eve (*AtS* "Soul Purpose"). Lindsey tried to kill Angel to gain entrance to the Circle of the Black Thorn and become the Senior Partners' instrument on Earth, but Angel beat him at that as well. As a result, the Senior Partners sent Lindsey to a hellish Holding Dimension as punishment (*AtS* "Underneath"). After being rescued by Angel, Lindsey eventually agreed to help Angel fight the Circle and was promised the keys to Wolfram & Hart if he survived. Instead Angel double-crossed him and had Lorne shoot Lindsey after the battle. Lindsey died, furious that Angel wasn't the one to finally kill him (*AtS* "Not Fade Away").

MCKELLER, DR. | Pediatrician at Sunnydale Memorial Hospital (*BtVS* "Triangle").

MCMANUS | Man who abandoned his family after he was turned into a werewolf. He bit Nina Ash before Angel stabbed him to death with Wesley's silver pen (*AtS* "Unleashed").

MCNAMARA, COLONEL | **CONOR O'FARRELL** | Officer brought in to head up the Initiative after the death of Maggie Walsh (*BtVS* "New Moon Rising"). A strict military man, McNamara had no use for the Slayer and the Scoobies, referring to them as "anarchists" in his reports (*BtVS* "The Yoko Factor," "Primeval").

MCPECK, CLARISSA | Reporter who worked for the *Sunnydale Press* for decades. She filed the following stories: "Sunnydale High Jock Kills Lover, Self" (*BtVS* "I Only Have Eyes for You"), "Tragic Accident Kills Three" (*BtVS* "Some Assembly Required"), and "Mysterious Obelisk Unearthed: Excavators Discover Ancient Artifact" (*BtVS* "Becoming, Part 1").

MEARS, WARREN | **ADAM BUSCH** | Misogynistic technological genius who pitted himself against Buffy after she saved him from the robot girlfriend he'd made for himself (*BtVS* "I Was Made to Love You"). Under duress, he later made a robot in the form of Buffy as a girlfriend for Spike (*BtVS* "Intervention"). Warren was the *de facto* head of the Trio, an evil—though generally unsuccessful—organization that included Jonathan and Andrew. Warren tried to force his ex-girlfriend, Katrina Silber, to obey him and accidentally murdered her in the process. He blamed Buffy for the continued failure of his plans and went after her with a gun, accidentally killing Willow's girlfriend, Tara (*BtVS* "Seeing Red"). Willow flayed him alive (*BtVS* "Villains") but Amy Madison saved him with magic (*Buffy* "The Long Way Home"). Although still skinless, Warren allied himself with the US Army and Twilight against Buffy, but ultimately died when the Seed of Wonder was destroyed (*Buffy* "Last Gleaming").

MEATPIE | Sheila Martini's boyfriend (*BtVS* "School Hard").

MECHA DAWN | Giant robot built by the Japanese Goth vampires to fight Giantess Dawn in the streets of Tokyo. Dawn ripped its head off (*Buffy* "Wolves at the Gate").

MEEKS, ROLAND | **JOHN KAPELOS** | Last concierge at the Hyperion Hotel. On December 16, 1979, he made his morning wake-up calls going room to room with a twelve-gauge shotgun (*AtS* "Are You Now or Have You Ever Been").

MELINDA | Neighbor who used to live across the street from the Summers' house. She was a bad influence on Dawn (*BtVS* "Family").

MELLISH | **MARC ROSE** | Demon fighter at XXI who had two kills in the ring before Trepkos finished him (*AtS* "The Ring").

MELMAN REALTY & DEVELOPMENT | Previous owner of the Hyperion Hotel (*AtS* "Are You Now or Have You Ever Been").

MELTZER, DR. RONALD | **ANDY UMBERGER** | Neurosurgeon known for performing risky surgeries. The Wolfram & Hart client was able to separate and reattach pieces of his body so he could stalk his patient Melissa Burns. Angel believed that if his parts were kept separate long enough, the lack of oxygen would atrophy them. Angel buried him in twelve steel boxes in twenty cubic feet of concrete in the floor of Los Angeles's newest subway station (*AtS* "I Fall to Pieces").

MENLO, M. JAMES | **W. EARL BROWN** | Demon who drove a reinforced station wagon and planned the heist at the Natural History Museum (*AtS* "The Shroud of Rahmon").

MENTAL HOSPITAL PATIENT | KEITH ALLAN | After begging the nurse (whom he called a barn owl) not to go, he was attacked and killed by a Queller Demon (*BtVS* "Listening to Fear").

MEREDITH | Mean girl at St. Cuthbert's Private School, who unknowingly dated a vampire and really had it in for the shy Mary. Meredith was killed in the locker room (*Angel and Faith* "A Little More than Kin").

MERENSHTADT TEXT, THE | Writings that contained a reference to the journal of Desmond Kane, pastor of Sharpesville, a town where an Ascension occurred on May 27, 1723 (*BtVS* "Enemies").

MERCER, LEE | THOMAS BURR | Associate at Wolfram & Hart who represented Tony Papazian (*AtS* "Sense and Sensitivity"). Mind readers revealed he was being courted by another a firm and planned to take clients with him. Mercer claimed he was stringing them along, but Holland ordered him shot as an example to other employees (*AtS* "Blind Date").

MERL (ED SILVERMAN) | MATTHEW JAMES | Parasite demon who hung out at Caritas and was one of Angel's go-to snitches. Merl provided information on several cases before warning Angel about the annual Wolfram & Hart Review and then leaving town (*AtS* "The Thin Dead Line"). When Merl got back from Akron, he refused to deal with Angel, but would speak with Wesley and Gunn (*AtS* "Heartthrob"). Merl spent three months in therapy after Angel hung him upside down in water to torture information out of him. He was not impressed with Angel's scripted apology. Gio killed Merl while leading Gunn's old crew on a vendetta against all demons regardless of affiliation (*AtS* "That Old Gang of Mine").

MERRICK | RICHARD RIEHLE | Buffy's first Watcher. He approached her at Hemery High School in Los Angeles when she was fifteen, told her she was the Chosen One, and trained her to fight vampires. He was killed while protecting her (*BtVS* "Becoming, Part 1").

MESEKTET (LITTLE GIRL IN THE WHITE ROOM) | KAY PANABAKER | Totem that was the evilest of the five enormously powerful beings linked to an embodiment of the ancient god Ra (*AtS* "Long Day's Journey"). Mesektet served as Wolfram & Hart's conduit to the Senior Partners. The occupant of the White Room who took the form of a little girl and gave Angel the ritual to manifest the Granok Demon Sahjhan (*AtS* "Forgiving"). She also provided an important clue to the team's fight with the Beast and teleported them safely away before the Beast killed her when he attacked Wolfram & Hart (*AtS* "Habeas Corpses").

MEYER'S BAIT AND TACKLE SHOP | Store in Sunnydale that Faith and Buffy broke in to to steal weapons (*BtVS* "Bad Girls").

M'FASHNIK DEMON | TODD STASHWICK | Mercenary demon hired by the Trio to attack Buffy. She killed him in her flooded basement (*BtVS* "Flooded").

MIAMI, FLORIDA: THREE SECONDS IN THE FUTURE | Location of Twilight's headquarters (*Buffy* "Twilight").

MICHELLE | TORI MCPETRIE | Sunnydale High student who tied for homecoming queen, beating both Buffy and Cordelia (*BtVS* "Homecoming").

MIGGINS, MRS. | Parker's neighbor. After the plague ball exploded, the men who lived across the hall from her ate her and hung her bones in the hallway (*Angel and Faith* "Where the River Meets the Sea").

MIKE | Dave Peck's friend with the '82 V6 Mustang. Lysette dated him (*BtVS* "The Zeppo").

MIKE | Another guy Lysette dated. He had a Mercedes (*BtVS* "The Zeppo").

MIKE | DANNY LACAVA | Lab assistant who studied carpet mold in Gene's Rainey's department (*AtS* "Happy Anniversary").

MIKE, DR. | Xander's San Francisco therapist who helped him with his anger issues (*Buffy* "I Wish," "Love Dares You").

MILKBAR | Candy bars that Ethan Rayne manufactured for the Mayor. They turned adults into irresponsible teenagers as a distraction so that the Mayor could deliver his tribute to the demon Lurconis (*BtVS* "Band Candy").

MILLAN, CESAR | Dog whisperer. Harmony had trouble finding dog sitters because her dogs were mean to him (*Angel and Faith* "In Perfect Harmony").

MILLER, DR. | Physician at Sunnydale Memorial Hospital (*BtVS* "Graduation Day, Part 2").

MILLER, GRAHAM | **BAILEY CHASE** | Member of the Initiative (*BtVS* "The Initiative") who testified on Riley Finn's behalf during the debriefing of the organization. He became a supernatural analyst for the government (*Buffy* "In Pieces on the Ground").

MILLER, MR. | **JAMES LURIE** | Sunnydale High teacher who taught at both the old and new campuses. He was briefly possessed by James Straley (*BtVS* "I Only Have Eyes for You") and later made the students wait until the bell on the last day of school by playing Hangman (*BtVS* "Graduation Day, Part 1"). He also taught the New Slayer Amanda (*BtVS* "Help").

MILLER, MRS. | **DENISE DOWSE** | Sunnydale High School teacher who failed to call on Marcie Ross while discussing *The Merchant of Venice*. In retaliation, Marcie attempted to suffocate her (*BtVS* "Out of Mind, Out of Sight").

MILLER SISTERS, THE (ABBY AND ZOEY) | Zompire attack victims who were rescued by Willow and Dawn. Billy Lane, Anaheed, and Devon promised to take them to their mother (*Buffy* "New Rules").

MIND READERS | **KEILANA SMITH AND DAWN SUGGS** | Employed by Wolfram & Hart to test the employees (*AtS* "To Shanshu in LA").

MINERVA | Goddess Willow called upon while casting a protective barrier spell: "*Careimonia, Minerva. Saepio, sapire, saepsi. Saepio impedimentum*" (*BtVS* "Showtime").

MISHUPASHUP | Where the Chumash First People dwelled (*BtVS* "Pangs").

MISS EDITH | Doll owned by Drusilla. The insane vampire used to gag and blindfold Miss Edith as punishments when it misbehaved. Drusilla also turned Edith's face to the wall and withheld cakes when it set a bad example for the other dolls (*BtVS* "School Hard").

MISS KITTY FANTASTICO | Willow and Tara's pet cat who experienced an unfortunate incident with Dawn's crossbow (*BtVS* "Family," "The Yoko Factor").

MISS PORTER'S | Joyce briefly considered sending Buffy to this private girls' school when Principal Snyder balked at readmitting her (*BtVS* "Dead Man's Party").

MISS SUNSHINE | Puppy that Drusilla brought to Spike to whet his appetite after she killed the dog's owner (*BtVS* "Passion").

MISTER DONUT | Local Sunnydale donut shop (*BtVS* "Beauty and the Beasts").

MISTRESS, THE | Part scaled woman and part tentacled fish, the Mistress was a Siren who lived in San Francisco, where her minion Sirens lured and devoured men they picked up in bars and clubs. Xander and Spike succumbed to their enchanting song but were freed partially by the "ghost" of Anya. The Mistress formed a pact with the Soul Glutton and the Sculptor to stop Buffy and D'Hoffryn from writing the rules of magic (*Buffy* "I Wish") but D'Hoffryn ultimately killed the Mistress and her partners (*Buffy* "In Pieces on the Ground").

MITCH | Owner of Helen's Kitchen (*BtVS* "Anne").

MITCH | Cordelia's date for the Spring Fling (*BtVS* "Out of Mind, Out of Sight").

MITCHELL, CYRUS | Human son of Tom Mitchell. Cyrus was estranged from his father for fifty years after Tom—who had been sired—killed Cyrus's mother-in-law. They reconciled when it became clear that Cyrus would die soon of old age (*Tales* "Father").

MITCHELL, TOM | Vampire father of Cyrus, sired outside the Club du Jazz. A Slayer dusted him when he was caring for his aged son (*Tales* "Father").

MITFORD, NANCY | Author. Nancy's Petticoat, a rare rose, is named after her (*AtS* "She").

MOAI | Guardians of the Easter Island Hellmouth. They appeared as the famous statues on the island, with their bodies submerged under the ground. Spike's bug crew killed them, causing the destruction of Spike's ship (*Spike* "A Dark Place").

MODERN PHYSICS REVIEW | Journal that published Fred's article on supersymmetry and P-dimensional subspace (*AtS* "Supersymmetry").

MOHRA DEMON | Member of a green-skinned, samurai-like demon species with a red jewel in his forehead. Mohra Demons are powerful assassins and soldiers of darkness who take out warriors like Angel and Buffy. They need vast amounts of salt to live and their veins run with the "blood of eternity," which has regenerative properties. When the demon's blood mixed with Angel's it rendered the vampire human. Angel killed it, but it regenerated even bigger and headed to a saline plant for more salt. Buffy broke the jewel in its forehead to destroy the demon (*AtS* "I Will Remember You").

MOK'TAGAR DEMON | Transdimensional being with fissured skin and glowing eyes. Buffy briefly roomed with one at UC Sunnydale (*BtVS* "Living Conditions").

MOLL, BLAYNE | **JACKSON PRICE** | Sunnydale High School student captured by the She-Mantis to fertilize her eggs. He was outed as a virgin despite acting like a player (*BtVS* "Teacher's Pet").

MOLLY | Wife of a Elliot, a wealthy artifact collector (*AtS* "Ground State").

MOLOCH THE CORRUPTOR (MALCOLM BLACK) | **MARK DEAKINS** | Horned demon who was bound into a book by the monk Thelonius and his circle, then released into the Internet by Willow when she scanned the book into a computer. Moloch attempted to have Buffy killed while he wooed Willow via e-mail. Jenny Calendar and Giles joined forces with technopagans to curse him, and Buffy electrocuted the robot body he had entered (*BtVS* "I Robot . . . You Jane").

MONK OF DAGON | **RAVIL ISYANOV** | Protector of the Key. Prior to his death, the monk revealed to Buffy that Dawn had been created to hide the Key and was not truly the Slayer's sister (*BtVS* "No Place like Home").

MONROE | Englishman who came to Oz's enclave in Tibet to be cured, but ultimately failed to change and led a violent werewolf pack that attacked the monastery. He brought his werewolves to fight against Twilight and the army (*Buffy* "Retreat").

MOON FROGS | Species of frog-like demons that live on the moon. Spike and his bug crew encountered them after Spike left San Francisco to get over Buffy and spent time on the dark side of the moon (*Spike* "A Dark Place").

MORAN, MS. | JENNIFER HETRICK | Sunnydale High School teacher whom Buffy hoped would provide her with a letter of recommendation to allow her to reenroll. Ms. Moran's class on contemporary American heroes supposedly changed Buffy's life (*BtVS* "Homecoming").

MORDAR THE BENTBACK | EJ GAGE | Furry, horned demon who sang at Caritas (*AtS* "Judgment").

MORGAN | Courtesan demon who took the shards of the Seed of Wonder in an effort to return to her home world. Morgan began a ritual to open the Easter Island Hellmouth but was ultimately stopped by Spike and his bug crew (*Spike* "A Dark Place").

MORGOG DEMON | A demon worshipped by a garage mechanic even though the supernatural being "couldn't find his way to his hairy spine-hump without a road map," according to Angel (*AtS* "Reunion").

MORIMOTO, AIKO | HOPE SHIN | Daughter of Takeshi Morimoto; she was used in a ploy by Gwen Raiden to distract Gunn (*AtS* "Players").

MORIMOTO, TAKESHI | DANA LEE | Businessman with numerous honorary degrees who is known for all kinds of charity work. He is also somewhat known for his work in bank fraud, smuggling, and money laundering. Gwen Raiden stole the LISA device from him (*AtS* "Players").

MORLEY CIGARETTES | Spike's brand of choice (*BtVS* "School Hard").

MORRIS, RYAN | RICK GARCIA | Reporter for KOUS who covered the story of the frozen guard at the Sunnydale museum after the Trio's attack (*BtVS* "Smashed").

MORT | BRIAN TURK | Duplicitous member of Harmony's vampire gang. Buffy staked him with the horn of one of Harmony's unicorn statues (*BtVS* "Real Me").

Morgan, Lilah

| STEPHANIE ROMANOV |

Ambitious lawyer at Wolfram & Hart who was once Lindsey's rival, before being partnered with him against her will. Lilah oversaw many attempts to kill or corrupt Angel, including hiring Faith to end his life (*AtS* "Five by Five").

When the law firm changed strategy to keeping Angel alive, she frequently tried to get around the new edict. After Lindsey left and recommended her for promotion, she was assigned a new associate, but his plans to undo Angel with paperwork annoyed her and she tried to help Angel (*AtS* "Carpe Noctem"). Rebuffed by the Angel Investigations team, she plotted against Angel again, and helped Sahjhan kidnap the baby Connor (*AtS* "Sleep Tight"). When Angel was buried at sea, Lilah tried to seduce Wesley for information, but they ended up falling in love (*AtS* "A New World"). Injured by the Beast, she was taken in by Wesley, but stabbed to death by Cordelia, who was acting under Jasmine's influence to frame Angelus (*AtS* "Calvary"). As her contract with Wolfram & Hart extended beyond death, Lilah was sent back from hell to give Angel and the team the keys to the Wolfram & Hart offices. Wesley tried to destroy her contract, but she admitted that she'd known what she was signing at the time (*AtS* "Home"), and she continued to do the law firm's bid-

MOSAIC WELLNESS CENTER | Rehabilitation center/asylum for supernatural beings (*Angel* "After the Fall").

MOTEL MANAGER | JOHN ENNIS | Warned Faith that roommates cost extra (*BtVS* "Faith, Hope & Trick").

MOTHERS OPPOSED TO THE OCCULT (MOO) | Antiwitch group founded by Joyce Summers after she was traumatized by the apparent deaths of two small children who mirrored the Hansel and Gretel folk tale (*BtVS* "Gingerbread").

MOTHER SUPERIOR | Drusilla's title when, while sane, she encouraged her followers to feed their despair to a Lorophage Demon (*Angel and Faith* "Daddy Issues").

MOULTER, LIEUTENANT | Minion of Twilight who met her leader at Devil's Tower to debrief regarding the deaths of Roden and Lady Genevieve (*Buffy* "No Future for You").

MOUNT WALMORE | Twenty-third-century name for Mount Rushmore (*Buffy* "Time of Your Life").

MR. GORDO | Buffy's plushy pig stuffed animal (*BtVS* "What's My Line? Part 1").

MR. POINTY | Kendra's name for her "lucky" stake. She bequeathed it to Buffy before her death (*BtVS* "Becoming, Part 1").

MUELLER, KARL | OSS agent whom Slayer Rachel O'Connor defeated on a train headed for Great Neck in 1937 (*Tales* "Broken Bottle of Djinn").

MUFFITT | Steampunk in appearance, a goggle-wearing, wheelchair-using companion of Aluwyn offered to Willow as walkabout guide (*Buffy* "Guarded").

MULIX DEMON | Species whose members can be "marginally attractive," according to Lorne (*AtS* "Dad").

MULLIGAN, JIMMY (HANDSOME JIMMY) | Irish mobster whom Faith's father owed money to. Angel paid him off and warned him to leave town (*Angel and Faith* "Daddy Issues").

MULVIHILL, C. | TOMMY HINKLEY | Private investigator who hunted for Judy Kovacs at the Hyperion Hotel in 1952 (*AtS* "Are You Now or Have You Ever Been").

MUNROE | JUSTIN SHILTON | Corrupt cop who tried to kill Faith. Buffy intervened when Faith almost killed him (*BtVS* "Empty Places").

MUNSON, RODNEY | JOEY CRAWFORD| Sunnydale High student that Willow tutored in chemistry. He had the life sucked out of him while messing with the artifacts at the *Culture Exchange Special Exhibit: Treasures of South America* at the Sunnydale Natural History Museum (*BtVS* "Inca Mummy Girl").

MUO PING | Vessel with the power to hold souls—including Angel's—when the team had it removed so they could question Angelus (*AtS* "Awakening"). The glass jar was stolen from the office safe (*AtS* "Soulless"). Cordelia—under Jasmine's influence—hid the jar to stop Angel from returning, but Willow's spell broke it, freeing the soul (*AtS* "Orpheus").

MU-RITE DEMON | Subspecies of Lu-rite Demon. Males sport a small, telltale fin just behind the third shoulder (*AtS* "Heartthrob").

MURPHY'S | Singles bar in San Francisco that specializes in speed dating for humans and vampires (*Buffy* "Love Dares You").

MURRAY | Spa employee who called Angel Investigations to stop a demon from hatching a litter (*AtS* "Slouching toward Bethlehem").

MURRAY, MS. | MOLLY BRYANT | Teacher at Sunnydale High who got very excited when Buffy parroted back a variation of her dissertation during the time that the Slayer could read people's minds (*BtVS* "Earshot").

MURROW, LINWOOD | JOHN RUBINSTEIN | Lawyer at Wolfram & Hart who got involved with Special Projects when a pregnant Darla appeared, as he wanted to get the scoop before the Senior Partners found out (*AtS* "Quickening"). Angel named Murrow as Connor's godfather because of the threat the lawyer had placed on Connor's life. The vampire then made it clear that whatever happened to Connor would happen to Murrow and then some (*AtS* "Dad"). Murrow tried to remove Lilah from his team because she was sleeping with Wesley, but she had him beheaded with a Senior Partner's blessing (*AtS* "Deep Down").

MURSHAN DYNASTY | Sixteenth-century ruling class. Made good knives (*AtS* "Heartthrob").

MUSELOK TRANCING AMALGAM | Potion that when viewed under a microscope is virtually indistinguishable from GHB, the date rape drug (*AtS* "Offspring").

MUSTARD MAN, THE | DAVID FURY | Singing man ecstatic that the dry cleaners got the mustard out of his shirt (*BtVS* "Once More with Feeling").

MUTARI GENERATOR | Laser cannon that created a pinhole to an infinite extradimensional space, a negatively charged pocket universe that drew Illyria's excess power into it without killing her (*AtS* "Time Bomb").

MYRNA, MISTRESS | DEBORAH ZOE | Lorne's blue-haired friend who specialized in dimensional magic (which meant she also

had a bad habit of jumping from place to place). She determined that a disturbance in the Hyperion Hotel lobby wasn't a portal, but a rip in reality leading to Quor'toth before she closed it (*AtS* "A New World").

MYSTERY OF ACATHLA | Library book Buffy consulted when Angel returned from hell (*BtVS* "Beauty and the Beasts").

"MY TREK THROUGH NEPAL" | Title of a Sunnydale High School alumni lecture. Cordelia and her friends mocked the speaker while simultaneously excluding Marcie Ross from their conversation (*BtVS* "Out of Mind, Out of Sight").

NAAYÉÉ'NEIZGHÁNI | Native American Slayer whose Watcher was killed by the half-Navajo vampire Tó Bájishcini. While tracking the vampire, the Slayer discovered a town completely occupied by vampires and demons. She killed Tó and many, if not all, of the inhabitants. This land would eventually become the site of Sunnydale (*Tales* "The Glittering World").

NABBIT, DAVID | DAVID HERMAN | Socially awkward billionaire software developer who paid people to come to his parties. Nabbit hired Angel Investigations when he was blackmailed with photos of his visit to a demon brothel (*AtS* "War Zone"). He was in Kuala Lumpur for a hostile takeover before returning to give Angel financial advice that allowed him to buy the Hyperion Hotel. Nabbit made his first million developing software that assists the blind in surfing the web. He also set up a foundation that donated twenty billion dollars a year to countless charitable causes (*AtS* "First Impressions").

NADIRA | New Slayer originally based in the Azores. Most of her squad was killed during the Twilight crisis and she swore vengeance on Angel, Pearl, and Nash (*Angel and Faith* "Live through This"). When the plague ball exploded, Nadira mutated into a magical being and became the guardian of the mutants in Magic Town (*Angel and Faith* "What You Want, Not What You Need"). She has made peace with Angel and assists him and Faith to this day (*Angel and Faith* "A Tale of Two Families").

NAHDRAHS | Gray demons who wear long robes and silver facemasks and speak a language that is mostly clicks, whirs, and popping sounds. They are not so much born as disgorged. A group of Nahdrahs offered to pay Angel to solve a problem for them as a present for their prince's birthday, but changed their mind when they met Fred. When she solved their puzzle, they tried to cut off her head to swap it for their dying prince's, which they do whenever their leader's head wears out. Angel and company disrupted this plan and kept the demons' money (*AtS* "Provider").

NAJAKOT DEMON | Being who preys on magic practitioners. Alasdair Coames gave Angel one of these demons to combat Amy Madison (*Angel and Faith* "Lost and Found").

NANCY | KAARINA AUFRANC | Young woman who made a wish to Anya that accidentally led to her boyfriend Ronnie being turned into a worm monster. She lost her dog, Rocky, to him (*BtVS* "Beneath You").

NANCY | MARIAN O'BRIEN | In the Wishverse, she, Giles, and Larry Blaisdell made up a team of unofficial vampire slayers. They collected Cordelia's body in a van driven by Oz (*BtVS* "The Wish").

NANJIN | Order of cave-dwelling monks in Pajaur that believes enlightenment is seeing with the heart, not the mind (*AtS* "Blind Date").

NARWEK, CONSTABLE | BRIAN TAHASH | Pylean hunter of fugitive slaves (*AtS* "Over the Rainbow").

NASH | Twin brother of Pearl, and a half demon whose human mother taught him that they were the next step in evolution. Resembling David Bowie, he could set people on fire with his green laser vision and was once engaged to both of Rupert

Giles's great-aunts (*Angel and Faith* "Family Reunion"). He worshipped Twilight (*Angel and Faith* "Live through This") and allied himself with Whistler to release the plague ball. Faith killed him (*Angel and Faith* "What You Want, Not What You Need").

NATPUDAN, DR. VINPUR | CARLOS CARRASCO | Author of *Anything's Possible* who believed we are everywhere at once. He introduced Dr. Meltzer to psychic surgeons—yogis who can shut down their somatic system for days at a time (*AtS* "I Fall to Pieces").

NDUO | Wesley's shorthand description for "nasty demon, unknown origin" (*AtS* "Judgment").

NEAL | One of Ted Buchanan's coworkers. He spilled the beans that Ted was planning to marry Joyce Summers (*BtVS* "Ted").

NELLINS, ERNIE | ANTHONY GUIDERA | Bookie who worked out of a sports bar called Shots. Under duress, he gave Wesley information about the demon fight club XXI (*AtS* "The Ring").

NESTER DEMON | Species that likes to live in the walls of homes. They hatch several times a year. The only way to destroy them is to kill their queen (*AtS* "Heartthrob").

NEV | PATRICK BREEN | Cordelia's underpaid personal assistant in the alternate universe created by Skip (*AtS* "Birthday").

NEWMAN, GRACE | MEREDITH SALINGER | Sunnydale High School teacher in 1955 who had an affair with a student named James Stanley. When she tried to break off their relationship, he shot and killed her. Both their ghosts were stuck in a loop repeating this tragedy until Buffy and Angel reenacted it, and "Grace" survived. It was implied that their ghosts then moved on (*BtVS* "I Only Have Eyes for You").

NEWMAN, KATHY | DAGNEY KERR | Buffy's upbeat college roommate (*BtVS* "The Freshman") who was actually a Mok'tagar Demon who had run away from home. Kathy attempted to steal Buffy's soul in order to live in Sunnydale undetected (*BtVS* "Living Conditions").

NEWTON, CASSIE | AZURA SKYE | Student at the new Sunnydale High whom Buffy rescued from being sacrificed to Avilas. The Slayer was tragically powerless to prevent the young woman's

death from a heart condition (*BtVS* "Help"). The First appeared as Cassie in an attempt to convince Willow to commit suicide (*BtVS* "Conversations with Dead People").

NEWTON, MR. | GLENN MORSHOWER | Cassie Newton's father, whom Buffy suspected of abusing his daughter (*BtVS* "Help").

NEW VAMPIRES | After the replacement Seed of Wonder was created, newly sired vampires now possess more powers than previous vampires (except for Dracula). These powers include being able to walk in the daylight and transform into bats, wolves, bees, panthers and mist. Vicki, a prominent New Vampire, has worked with Buffy to keep the peace by magically limiting her peoples' power, much to the annoyance of Harmony (*Buffy* "In Pieces on the Ground").

NEZZLA DEMON (NEZZA) | TROY BRENNA | Bulky, smelly demon with a thick neck and a webbed body. The Trio killed it and Jonathan wore its body to get past the wards that guarded its orbs (*BtVS* "Seeing Red").

NICK | Roommate of Kenny the Thricewise; Dawn slept with him (*Buffy* "No Future for You").

NICOLE | BROOKE BLOOM | Leader of the UC Sunnydale Wiccan group. She made an "empowering" lemon Bundt (*BtVS* "Hush").

NICHOLS, LORD | Horrid little man who dickered over the price of streetwalkers. Darla killed him (*AtS* "Dear Boy").

NICOLS, PETER | ZACHERY TY BRYAN | Leader of the cult that worshipped Avilas and planned to kill Cassie Newton as tribute. Avilas killed him (*BtVS* "Help").

NIGEL | KRIS IYER | Watcher who came with Quentin Travers to test Buffy to determine if she was worthy to receive the Council's information on the Hellgod Glorificus (*BtVS* "Checkpoint"). It is assumed that he died in the explosion Caleb set to destroy the Council (*BtVS* "Never Leave Me").

NIGHTHAWK | Xander's code name, used for team vampire slaying that was conducted in Buffy's absence (*BtVS* "Dead Man's Party").

NINNY | San Francisco Siren who captivated Spike and Xander (*Buffy* "I Wish").

NISANTI DEMON | Faith assumed the generous reward of a passport and retirement was incentive for her to kill something as dangerous as one of these (*Buffy* "No Future for You").

NISHA | New Slayer who was Simone Doffler's lieutenant (*Buffy* "Predators and Prey").

NOELLE | Telepathic Sadecki Demon who kept Non's followers in thrall (*Spike* "After the Fall").

NOLAN, HEATHER | Paralegal who vanished after leaving a downtown bar called D'Oblique. She was possessed by the demon Talamour (*AtS* "Lonely Heart").

NON | Powerful demon who could drain the life out of mammals (including humans) and return it as well, as a form of healing and regeneration. Spike and Illyria usurped her position as the Demon Lord of Beverly Hills. When time was reset, she revived Gunn from his coma so they could fight side by side (*Spike* "After the Fall", *Angel* "Last Angel in Hell").

NORA | LINDA CHRISTOPHER | British Potential who was murdered by the Bringers while under the mentorship of Robson, her Watcher (*BtVS* "Sleeper").

NOSTROYEV | BART MCCARTHY | Russian vampire who dressed in late-nineteenth-century aristocratic fashion. While held by Nazis on a submarine in 1943, he claimed to be known as the scourge of Siberia and butcher of Alexander Palace and that he was Rasputin's lover. Angel staked Nostroyev when the vampire tried to kill the rest of the Allied crew (*AtS* "Why We Fight").

NOVAC | JOSHUA HUTCHINSON | Former head of the grave-robbing division at Wolfram & Hart. When Angel shuttered the department, he sent Novac to tell their top client. Novac's body was returned in buckets (*AtS* "Just Rewards").

***NUMERO CINCO* (NUMBER FIVE) | DANNY MORA |** Silent mailman at Wolfram & Hart who wore a face mask sporting the number five in honor of his past as a Mexican wrestler and a fighter of evil. Together, he and his four brothers were known as *Los Hermanos Numero*. Tezcatcatl lured *Numero Cinco* to the cemetery, where he was mortally wounded and joined his brothers in the afterlife (*AtS* "The Cautionary Tale of Numero Cinco").

NUMFAR | JOSS WHEDON | Lorne's brother. Numfar is able to do the Dance of Joy for three moons. He also performed the Dance of Honor for Angel (*AtS* "Through the Looking Glass") and the Dance of Shame when Lorne left Pylea (*AtS* "There's No Place like Plrtz Glrb").

NUNASHUSH | Chumash "spirits from below, spirits of the night" invoked by Hus (*BtVS* "Pangs").

NYAZIAN SCROLLS | Texts that contain a math-based prophecy that predicted the arrival (or arising) of the Tro-Clon that would bring about the purification (or ruination) of humankind (*AtS* "Offspring"). As the text described, "For surely in that time, when the sky opens and the heavens weep, there will be no birth, only death" (*AtS* "Lullaby"). Sahjhan revised his own prophesied death at Connor's hands to imply Angel would kill Connor, causing Wesley to try to make a deal with Holtz, and then run away with Connor (*AtS* "Loyalty"). Cyvus Vail referred to the prophecy when he brought Connor to LA to open the urn and kill Sahjhan (*AtS* "Origin").

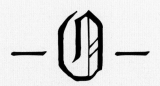

OBSCURING SPELL | Magic that Tara used against a demon Jonathan conjured. To cast the spell, she blew smoke into its face and chanted, "*Sensus confundantur et aer appleatur. Obscuratam*" (*BtVS* "Superstar").

O'CONNOR, RACHEL | Slayer during 1937 who pretended to be a blind pencil seller to attract and dust vampires. The OSS (Office of Strategic Services) recruited her to thwart a Nazi attempt to obtain a Djinn (*Tales* "Broken Bottle of Djinn").

OCTARUS | Member of the Order of Taraka—assassins sent by Spike to kill Buffy—who attacked the Slayer during her ice-skating date with Angel. Buffy cut his throat with the blade of her skate (*BtVS* "What's My Line? Part 2").

ODEN-TAL | Alternate dimension in which the Vigories control women by removing their Ko. Oden-Tal connected to Earth via a portal (*AtS* "She").

O'DONNELL | YAN ENGLAND | R.J. Brooks's rival as a QB starter on the Sunnydale High football team. Dawn pushed him down the stairs (*BtVS* "Him").

OF HUMAN BONDAGE | Book that UC Sunnydale freshman Eddie always kept with him. The fact that he left it in his dorm room when he supposedly left school tipped Buffy off that he had been murdered (*BtVS* "The Freshman").

O'KEEFE | A. J. WEDDING | Sunnydale High student and follower of Avilas (*BtVS* "Help").

OLAF'S HAMMER | Magical weapon belonging to Olaf the Troll God and employed by Buffy against Glory. The heavy hammer was difficult for those without Slayer strength to wield (*BtVS* "The Gift").

OLAF THE TROLL GOD | ABRAHAM BENRUBI | Viking warrior who cheated on Aud, which inspired her to turn him into a troll (*BtVS* "Selfless"). Olaf was imprisoned inside a crystal with his magic hammer until Willow accidentally released him in 2001. He then went on a rampage before Willow sent him to an alternate dimension (*BtVS* "Triangle").

"OLD MAN" HUNTER | IAN ABERCROMBIE | Participant in SlayerFest '98 who remotely guided the Gruenstahler twins (*BtVS* "Homecoming").

OLD ONES | Pure demons who walked the Earth before humans took it from them (*BtVS* "The Harvest"). The greater ones were interred, for death was not always their end (*AtS* "A Hole in the World"). The Old Ones came with the Seed of Wonder (*Buffy* "The Core") and shared the earth with higher beings known as the Powers That Be (*AtS* "City of"). Old Ones include Lohesh, Boluz, Vrill, Neauth, Illyria, Arsgomor, Sephrilian, Quor'toth, and Maloker. Many have been entombed in the Deeper Well (*Buffy* "The Core").

OLIVIA | PHINA ORUCHE | British girlfriend of Giles who saw the Gentlemen and lived to tell the tale (*BtVS* "Hush"). She was devastated by Giles's death (*Angel and Faith* "Death and Consquences") until she learned of his resurrection. They got together on the day he magically re-aged, when it was discovered that she had become a liaison to the San Francisco Police Department's supernatural crimes unit (*Buffy* "Old Demons").

OLVIKAN | The Old One that Mayor Wilkins became upon his Ascension, appearing as a giant demonic snake (*BtVS* "Graduation Day, Part 2").

ONI DEMON | Japanese demon who gave Sachiko her Vampy Cat (*Buffy* "Predators and Prey").

ORACLES (THE KNOWING ONES) | CAREY CANNON AND RANDALL SLAVIN | Conduits for the Powers That Be that served as guides for champions and lived in the Netherworld of Eternal Watching. They could be accessed through the Gateway for Lost Souls, under the post office. According to Doyle, they were "finicky and unpredictable," and a supplicant seeking their audience was required to bring them a gift and greet them in the following manner: "*We beseech access to the Knowing Ones.*" It was not their place to grant life or death and matters of love did not concern them, although they could create temporal folds and undo what had been done, but not for lower beings. They believed

Angel's sacrifice for Buffy elevated his status, and they undid the day and events with the Mohra Demon that allowed him to be with Buffy (*AtS* "I Will Remember You"). The Oracles were slaughtered by Vocah, but a trace of one Oracle remained on this plane long enough to tell Angel what he needed to know about Vocah and how to help Cordelia (*AtS* "To Shanshu in LA").

ORB OF RAMJARIN | Small glass ball needed to raise a Thesulac Demon in a spell that also required sacred herbs, divining powder, and incantations (*AtS* "Are You Now or Have You Ever Been").

ORB OF THESULAH | Magical artifact in which a soul can be kept until it is restored to the individual who lost it. Jenny Calendar purchased one for Angel (*BtVS* "Passion"), while Giles already had one that he'd been using as a paperweight (*BtVS* "Becoming, Part 2").

ORBS OF NEZZLA'KHAN | Pair of magical orbs that bestowed invulnerability on and enhanced the strength of their possessor. They are quite fragile (*BtVS* "Seeing Red").

ORDER OF AURELIUS, THE | Ancient vampiric order following the vampire prophet Aurelius for the retaking of the Earth by the Old Ones (*BtVS* "Never Kill a Boy on the First Date"). Members have included the Master, Darla, Absalom, the Anointed One, Big Ugly, Bob, Andrew Borba, Claw Guy, Jane, Lean Boy, Luke, Yuki Makimura, Jesse, Ned, Scylla, Tara, Terrence, Thomas, the Three, Walt, and Zachary.

ORDER OF DAGON, THE | Monastic order formed to protect the Key. Prior to their destruction by the Hellgod Glorificus, they sent the Key to Buffy in the form of her sister, Dawn (*BtVS* "No Place like Home").

ORDER OF TARAKA, THE | Society of deadly assassins dating back to the time of King Solomon. Their credo is "to sew discord and kill the unwary." Employed by Spike, three of them (Norman Pfister, Octarus, and Patrice) attempted unsuccessfully to kill Buffy (*BtVS* "What's My Line? Part 1"). They are described in *The Writings of Dramius*, Volume 6 (*BtVS* "What's My Line? Part 2").

ORKIN, JEFF | Student at the original Sunnydale High School who was mauled to death by Pete Clarner. His body was discovered in the woods (*BtVS* "Beauty and the Beasts").

ORLANDO | **JUSTIN GORENCE** | Knight of Byzantium sworn to destroy the Key. After arriving in Sunnydale (*BtVS* "Checkpoint"), he was tortured and rendered insane by Glory (*BtVS* "Blood Ties"). Fellow knight Dante killed Orlando to save him from further humiliation due to his failures (*BtVS* "Spiral").

ORLON WINDOW | Spell that allows its user to see the past as it once was. If the Orlon Window, which is housed in a glass cube, breaks around someone whose mind has been altered, then all that person's old memories will return. Wesley broke the window, releasing the team's original memories of their time with Connor in their lives (*AtS* "Origin").

Osbourne, Daniel

OZ | SETH GREEN |

Willow's ex-boyfriend and former member of the band Dingoes Ate My Baby (*BtVS* "Inca Mummy Girl"). Oz was changed into a werewolf when his cousin Jordy bit him (*BtVS* "Phases"). He and Wilow built a relationship together that weathered this change in him as well as her brief fling with Xander. The pair stayed together and made love for the first time in the lead up to the final confrontation with the Mayor at Graduation (*BtVS* "Graduation Day Parts 1 & 2"). Oz matriculated with Willow at UC Sunnydale, but after cheating on her with the murderous werewolf Veruca (*BtVS* "Wild at Heart"), he left Sunnydale.

Oz returned later, believing he could successfully control his wolf side and possibly reunite with Willow. Instead, he discovered that Willow was in love with Tara. He changed into the wolf again and was captured and tortured by the Initiative. After being freed, he left town again (*BtVS* "New Moon Rising"). While touring with his band, Oz went to LA for a gig and brought the Gem of Amarra with him as a gift from Buffy to Angel. His timely arrival with two crossbows and a van saved Angel, Cordelia, and Doyle from Spike and Marcus (*AtS* "In the Dark"). Oz was later seen in Tibet with his werewolf partner Bayarmaa and their son. He helped Buffy and the Slayers in their battle against Twilight and his forces. He is currently living in Tibet with his family (*Buffy* "Retreat").

ORPHEUS | Enchanted drug that humans inject themselves with so vampires can feed off them for a serious psychic trip. The more one takes of the drug, the deeper that person sinks into metaphorical hell (*AtS* "Orpheus").

OSIRIS | Egyptian god petitioned during resurrection spells; appearing as a giant, misty head, he refused to bring Tara back to life (*BtVS* "Villains").

OSWALD, BRITTANY | Junior at St. Michael's High School, who had been missing for a year by the time Buffy killed Machida. Brittany is assumed to have been a sacrifice (*BtVS* "Reptile Boy").

OSWALD, LEE HARVEY | Assassin of President Kennedy. According to Jasmine, he acted alone (*AtS* "Magic Bullet").

O'TOOLE, JACK | CHANNON ROE | Sunnydale High bully resurrected by his grandfather shortly after his death from multiple gunshot wounds. Jack raised his old gang and attempted to blow up the high school. While Oz was in werewolf form, he ate O'Toole (*BtVS* "The Zeppo").

OVERHEISER, DR. | TIME WINTERS | Surgeon summoned to operate on Riley Finn when the soldier withdrew from Maggie Walsh's drug regimen. Spike kidnapped the doctor to force him to remove the chip in Spike's head (*BtVS* "Out of My Mind").

OVERLORNE | Villainous character in the film *Last Angel in Hell* (*Angel* "After the Fall").

OVERSEER, THE | Priest and leader of the Nitobe Demons who was corrupted by Illyria. He framed Eldre Koh for murder (*Angel and Faith* "United").

OVU MOBANI (EVIL EYE) | Nigerian god of the undead, who—when summoned through an ancient mask—would take control of a body and raise the dead as zombies. Buffy destroyed the mask with a shovel while her mother's friend Pat wore it, which destroyed the demon possessing Pat's body at the time (*BtVS* "Dead Man's Party").

P

PACK, THE (HEIDI BARRIE, KYLE DUFOURS, TOR HAUER, RHONDA KELLEY) | JENNIFER SKY, EION BAILEY, BRIAN GROSS, MICHAEL MCCRAINE | Four students at the original Sunnydale High School who were possessed by hyena spirits. They ate Principal Flutie and Herbert the Pig (*BtVS* "The Pack").

PADRE | Catholic priest who told Mayor Richard Wilkins the story of Naayéé'neizghání the Vampire Slayer (*Tales* "The Glittering World").

PAGE, DEIDRE) | WENDY WAY | Member of Giles's occult circle during his youth in London. Together they raised the demon Eyghon. Years later, her distinctive tattoo drew Eyghon to her, and he killed her. Then Eyghon possessed her body, using it to kill Philip Henry (*BtVS* "The Dark Age").

PALMER, BILLY (LUCKY NINETEEN) | JEREMY FOLEY | Twelve-year-old Kiddie League baseball player who astrally projected and manifested other people's nightmares while he was in a coma due to a beating by his coach (*BtVS* "Nightmares").

PAPAL ENCYCLICAL, TWELFTH CENTURY | Document in Giles's collection (*BtVS* "Gingerbread").

PAPAZIAN, TONY (LITTLE TONY) | JOHN CAPODICE | Mob boss with a favorite drop spot for victims (and victim parts) at Pier 39 in San Pedro, CA. Represented by Lee Mercer at Wolfram & Hart, Papazian was suspected of putting the hit out on a county supervisor. His lawyers set up the sensitivity training at Kate's precinct to distract the police so he could get away. His attempt on Kate's life made him a liability to the firm, so they dropped him, leaving him in jail (*AtS* "Sense and Sensitivity").

PARANYCH GRIMOIRE | Book that revealed that the Beast's weakness was the Tooth of Light (*AtS* "Awakening").

PARGO DEMON | Leathery, red-skinned species with huge teeth and wispy white hair that can be killed only by drowning (*BtVS* "Something Blue").

PARK, GAVIN | DANIEL DAE KIM | Lawyer at Wolfram & Hart. Gavin moved from Real Estate to the Special Projects division and was immediately at odds with Lilah Morgan. He first encountered Angel when he notified the vampire of the firm's future purchase of the hotel (*AtS* "Over the Rainbow"). In addition to drowning Angel in red tape, Gavin started to pursue Angel's lack of official identity, but Lilah thwarted him (*AtS* "Carpe Noctem"). Once he became Linwood Murrow's right-hand man, Gavin began working with the psychics and uncovered Lilah's affair with Wesley. When Lilah dispatched Murrow, Gavin was cowed and made her subordinate (*AtS* "Deep Down"). When captured by Angel, Gavin wouldn't stop talking long enough for Angel to torture him and revealed they hadn't been able to decipher Lorne's reading of Cordelia (*AtS* "Rain of Fire"). The Beast killed Gavin and then he became a zombie under Wolfram & Hart's backup defense plan. Gunn cut off his head out of sympathy (*AtS* "Habeas Corpses").

PARKER | Resident of Magic Town and lover of mutated woman Tricia (*Angel and Faith* "Where the River Meets the Sea"). He died in Tricia's arms during the battle against Drusilla and Archaeus (*Angel and Faith* "A Tale of Two Families").

PARKER | DARIN HEAMES | One of Jack O'Toole's revenant buddies. Xander dragged him along the side of his car until Parker revealed that the bomb he and the others had built was in the school's boiler room. Then Xander accidentally decapitated him with a mailbox (*BtVS* "The Zeppo").

PARKER, MRS. | Sweet old lady who offered Halloween candy to Willow's band of trick-or-treaters before a spell turned them into demons that attacked her (*BtVS* "Halloween").

PARKING TICKET WOMAN | MARTI NOXON | Woman who tried to sing her way out of a ticket for illegally parking next to a fire hydrant by first offering excuses and then coming on to the officer (*BtVS* "Once More, with Feeling").

PARNELL | Evolved Vampire whose predatory activities during daytime alerted Angel to the fact that there was a new kind of vampire that could walk in sunlight (*Angel and Faith* "Where the River Meets the Sea").

PAROLE OFFICER | MIK SCRIBA | Representative who oversaw Bradley Scott's parole. He feared death more than he was afraid of Wolfram & Hart (*AtS* "Dead End").

PARTNEY, MATTHEW | Fred's friend from Lubbock, Texas (*AtS* "Home").

PARTY TOWN | Costume shop in Sunnydale. Costumes rented there during Halloween were not enchanted and the wearers remained themselves, unlike those who wore outfits purchased at Ethan's Costume Shop (*BtVS* "Halloween").

PASSIONS | Spike's favorite soap opera, a supernatural series that has since been canceled (*BtVS* "Something Blue").

PASTERNAK, LANA | Fake medium in San Francisco who was became possessed by a demon who could see ghosts. Before Giles exorcised her, she revealed that the "ghost" of Anya was not really Anya (*Buffy* "Old Demons").

PAT | NANCY LENEHAN | Joyce's friend from book club who was a source of support during the time that Buffy ran away from home. Pat was possessed by the demon Ovu Mobani after being murdered by zombies raised by the evil being. Buffy then killed her (again) with a shovel (*BtVS* "Dead Man's Party").

PATCHES | Oz's nickname for the zombie cat resurrected by Ovu Mobani (*BtVS* "Dead Man's Party").

PATRICE | SPICE WILLIAMS-CROSBY | Member of the Order of Taraka, a group of assassins sent by Spike to kill Buffy. Patrice disguised herself as a police officer and tried to kill Buffy during Sunnydale High School's career fair. It is assumed that she died in the fire that Spike set in the church (*BtVS* "What's My Line? Part 2").

PAVAYNE, MATTHIAS (REAPER, DARK SOUL #182) | SIMON TEMPLEMAN | Eighteenth-century European aristocrat and doctor who earned his nickname "the Reaper," by performing unnecessary surgery on his patients. Wolfram & Hart sacrificed him to deconsecrate missionary ground so they could build their LA office on it. Pavayne can bend reality to his will and has been feeding hell the souls of their dead employees ever since. He tried to send Spike to hell in his place, but the vampire forced Pavayne to become corporeal, and Angel locked him up in the permanent storage of Wolfram & Hart (*AtS* "Hellbound").

PAYMER, STEVE | Actor David Paymer's brother who lived in Cordelia's apartment complex (*AtS* "She").

PEACHES | FAITH S. ABRAHAMS | Member of Harmony's vampire gang who rebelled. Buffy staked her (*BtVS* "Real Me").

PEARL | Half demon twin sister of Nash, a former follower of Twilight, and an ally of Whistler. She survived Angel and Faith's attack during the detonation of the plague ball (*Angel and Faith* "Live through This"). Afterward, she worked for Corky Smallwood and was subsequently blinded by Angel with a bottle of magic. She escaped and continues her vendetta against Angel (*Angel and Faith* "Where the River Meets the Sea").

PEARSON, MAUDE | BETH GRANT | Former owner of the Pearson Arms apartment building. In 1946 she dropped dead of a heart attack at the age of fifty-seven. Her ghost chased away or killed any woman who tried to move in to her apartment and attempted to do the same to Cordelia. Angel thought Maude was killed by her son Dennis, but opening the wall in Cordelia's apartment revealed the son's body, leading the ghost to confess that she killed him by walling him in there to keep him with her before she died. Dennis's ghost destroyed her (*AtS* "Rm w/ a Vu").

PECK, DAVE | Lysette the car freak dated him. He had a completely tricked-out Thunderbird, but the upholstery was kind of shot (*BtVS* "The Zeppo").

PEGGY | Underage fan of Billy Rage who was unaware that the demon rock star planned to seduce her in his hotel room. Her father attempted to shoot him for preying on his teenage daughter (*Angel and Faith* "Where the River Meets the Sea").

PELLERIS SPELL | Cleansing and banishment spell that Ethan Rayne and Giles performed on their friend Randall to exorcise Eyghon, even though the spell was originally intended for objects and locations. The magic killed Randall as Giles had feared it would (*Angel and Faith* "Death and Consequences").

PELLETTI | JEFF DENTON | Newly risen vampire whom Buffy used to train Dawn in the ways of Slaying (*BtVS* "Lessons").

PENN | JEREMY RENNER | Puritan vampire sired by Angelus. Tabloids called him "the Pope" due to the cross he carved into his victims' cheeks with a silver fingernail, but the act was meant to mock God, not to praise him. Once turned, Penn drank his family's blood, specifically targeting his father as Angelus did his own. They lost touch when Angelus regained his soul. In the present day, Penn targeted victims that resembled his family. He

kidnapped Kate and planned to turn her so Angel would have to kill her, but Angel fought him, buying Kate enough time to drive a stake up through Angel's stomach into Penn's heart (*AtS* "Somnambulist").

PENSHAW, JANICE | AMBER TAMBLYN | Dawn Summers's best friend who snuck out with her on Halloween and was nearly killed by vampires (*BtVS* "All the Way").

PERCELL, KELLY | Sophomore at Grant High School who went missing and is presumed to have been sacrificed to Machida (*BtVS* "Reptile Boy").

PERGAMUM CODEX | Writings that contain the most complete prophecies about the Slayer's role in the end years. Angel obtained it for Giles (*BtVS* "Prophecy Girl").

PERKINS, DENISE | Victim of Russell Winters who knew Angel Investigations' first client, Tina. Angel tied Denise's disappearance to the discovery of a body with a rose tattoo (*AtS* "City of").

PERREN, DOUG | JACK MCGEE | Sunnydale Natural History Museum curator and archaeologist. Perren asked Giles to examine the stone sarcophagus containing Acathla because Lou Tabor at the Washington Institute told him that Giles was the foremost authority on obscure relics. Drusilla killed him (*BtVS* "Becoming, Part 1").

PERRY | Human who was changed into a pixie after the plague ball exploded (*Angel and Faith* "Where the River Meets the Sea"). He assisted Corky Smallwood and Amy Madison, but he ran off after Nadira changed Amy into a rat (*Angel and Faith* "Lost and Found").

PERUVIAN MAN | GIL BIRMINGHAM | "Bodyguard" of the Incan mummy, who attempted to return her to her tomb. She drained and killed him (*BtVS* "Inca Mummy Girl").

PETRONZI, GAGE | WENTWORTH MILLER | Smart-aleck member of the swim team at the original Sunnydale High School. Gage skated in Willow's computer class because he knew Principal Snyder wanted him to pass. Angelus attacked him but his blood was tainted with Coach Marin's secret formula, which turned the swim team members into Gill Monsters. Gage transformed into one of those creatures in front of Buffy (*BtVS* "Go Fish").

PFISTER, NORMAN | KELLY CONNELL | Assassin with the Order of Taraka who could shape-shift into hundreds of worms. He could be killed only in his disassembled (worm) state, so Xander and Cordelia immobilized the creepy crawlies with liquid adhesive and then stomped all the worms to death (*BtVS* "What's My Line? Part 2").

PHALANGOID DEMON | Creature that sucks brains out of the skull (*AtS* "To Shanshu in LA").

PHANTOM DENNIS (DENNIS PEARSON) | B. J. PORTER | Cordelia's roommate, the ghost son of the original owner, Maude Pearson (*AtS* "Rm w/ a Vu"). He coexisted with the current resident of his former home, looking after her on occasion.

PHIL | CHARLES CONSTANT | Security guard at Wolfram & Hart who killed people as assigned (*AtS* "Blind Date").

PHIL | MARC BRETT | Health-club employee who promised he could get Angel a great deal at the gym. He wanted to keep a lid on any rumors of steroid abuse, so he showed Angel their member files (*AtS* "Carpe Noctem").

PHILIP | Watcher-in-training and peer of Rupert Giles in 1972. He was killed by the Lorophage Demon thought to be the Highgate Vampire (*Angel and Faith* "Daddy Issues").

PHILIP | OLIVER MUIRHEAD | Watcher who accompanied Quentin Travers to test Buffy (*BtVS* "Checkpoint"). He died in the explosion Caleb set at Watcher headquarters in London (*BtVS* "Never Leave Me").

PHILLIP | DOUGLAS BENNETT | Doublemeat Palace employee who trained Buffy on the grill (*BtVS* "Doublemeat Palace").

PHISTO'S DICTIONARY OF DEMONS AND DIMENSIONAL SPIRITS | Book written in Gashundi (*AtS* "Forgiving").

PIANIST | CHRISTOPHE BECK | Musician who appeared in Giles's dream after the defeat of Adam (*BtVS* "Restless").

PIASCA DEMON | Flesh-eating Indian demon who entered its victims through the mouth and eviscerated them from within (*AtS* "Lonely Heart").

PICK ME UP | Coffeehouse in San Francisco where Buffy worked post-Seed (*Buffy* "Last Gleaming").

PIERCE | ROBERT HILLIS | Suitor who took Cordelia to La Petite Renard for a dinner date, but bored her with talk of corn futures. When confronted with a vengeful vampire outside the office, Pierce fled, leaving Cordelia behind (*AtS* "The Bachelor Party").

PINKY | Nickname Spike gave the Las Vegas monster made entirely of Elvis impersonators (*Spike* "Alone Together Now").

PIT, THE | Section of the Initiative laboratory where experiments were performed on demons (*BtVS* "The I in Team").

PLAGIARUS DEMON

PLACENTURIANS | Xander's term for the hordes of demons entering Earth's dimension after Buffy and Angel ascended (*Buffy* "Twilight").

PLAGIARUS DEMON | Tentacled, parasitic demon who can be induced to leave its host body if it believes the host is about to be killed. By saying "stamata!" it is possible to give up a day of happy memories in return for its defeat (*Angel and Faith* "Live through This").

PLAGUE BALL | Magical sphere created by Whistler, Pearl, and Nash to spread magic throughout the world after the destruction of the Seed of Wonder. When it exploded over the Hackney area of London, it caused magical mutations in many of the inhabitants, the result being the current district called Magic Town (*Angel and Faith* "What You Want, Not What You Need").

PLAKTICINE | Harmless yellow mucus secreted by an Ethros Demon (*AtS* "I've Got You under My Skin").

PLASMA AND FLUID TURBULENCE | Book that contains information on demons and opening portals to other dimensions. It should not have been shelved alongside the neutrino books in Professor Seidel's bookcase (*AtS* "Supersymmetry").

PLATT, STEPHEN | **PHIL LEWIS** | Sunnydale High School guidance counselor. Buffy was required to see him as a condition of returning to school after the death of Kendra. Mr. Platt asked another student, Debbie Foley, to keep a dream journal. Pete Clarner, Debbie's boyfriend, was jealous of the counselor's influence over his girlfriend and killed him (*BtVS* "Beauty and the Beasts").

PLAZA INN | Location of the first meeting of the newly re-formed Magic Council (*Buffy* "Own It").

POCKLA DEMON | **ROBIN ATKIN DOWNES** | Robed demon healer who used mystical powders and chanting to aid in healing and regeneration (*AtS* "Dead End").

PODELLE, BRITTANY | While searching for a werewolf, Buffy spotted her making out with Owen Stadeal even though she was the girlfriend of Bara Williams (*BtVS* "Phases").

POKER GAME SPELL | Cheating spell chanted by Willow: "*I implore you, Neisa, blessed goddess of chance and fortune, heed my call. Send to me the heart I desire*" (*BtVS* "The I in Team").

POLGARA DEMON | Keen-sighted demon species with distinctive razor blade arms. Dr. Walsh sent Buffy and Riley's team out to retrieve one (*BtVS* "The I in Team"). It had escaped through Tunnel 72 of the Initiative headquarters (*BtVS* "Goodbye Iowa").

POLO | **VICTOR YERRID** | Demonic lead puppet from the *Smile Time* children's television program. Polo smoked, drank whiskey, and turned the human staff at the studio into zombies. He worked with Groofus, Ratio Hornblower, and Flora to drain the life force of each child that watched the show. They planned to sell that lifeforce down in hell and become very rich. Puppet Angel cut him to pieces (*AtS* "Smile Time").

POP'S PUMPKIN PATCH | Local Sunnydale pumpkin patch. Spike viewed video footage filmed at that location of Buffy's battle with a vampire (*BtVS* "Halloween").

PORTAL | A geographical area—like Caritas, the public library, Dr. Seidel's office, and the Hyperion lobby—that is rife with psychic energy. Portals can function as dimensional hotspots; natural gateways between worlds. Creating a portal tends to deplete a hotspot of its psychic energy. If one has been used, it goes cold for a while and can't be used again until it recharges. When multiple entities enter a dimensional portal, they sometimes separate on the other side (*AtS* "Over the Rainbow").

PORTER, NURSE | SARA VAN HORN | Hospital employee who took care of Faith while she was in a coma. Porter called the Watchers Council when Faith escaped from the hospital and told them to "send the team" (*BtVS* "This Year's Girl").

POSEY | New Slayer in the Roman squad who could read Latin. Demon goatmen killed her in an ambush by Warren Mears and Amy Madison (*Buffy* "Retreat").

POST | Santa Rosa school bully turned zompire who was dusted by Billy Lane to save his boyfriend Devon (*Buffy* "Guarded").

POST, GWENDOLYN | SERENA SCOTT THOMAS | Woman who arrived in Sunnydale posing as Faith's new Watcher although she had been kicked out of the Watchers Council for misuses of dark power. Post put on the Glove of Myhnegon and after Buffy cut off her arm, the magical lightning she had called down killed her. (*BtVS* "Revelations").

POWELL, DR. | PAULO ANDRES | Doctor who tended to Buffy when Angel brought her to the hospital after he drained her (*BtVS* "Graduation Day, Part 2").

POWER GIRL | Eight-year-old Buffy's play name when "rescuing" her little cousin Celia from imagined dangers (*BtVS* "Killed by Death").

POWERS THAT BE, THE (PTB) | Immensely powerful beings that were the first life to exist in Earth's dimension. Inside every living thing there is a connection to the Powers That Be. Some call it instinct or intuition, but deep down it is how lesser beings know their purpose in this world (*AtS* "Birthday").

PRATT, ANNE | CAROLINE LAGERFELT | Spike's doting but consumptive mother. After Drusilla sired him, he sired his mother, and she became vindictive and cruel. Spike staked her (*BtVS* "Lies My Parents Told Me").

Potentials

Girls identified as possible Slayers and part of the Slayer line. After Willow performed the spell that shared Buffy's (and Faith's) power with the Potentials, they were all made Slayers at the final Battle of the Hellmouth (*BtVS* "Showtime" and others).

They include:

Ally Roads	**Eve**
Amanda	**Kennedy**
Annabelle	Molly
Caridad	**Nora**
Chao-Ahn	**Rona**
Chloe	**Shannon**
Colleen	**Soledad**
Dianne	Violet
Dominique	

PREGGOTHIAN DEMON | Wolfram & Hart employed a member of this species to guard their vault. It can be rendered inert with mystical powder (*AtS* "Blind Date").

PREKIAN DEMON | Species known for traveling in roving bands and ritualistic slayings (*AtS* "The Thin Dead Line").

PRICE, ROBERT | Former lawyer with Wolfram & Hart. When he let down the Senior Partners, they made him eat his own liver (*AtS* "To Shanshu in LA").

PRIEST | LARRY CLARKE | Holy man who revealed to Spike and Andrew that Caleb had massacred the rest of his religious order after uncovering an inscription in their monastery saying "It is not for thee. It is for her alone to wield" (*BtVS* "Empty Places").

PRIMA BALLERINA | SUMMER GLAU | Dancer who had been trapped in the Blinnikov World Ballet Corps since the nineteenth century. She fell in love with Stefan, but was too afraid to run away with him and give up the ballet. A jealous Count Kurskov trapped her in a time spell, forcing her to perform the exact same dance forever. At Angel's request, she committed a new mistake in her dance, which upset the count, loosening his hold on her and allowing her to pass away (*AtS* "Waiting in the Wings").

PRIMALS, THE | African Masai sect that worshipped predatory animals such as hyenas and sought to accept their souls into their bodies (*BtVS* "The Pack").

PRIMITIVE, THE | See Sineya.

PRINCE OF LIES | CAMDEN TOY | Bald, pale vampire who was held prisoner on a German submarine in 1943. He claimed that he was older than darkness, and his pointed ears, odd teeth, long fingernails, and bony fingers demonstrated his age. He'd discovered that the Nazis were experimenting on vampires, planning to create an army from the best of them. Angel staked him before he could kill the Nazi prisoner (*AtS* "Why We Fight").

PRIO MOTU | Ancient Ofga-beast bred to maim and massacre (*AtS* "Judgment").

PROKAYROTE STONE | Smooth, brown stone that can transform into a metallic wormlike creature that bores into the subject's optic nerve and reveals suppressed or forgotten ideas, images, and memories. Used by Rupert Giles on Spike with the accompanying chant: "*Kun'ati belek sup'sion. Bok'vata im / kele'beshus. Ta'li ta'li ek'vota. / Mor'osh boota'ke. . . .*" (*BtVS* "Lies My Parents Told Me").

PROPHECIES OF ABERJIAN, THE (WORDS OF ANATOLE) | Scroll written in a dozen different languages over the course of the last four thousand years. It foretold the coming of the Seers and had an entire passage about the vampire with a soul (*AtS* "Blind Date"). The prophecies saved Cordelia from the Mark of Vocah and foretold that Wolfram & Hart would sever all of Angel's connections to the Powers That Be. It also contained information about the Raising ritual and would connect Angel to the Powers That Be if he could translate it (*AtS* "To Shanshu in LA").

PROSERPEXA | Sister of the Dark Demon whose followers attempted to destroy the world in 1932, causing an earthquake that buried her temple. Her statue depicts her as a woman with a forked tongue and taloned fingers. She was called again by Willow, but the ritual required for her to destroy the world was aborted (*BtVS* "Grave").

PROTHGORIAN BROADSWORD | Weapon in the arsenal at the Hyperion (*AtS* "Fredless").

PSI THETA | Fraternity at UC Sunnydale that lost its charter. The vampire Sunday used its abandoned frat house as her lair (*BtVS* "The Freshman").

PSYCH 105 | Dr. Walsh's class at UC Sunnydale in which Buffy and Willow were students during freshman year and Riley served as TA (*BtVS* "The Freshman").

PSYCHON WAVE | Warren re-created this death-trap machine that Darkseid made in an X-Men/Teen Titans crossover comic book (*Buffy* "Twilight").

PUSLEAK | Anharrans Demon who worshipped the god-king Kerberon until his fall; then he worshipped Dawn (*Buffy* "Own It").

PYLEA | Planet orbiting two suns in another dimension. As Lorne described it, "A world of only good and evil, black and white, no gray. No music, no art, just champions roaming the countryside fighting for justice . . . You got a problem, solve it with a sword. No one ever admits to having actual feelings and emotions, let alone talks about them." Standard vampire rules do not apply there, meaning Angel could be in the sun and had a reflection while in the world (*AtS* "Belonging"). The humans on Pylea were considered cows and used for slave labor. They wore restraining collars that tortured them if they didn't follow their owner's instructions. If the collar was tampered with, the slave's head exploded (*AtS* "Over the Rainbow"). Cordelia set the slaves free before returning to Earth (*AtS* "There's No Place like Plrtz Glrb").

BACHNAL Ritual for executing fugitive slaves (*AtS* "Through the Looking Glass").

BLEAUCHA Demon that resembles the *Senih'd* and nests in the scum pits of *Ur*. Groo has killed many (*AtS* "Couplet").

COM-SHUK The act of mating (*AtS* "Through the Looking Glass").

CREBBIL | Axe used in Bachnal (*AtS* "Through the Looking Glass").

GROOSALUGG Brave; Undefeated. A name befitting a Champion (*AtS* "Through the Looking Glass").

KALLA BERRIES Fruit used to sweeten cug-grain and thistles (*AtS* "There's No Place like Plrtz Glrb").

KAYA-NO-M'TEK "May you orally please the gods." It is very close to the phrase "May your words please the gods" (*AtS* "Spin the Bottle").

KYE-RUMPTION The meeting of two great heroes on the field of battle, and specifically the point when they recognize their mutual fate. It's also a kind of grog made out of the ox dung, but that's archaic, according to Fred (*AtS* "Offspring").

LO-LATH CH-OWRNG NE BRUUN "I may be prepared to shout a joyful chant" (*AtS* "Spin the Bottle").

MOCK-NA Soothing Pylean brew that can release tension. Ingredients include mud and Plockweed, but creeping fig and sour cress may be substituted in a pinch (*AtS* "Tomorrow").

MOIRA The gut physical attraction between two larger than life souls (*AtS* "Offspring").

SCHLUG-TEE Tense neck muscle (*AtS* "Tomorrow").

SEEKUL Hunting, doglike demon (*AtS* "Over the Rainbow").

SHIV-ROTH The Vigil of the Bereaved (*AtS* "Double or Nothing").

TARKNA Pylean version of hell (*AtS* "There's No Place like Plrtz Glrb").

VAN-TAL Vampire (*AtS* "There's No Place like Plrtz Glrb").

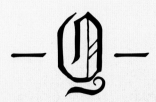

QUEEN C | Vanity license plate on Cordelia's car while she was in high school (*BtVS* "Reptile Boy").

QUEEN PUFFLES OF POMERANIA | Harmony's dog that appeared with her on Anderson Cooper's talk show (*Buffy* "Predators and Prey").

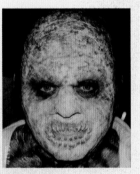

QUELLER DEMON | BARBARA C. ADSIDE AND DEBBIE LEE CARRINGTON | Insectoid demon species with a white face, black-ringed eyes, and fangs. It lived inside a meteor and killed the mentally ill by suffocating them with its viscous mucous. Ben Wilkinson summoned one to deal with the victims of Glory's "brain suck," and it targeted Joyce Summers because she had a brain tumor (*BtVS* "Listening to Fear").

QUIET MAN, THE | Demonic member of D'Hoffryn's Magic Council whose mouth and eyes were sewn shut. His designated magical power was the ability to return any being to its home dimension. D'Hoffryn killed him (*Buffy* "In Pieces on the Ground").

QUINTESSA, THE | Cargo ship with a captain who owed Angel a favor. Angel used the freighter to transport Lister Demons to Briole (*AtS* "Hero").

QUOR'TOTH (DIMENSION) | Darkest of the dark worlds. Sahjhan opened a passageway to this hell dimension as a threat, but Holtz jumped through with baby Connor before it closed. Although they only stayed in the hell dimension for a relatively short time by human standards, they were gone for sixteen years in Quor'toth's time (*AtS* "Sleep Tight"). There are no portals to Quor'toth; the only way in is to rip right through the fabric of reality, which requires dark, dark magic (*AtS* "Forgiving"). Anything

that comes out of Quor'toth leaves behind a kind of para-plasmic radioactivity (*AtS* "Benediction"). The dimension is named for the Old One who rules it (*Angel and Faith* "Family Reunion").

QUOR'TOTH (OLD ONE) | An immense being with huge, four-hoofed limbs, an upper jaw of fangs, an exposed brain mass, and cichlid-like armor on its back. Connor's loving nature started a cult of followers when he returned to the dimension as an adult, and Quor'toth woke from his multi-millennial slumber to eradicate them with his breath attack (*Angel and Faith* "Family Reunion").

QWA'HA XAHN | Priest for Illyria that serves as her guide in this world. He sewed her sacraments up inside him according to ancient ways. Knox served this role when she returned in Fred's body (*AtS* "Shells").

RABINAW, DR. | KEVIN QUIGLEY | Doctor at the psychiatric hospital who treated Dana, a Slayer with mental issues. He videotaped their sessions and planned to write a book about her, so he kept her escape from the hospital quiet (*AtS* "Damage").

RACHEL | JENNIFER SHON | UC Sunnydale student in Willow's sociology class (*BtVS* "Life Serial") who made a wish Anyanka acted on, tearing the hearts out of some fraternity boys by means of a Grimslaw Demon (*BtVS* "Selfless").

RACHEL | MALIA MATHIS | Angel Investigations client who hired the team to stop her abusive boyfriend (*AtS* "In the Dark").

RACK (MARRAK) | JEFF KOBER | Powerful warlock who dispensed magic like drugs, getting both Willow and Amy Madison hooked on it (*BtVS* "Wrecked"). Warren Mears sought magical aid from him when Dark Willow came after him (*BtVS* "Villains"), and the witch out for vengeance sucked the magic out of Rack as payback (*BtVS* "Two to Go"). When Willow went in search of the restoration of magic, he appeared to her as "Marrak." At first he seemed to be guiding her, but he eventually dropped his cover and attacked her. He was destroyed (*Willow: Wonderland*).

RADIE | Twenty-third-century slang term for people suffering mutations due to solar radiation (*Fray* "Big City Girl").

RAGE, BILLY | Rock-star client of Deepscan. He turned out to be a demon who fed on the obsessive love of his young fans. In demon form his skin was fuchsia and he had the head of a bird. Faith tried to kill him, but Kennedy (who had not known about his demonic proclivities) stopped her. Rage ultimately fired Deepscan (*Angel and Faith* "Where the River Meets the Sea").

RAGLAN, WOODROW (WOODY) | PAUL LOGAN | Gym rat whose body was switched with Marcus Roscoe. He melted into a puddle of skin when Roscoe's spirit left him (*AtS* "Carpe Noctem").

RAGNA DEMON | Once-extinct spiderlike creature that Andrew Wells brought back in a steampunk version with recombinant DNA. Simone Doffler offered the demon to Buffy in exchange for Andrew (*Buffy* "Predators and Prey").

RAIDEN, GWEN | ALEXA DAVALOS | Self-described freak who conducts electricity with her hands. Gwen's wealthy parents deposited her at Thorpe's Academy when she was young so she could attend a school that accommodated her special needs. She now wears gloves most of the time to contain her powers, which she uses in her job as a cat burglar. She inadvertently started Angel's heart when the two fought over the Axis of Pythia (*AtS* "Ground State"). She later needed Gunn's help so she could steal technology that would neutralize her powers. She and Gunn had sex, once those powers were suppressed and she could touch another person and be touched as well (*AtS* "Players"). When Los Angeles was sent to hell, the device no longer worked. She allied herself for a time with the sired version of Gunn and later helped Connor and Nina Ash give sanctuary to humans and good demons at the Hyperion Hotel. She sacrificed herself while battling the Wolfram & Hart legions of dragons, and was resurrected when time was reset (*Angel* "After the Fall").

RAIDEN, MR. AND MRS. | MICHAEL MEDICO AND HEIDI FECHT | Wealthy couple that abandoned their daughter at Thorpe's Academy, believing the school could accommodate her special needs (*AtS* "Ground State").

RAIDON | Japanese vampire follower of Toru. Satsu dusted him (*Buffy* "Wolves at the Gate").

"RAINDROPS KEEP FALLING ON MY HEAD" | Song by B.J. Thomas. Angelus sang it to Lorne as "proof" that he was Angel (*AtS* "Calvary").

RAINEY, GENE | MATT CHAMPAGNE | Physicist grad student who sang at Caritas, revealing that he had no future when Lorne read him. Rainey's work on time paradox with Professor Orfalla earned the professor a Nobel Prize nomination. He tried to freeze time with his unhappy girlfriend, but was genuinely sorry when Angel explained the dire consequences of the act (*AtS* "Happy Anniversary").

RAISING, THE | Ritual designed to bring Angel "down" to Wolfram & Hart and tear him from the Powers That Be by returning Darla from the dead (*AtS* "To Shanshu in LA").

RAMADAN EFFIGY | Statue in the Magic Box that Anya assumed was part of the store inventory. Rupert Giles insisted that it belonged in his personal collection (*BtVS* "Bargaining, Part 1").

RAMONE | Former bartender at Caritas who told the fake T'ish Magev that Angel would be coming by (*AtS* "Guise Will Be Guise").

RANCIDUS | Anharrans Demon who became an architect after Dawn Summers killed his god-king, Herberon (*Buffy* "Own It").

RANDALL | DANIEL HENRY MURRAY | Member of Giles's occult circle during his "Ripper" days. Eyghon "took him whole" and when the group tried to perform an exorcism, Randall died (*BtVS* "The Dark Age").

RANNVEIG | Barmaid in Sjornjost, Sweden with whom Olaf cheated on Aud (*BtVS* "Selfless").

RATCATCHER, THE (SILENT DEATH) | Priest sired as a vampire in the fifteenth century during the Spanish Inquisition in retaliation for executing a witch. He had a sweet tooth and he preyed on the religious—nuns, ministers, rabbis, and priests—to punish them for their arrogance. Avery Holls persuaded him to die by exposure to sunlight (*Tales* "Taking Care of Business").

RATCATCHER'S SIRE, THE | Vampire who slaughtered all the inquisitors in the fifteenth-century, save the Ratcatcher, who had tortured his witch ally. That lone priest he sired as punishment (*Tales* "Taking Care of Business").

RA-TET | Mystical order composed of Mesektet, Ashet, Ma'at, Manjet, and Semkhet, five enormously powerful beings that were linked to an embodiment of the ancient god Ra. They were totems, symbolic manifestations whose origins had been shrouded in mystery since the dawn of time. Only the totems themselves knew their true purpose. The Beast killed them all to remove the artifacts necessary to put out the sun (*AtS* "Long Day's Journey").

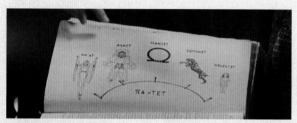

RAT-FACED DEMON | DAVID J. MILLER | Being who used his X-ray vision while playing poker for kittens with Spike (*BtVS* "Life Serial").

RAT TRANSFORMATION SPELL (AND COUNTERSPELL) | Magic used to turn Amy Madison into a rat: "*Goddess Hecate, work thy will. Before thee let the unclean thing crawl!*" (*BtVS* "Gingerbread"). Also used to turn her and Buffy back into their human forms: "*Diana! Hecate! I hereby license thee to depart. Goddess of creatures great and small—I conjure thee to withdraw!*" (*BtVS* "Bewitched, Bothered and Bewildered," "Gingerbread").

RAWLS, KETTIE | Human from the Versi district of Haddyn who bullied Loo and taunted Melaka Fray. He ultimately sided with Melaka when Harth attacked (*Fray* "Ready, Steady . . . ," "The Gateway").

RAY | CORY C. HARDRICT | Teen drug dealer at East Hills Teen Center who knew Gunn (*AtS* "The Thin Dead Line").

RAYNE, ETHAN | ROBIN SACHS | Sorcerer who worshiped chaos. Ethan was a mate of Rupert Giles in the '70s, when their occult circle summoned the demon Eyghon, killing one of their own in the process (*BtVS* "The Dark Age"). He visited Sunnydale a total of four times, the first being to use Giles as bait for the revenge-seeking Eyghon. He also rented enchanted Halloween costumes to Buffy and most of her friends that endangered their lives (*BtVS* "Halloween"). Ethan later created magic candy for the Mayor, which made the adults of Sunnydale act like teenagers (*BtVS* "Band Candy"). After he changed Giles into a Fyral Demon, Ethan was apprehended by the US military and sent to a secret facility (*Buffy* "A New Man"). While there, he entered Buffy's dreamscape created by Amy Madison's magical slumber spell. He was subsequently shot, and died in his cell (*Buffy* "The Long Way Home").

REAPER OF THE TIGRIS | Weapon named after the Tigris River (*BtVS* "End of Days").

REBEL LEADER | **ADONI MAROPIS** | Pylean slave who tried to kill the princess. He later captured Wesley and Gunn and when he learned they were friends of hers, ordered their deaths (*AtS* "Through the Looking Glass"). Castle guards killed him (*AtS* "There's No Place like Plrtz Glrb").

RED, JOHNNY | **JIMMY SHUBERT** | One of Doyle's sources. He led a spin class at a gym (*AtS* "Sense and Sensitivity").

REED, NATHAN | **GERRY BECKER** | Lawyer at Wolfram & Hart who supervised Lilah and Lindsey. He attended the teen shelter fundraiser, where he could witness their failure. (*AtS* "Blood Money"). Reed promoted Lilah when Lindsey left the firm (*AtS* "Dead End").

REFORM VAMPIRISM | Vampiric movement with three main tenets: Only drain blood with permission; never take enough to kill; and no siring. Harmony Kendall is its leading advocate (*Angel and Faith* "In Perfect Harmony").

REG | **RANDALL RAPSTINE** | Occult bookshop owner Angelus tortured for information on the Beast's master (*AtS* "Release").

REGGIE | Husband of one of the New Vampire Parnell's victims (*Angel and Faith* "Where the River Meets the Sea").

RENEE | New Slayer who had a crush on Xander (*Buffy* "The Long Way Home"). Renee accompanied him to consult with Dracula and died in Tokyo when Toru stabbed her with the Scythe (*Buffy* "Wolves at the Gate").

REPO MAN | **JASON CARTER** | Demon who was considered casino-owner Jenoff's right-hand man (*AtS* "Double or Nothing").

RESIKIAN URN | Notoriously fragile artifact with the power to trap a dimensional essence (*AtS* "Loyalty"). Justine trapped Sahjhan in it, but Connor later opened the urn to release the demon before killing him (*AtS* "Origin").

RESTFIELD CEMETERY | One of twelve cemeteries in Sunnydale and the original location of the Glove of Myhnegon (*BtVS* "Revelations"). It is also where Giles approached the Spirit Guides (*BtVS* "The Zeppo").

RESURRECTION SPELLS | Form of magic that has always existed as a means of bringing back the dead. These spells aren't used much because they're difficult and dangerous and they work only on the body, not the soul. Often a resurrection spell results in a zombie, or something worse (*BtVS* "Forever"). When one dies naturally, the soul moves on, out of reach. But if magic is involved, there can be a spiritual connection to the soul (*Angel and Faith* "Live through This").

REVELLO DRIVE | Sunnydale street on which the Summers family lived before the town was consumed by the Hellmouth (*BtVS* "Angel").

REVIVIFICATION RITUAL (TO BRING BACK JACK O'TOOLE'S FRIENDS) | Spell that requires ingredients that include a chicken foot and human blood. While the spellcaster waves the chicken foot, the following chant is spoken: *"He calls forth the spirit of Uurthu, the Restless. No one shall speak. He shall arise! Hear me! The blood of the earth shall restore him."* (Speaker kneels by the grave, cuts the palm of their hand, and allows the blood to drip onto the grave.) *"He shall arise! Shall arise!"* (*BtVS* "The Zeppo").

REVIVIFICATION RITUAL (TO BRING BACK THE MASTER) | Spell written in Latin that was originally translated from Sumerian. A required element of the ritual was those who were *physically* closest to the Master at the time of his death (*BtVS* "When She Was Bad").

RHINEHARDT'S COMPENDIUM | Book in Wesley's collection that identified the Ra-Tet (*AtS* "Long Day's Journey"). Lilah had a version of the tome as well, but she had to pull some favors to get it on the pan-dimensional black market. Her edition had material on the Beast that was omitted from Wesley's copy (*AtS* "Long Day's Journey").

RHONDA | **ANDREA BAKER** | Sales clerk at April Fools who witnessed the Hellhound attack and later informed Cordelia that someone had paid for her prom dress (*BtVS* "The Prom").

RICHARD | **IRA STECK** | Vampire whom Buffy killed right after he rose (*BtVS* "Lies My Parents Told Me").

RICHARD | **RYAN BROWNING** | Buffy's blind date—arranged by Xander and Anya—for her twenty-first birthday party. A demon stabbed him (*BtVS* "Older and Far Away").

RICHLER, SHARON | **LILLI BIRDSELL** | Plain woman whom Cordelia believed either had or came from money to explain how she snagged Kevin's attention in D'Oblique. Kevin transmitted the Burrower Demon to her, and she returned to the bar the next night to pick up another victim. She had sex with him, passing on the Burrower, and then died (*AtS* "Lonely Heart").

RIEFF | **TONY DENMAN** | Young Lister Demon who was tired of being feared and hated. The only day he was ever able to go outside and play was Halloween, because he blended with the children in costume. He didn't believe Angel was the Promised One prophesied to save his people (*AtS* "Hero").

RIPPER | Giles's nickname from his youth (*BtVS* "The Dark Age").

RITUAL FLAYING OF THE DEMON AZORATH | Giles confirmed that the Mayor's Ascension was not this event (*BtVS* "Earshot").

RIVALLI, MONSIGNOR | **SERGIO PREMOLI** | Excommunicated holy man in the eighteenth century who founded the Inquisitore, an order that adhered to the old beliefs. They were traditionalists and quite good at their work. The monsignor performed Holtz's wedding to Caroline and helped Holtz capture and torture Angelus in Rome in 1771. He was either injured or (more likely) killed by Darla when she rescued Angelus (*AtS* "Offspring").

ROBIN | Chosen Minder of the demon Sephrilian's reality field. Robin was able to help Buffy determine that someone close to her would betray her (*Buffy* "No Future for You").

ROBSON | **ROB NAGLE** | Nora's Watcher who was attacked by a Bringer (*BtVS* "Sleeper"). Robson called Buffy because he suspected that Bringers had killed Rupert Giles and that the First was masquerading as him (*BtVS* "First Date").

ROCHA, MANNY | **BRENT HINKLEY** | Buffy's first manager at the Doublemeat Palace. He was killed and devoured by the Wig Lady (*BtVS* "Doublemeat Palace").

ROCHE | Vampire in chains who told stories to the Watchers Academy students. Sophie Downs sired him, and she masqueraded as one of the students to release him. He referred to her as *"Die Einsame,"* "the Lonely" (*Tales* "Tales of the Vampires Parts 1 through 6").

ROCKET CAFÉ | Student hangout at UC Sunnydale (*BtVS* "The I in Team").

ROCKY | Yorkshire terrier that was devoured by his owner's ex-boyfriend when Anya accidentally changed the guy into a Sluggoth Demon (*BtVS* "Beneath You").

RODEN | Irish warlock from Belfast who became the Watcher of Lady Genevieve Savidge. He believed he was following Twilight's orders to train the "Slayer to end all Slayers," not realizing Twilight meant Buffy. Giles blew up his head (*Buffy* "No Future for You").

ROG | Vampire who was going to "drain the tap" of a human hung upside down in a playground. Harmony attacked him after he said that she had a fat arse (*Angel and Faith* "Live through This").

ROGER | Husky red demon resident of Magic Town who brawled with Eldre Koh at Rory's Pub (*Angel and Faith* "United").

ROME SQUAD LEAD SLAYER | New Slayer who, along with her squad, saved Buffy and Andrew when they went up against Simone Doffler (*Buffy* "Predators and Prey").

RON | DERRICK MCMILLON | Member of Xander's construction crew who told Buffy to slow down because they got paid by the hour (*BtVS* "Life Serial").

RONA | INDIGO | Potential who became a New Slayer that fought at the Battle of the Hellmouth even though she was already injured at the time (*BtVS* "Chosen"). She later became leader of the Chicago squad and sent Simone Doffler to Andrew so he could "soften Simone's rough edges" (*Buffy* "The Long Way Home").

RONDELL | JARROD CRAWFORD | Gunn's friend who took over the crew of demon-fighting friends when Gunn joined Angel Investigations (*AtS* "The Thin Dead Line"). He could not believe that Gunn was associating with demons, no matter their affiliation. After the shootout at Caritas, he and Gunn parted ways (*AtS* "That Old Gang of Mine").

RONNIE | Faith's deadbeat ex-boyfriend (*BtVS* "Revelations").

RONNIE | JACK SUNDMACHER | Nancy's boyfriend whom Anya accidentally turned into a Sluggoth Demon (*BtVS* "Beneath You").

RONOK (THE GREAT RONOK) | Demon who resembles a leaf blower. He had a beef with the demon Ganderfleb (*Buffy* "Goddesses and Monsters").

ROOKIE | MIKE RAD | Member of Sunday's vampire gang who sounded like a stoner (*BtVS* "The Freshman").

ROOT | Buffy's boss at the Pick Me Up coffeehouse in San Francisco (*Buffy* "Last Gleaming").

RORY | Demon informant who owns a pub in Magic Town and was willing to help Angel locate Corky Smallwood anonymously (*Angel and Faith* "Where the River Meets the Sea"). Vampires trashed his bar so they could follow Angel and Faith back to Nadira to kidnap her (*Angel and Faith* "A Little More than Kin"). Rory rallied London towners to stand with Angel when Archaeus and Drusilla attacked (*Angel and Faith* "A Tale of Two Families").

ROSARIA | ADDIE DADDIO | Vampire who knew Angelus in Tuscany in 1845. Over a century later she was lured to LA by the promise of eternal night. After she arrived, Angelus staked her (*AtS* "Salvage").

ROSCOE, MARCUS | RANCE HOWARD | Elderly man who used a spell to switch bodies with young men who eventually died when he switched back to his true form. Roscoe lived at the Monserrat Retirement Home, and his room overlooked a health club where he found his victims. He switched bodies with Angel and left the home before realizing he was in the body of a vampire. This sent him back to the retirement home to kill his old body, with Angel in it. The gang cornered Roscoe as he was about to kill Angel, and Wesley reversed the spell. Roscoe, back in his old body, began to have heart palpitations, and Angel told him the reason his heart didn't work was because he never used it (*AtS* "Carpe Noctem").

ROSENBERG, IRA | Willow's father (*BtVS* "I Robot . . . You Jane"). He was so devout about preserving Jewish tradition in the home that Willow had to go over to Xander's to watch *A Charlie Brown Christmas* (*BtVS* "Amends") and she was nervous about hanging up a cross on her wall (*BtVS* "Passion").

ROSENBERG, SHEILA | JORDAN BAKER | Willow's mother, an intellectual who studied adolescent behavior while ignoring her own daughter (*BtVS* "Gingerbread").

ROSENBERG, WILLOW | ALYSON HANNIGAN | See following page.

ROSS, LORRAINE | KIRSTEN NELSON | Manager of the Doublemeat Palace who revealed the secret ingredient to Buffy and agreed to hire Buffy back if she promised to keep that secret ingredient a secret (*BtVS* "Doublemeat Palace," "Normal Again").

ROSS, MARCIE | CLEA DUVALL | Sunnydale High student who was completely ignored by teachers and students to the point that she became invisible. Buffy stopped Marcie from attacking students and potentially disfiguring Cordelia, before the FBI took her away to a special assassins' school with other invisible kids (*BtVS* "Out of Mind, Out of Sight").

ROWENA | New Slayer stationed in Scotland and one of Buffy's most trusted allies (*Buffy* "The Long Way Home"). She took over Buffy's squad when Buffy went to Japan (*Buffy* "Wolves at the Gate"). Rowena evacuated Command Central when it was hit by a missile and led the battle against the serpent fighters deployed by the missile (*Buffy* "Predators and Prey"). After the end of magic, she began working for Deepscan (*Buffy* "Guarded").

ROY | BRYAN CUPRILL | UC Sunnydale student who got drunk on Black Frost Beer and turned into a Neanderthal (*BtVS* "Beer Bad"). He later fell under the influence of the Lowell House poltergeist at a frat party (*BtVS* "Where the Wild Things Are").

ROYAL CROWN REVUE | Jonathan's backup band in an alternate universe created by a spell (*BtVS* "Superstar").

Rosenberg, Willow

DARK WILLOW | ALYSON HANNIGAN |

Best friend of the Slayer and one of the most powerful witches of all time. Willow was born and raised in Sunnydale, along with her other best friend, Xander (*BtVS* "Welcome to the Hellmouth"). A shy and bookish young woman, Willow easily fell under the influence of a demon posing as a boy on the Internet (*BtVS* "I Robot . . . You Jane"). She grew more confident when Buffy chose her and Xander to be her core friends, Giles became something of a mentor to her, and she bonded with her computer teacher, Ms. Calendar. In her junior year at Sunnydale High School, Willow started dating Oz (*BtVS* "Surprise"), a young man who was soon thereafter bitten by a werewolf and turned (*BtVS* "Phases"). They eventually broke up.

Willow herself began to dabble more personally with the occult when she connected with strong magical forces to restore Angel's soul (*BtVS* "Becoming, Part 2"). In college, she joined a Wiccan group that turned out to be all talk and little spell casting, but there she met a young woman, Tara Maclay, who would soon become her deepest love (*BtVS* "Hush"). The pair began a relationship that withstood the test of Oz's brief return to Sunnydale but grew strained as Willow dabbled with darker and darker magic. Willow's powers grew over time until she was able to injure the Hellgod Glory (*BtVS* "Tough Love") and raise Buffy from the dead (*BtVS* "Bargaining, Parts 1 & 2"). Willow briefly stopped using magic after she developed an addiction to it. However, when Tara was murdered, Willow absorbed as much magical power

as she possibly could, causing a transformation in which her hair, eyes, and clothing grew dark, and black veins rose on her face (*BtVS* "Villains," "Two to Go"). She adopted the persona of "Dark Willow" and sought vengeance on anyone associated with Tara's death.

After Xander talked her out of the violence, Willow worked hard to divorce herself from that side of magic. As Willow began to regain her control over magic, Fred called her to LA because Angelus had returned and the witch was the only person who had ever successfully restored Angel's soul. Willow successfully fought off Cordelia's spells, broke the Muo Ping, and used the Orb of Thesulah to summon Angel's soul back from the ether. She then returned to Sunnydale with Faith to help battle the First Evil (*AtS* "Orpheus"). With the support of her new girlfriend, Kennedy, Willow allowed herself to tap into powerful forces once again and awakened the power of the Slayer in every Potential, an act that helped save the world (*BtVS* "Chosen").

Willow went on to work with the Slayer Organization as well as the US military (*Buffy* "In Pieces on the Ground") and was devastated when Buffy destroyed the Seed of Wonder. After a walkabout (*Buffy* "Guarded") and a trip to Quor'toth, she restored magic to the universe (*Angel and Faith* "Family Reunion"). In an alternate future timeline where Melaka Fray was the Slayer, Willow went dark again and was called "the Madwoman." Buffy time-traveled to that point and killed her best friend but returned to assure present-day Willow that the future was never certain (*Buffy* "Time of Your Life"). She continues to work her magic to this day.

ROYCE, DR. | **BILLINGSLEY, JOHN** | Cryptozoologist for Wolfram & Hart who drank calendula to fool Lorne's singing test when he sang "Jessie's Girl." Royce turned over information about Nina Ash to a dining club that wanted to eat a werewolf. Nina bit Royce and left him with the dining club (*AtS* "Unleashed").

RUDY | **CHRISTOPHER GEHRMAN** | Wolfram & Hart lab tech responsible for testing the vampire employees' blood for evidence of human blood in their system (*AtS* "Harm's Way").

RUGGS FIELD | Park in Sunnydale where Riley invited Buffy to have a picnic (*BtVS* "Something Blue").

RU'SHUNDI | Is not Bu'shundi (*AtS* "Inside Out").

RUSKIN, VICTORIA | Sunnydale High student whose name was on Buffy's list of potential votes for homecoming queen (*BtVS* "Homecoming") and later in the UC Sunnydale student directory Spike consulted to find Buffy and Willow's dorm room (*BtVS* "The Initiative").

RUSTY | The Mayor's Irish setter (*BtVS* "Choices").

RUSTY | **JACK JOZEFSON** | Museum security guard who was frozen by the Trio when they stole the Illuminata diamond (*BtVS* "Smashed").

RWASUNDI DEMON | Black-robed creatures who can cause temporal distortions that result in vivid hallucinations (and a slightly tingly scalp). Three Rwasundi were used to convince Buffy she had killed Katrina Silber (*BtVS* "Dead Things").

RYAN | **ANDREW DUCOTE** | Young hospital patient who was nearly killed by Der Kindestod. Ryan gave Buffy information and survived an attack by the monster. He later commemorated the event with a drawing, which he sent to Buffy (*BtVS* "Killed by Death").

RYAN | **JORDAN BELFI** | Bronze patron who dissed Amy and Willow when the women danced together instead of with him and his friend Simon. The two witches magically transformed them into male go-go dancers (*BtVS* "Smashed").

RYAN | **STEVEN W. BAILEY** | Orderly at Monserrat Retirement Home who had his hands full keeping Marcus Roscoe in the building and alive (*AtS* "Carpe Noctem").

RYAN, CATHY | One of the three Fondren High pep squad car-crash victims. Chris Epps stole her corpse (*BtVS* "Some Assembly Required").

RYAN, SAM | **JEFFREY DEAN MORGAN** | Press foreman who impersonated his boss, Harlan Elster, to hire Angel to clean out a vampire nest as vengeance for the death of a friend (*AtS* "Provider").

S

SAABIRA | New Slayer in the Scotland squad. Saabira grew up under the Taliban and wasn't allowed to go to school, thus belonging to the Slayer Organization meant a lot to her. She was shot during the battle against Twilight in Tibet and died with Buffy holding her hand (*Buffy* "In Pieces on the Ground").

SACHIKO | Main character of the comic strip *Vampy Cat* (*Buffy* "Predators and Prey").

SACRIFICE OF THREE | Ancient ritual requiring the blood of a man, the bones of a child, and an amulet called the Word of Valios. Three Vahrall Demons would then sacrifice themselves to bring about an apocalypse (*BtVS* "Doomed").

SADECKI DEMON | Mind-reading demon species (*Spike* "After the Fall").

SADHU | Hindu holy person who raised a dead body from ashes in 1764 (*Angel and Faith* "Live through This").

SAHJHAN (THE TIMESHIFTER) | **JACK CONLEY** | Noncorporeal Granok Demon who summoned Holtz to LA in the twenty-first century, fulfilling the Tro-Clon part of the Nyazian prophecy. Sahjhan had the ability to navigate through other dimensions where time behaved differently. He could also manipulate his demon features to appear human (*AtS* "Quickening"). When

Connor went missing in Quor'toth, a grieving Angel summoned Sahjhan, making him corporeal. The demon then revealed to Angel that the prophecy actually foretold that Connor would kill Sahjhan. As Sahjhan was about to stake Angel, Justine trapped the demon in the Resikian Urn (*AtS* "Forgiving"). Cyvus Vail acquired the urn because his prophecy said Sahjhan would kill him, so he wanted Connor to tie up that loose end. When Connor returned as a teen he released Sahjhan from the urn and beheaded him (*AtS* "Origin").

SAHRVIN DEMON | Tall demons with tentacles coming out of their faces. They feuded with Vinji Demons (*AtS* "Harm's Way"). Lindsey killed them all (*AtS* "Not Fade Away").

SAL | Woman who attempted to aid the vampire Joe Cooper in western Kansas in 1933. Joe meant to sire her but drained her instead (*Tales* "Dust Bowl").

SANCTUARY SPELL | Magic used to protect Caritas and later the Hyperion with the incantation "*Violence restrained, demons disarmed. For mortals within these walls, no harm. Protection and safety this charm doth endow to make this shelter a sanctuary now.*" It had some loopholes (*AtS* "Salvage").

SANDERS, DOUG | **PAT HEALY** | Author of the book *Selective Slaughter: Turning a Bloodbath into a Blood Bank*. As a human he ran a financial pyramid scheme and was wanted by the Department of Justice. As a vampire he ran a deadly pyramid scheme that included siring two victims and making them kill the rest. His acolytes rose through the ranks with the more humans they brought in, and each level they earned was indicated by a different colored robe. Angel decapitated him (*AtS* "Disharmony").

SANDERSON, MR. | Vampire who worked at the bank in Sunnydale before he was turned. He helped Joyce Summers open an IRA account (*BtVS* "Gingerbread").

SANDY | **MEGAN GRAY** | Vampire sired by the Wishverse version of Willow (*BtVS* "Doppelgangland"). Riley let her feed off him (*BtVS* "Family") before Buffy dusted her (*BtVS* "Shadow").

SANTORIO CORP | Japanese company that produced *Vampy Cat* (*Buffy* "Predators and Prey").

SARACEN QUEEN | Being whom Willow called upon while cursing Oz and Veruca (*BtVS* "Wild at Heart").

SATAN | Villain in the film *Last Angel in Hell* (*Angel* "After the Fall").

SATANAS | Deity that Willow called upon when she began to curse Oz and Veruca (*BtVS* "Wild at Heart").

SATHARI | Clan of demon assassins that attacked Drogyn in LA. The poison from their blades drained Drogyn's power (*AtS* "Power Play").

SATSU | Japanese Slayer who was in love with Buffy. The pair slept together, but their relationship did not progress beyond friendship (*Buffy* "Wolves at the Gate"). Satsu and the Tokyo squad stole a Korean submarine from vampire hijackers and successfully launched a missile at the Swell (*Buffy* "Predators and Prey").

SAVIDGE, LADY GENEVIEVE (GIGI) | Evil New Slayer who intended to kill Buffy and take her place as leader of the Slayers. Faith accidentally killed her with an ax (*Buffy* "No Future for You").

SAVITSKY, KARL | **MICHAEL MERTON** | Bank loan officer who turned down Buffy's application (*BtVS* "Flooded").

SCAPULA | Bag of protective ingredients worn around the neck. Willow's first attempt at creating one resulted in a scapula that smelled like "grandpa breath" because she used sulfur (*BtVS* "I Only Have Eyes for You").

SCOOBY GANG, THE | Term coined by Xander to refer to Buffy's team of helpers. Originally consisting of Willow, Giles, and Xander, the group expanded over time to include Cordelia, Angel, Oz, Tara, Anya, Dawn, Spike, and Andrew (*BtVS* "What's My Line? Part 2").

SCOTT, BRADLEY (BRAD) | **STEVE DERELIAN** | Former Wolfram & Hart employee who started out in the mail room with Lindsey. Scott served two years at Soledad Correctional Facility for embezzling and dumping bearer bonds on the black market while he worked at the law firm. After his release, he "disappeared" and his body was kept at the Fairfield Clinic for organ harvesting. Lindsey ended up with his hand (*AtS* "Dead End").

SCOURGE, THE | Army of purebred demons who despised half-breeds and humans, and sought to annihilate them. They believed interbreeding with humans was a crime because it diluted the demon bloodline. They were hard to beat because they were prepared to die for their cause, but Doyle defeated them when he destroyed their bomb (*AtS* "Hero").

SCULPTOR, THE | Hulking demon with multiple eyes and a fleshy body from which body parts of its victims extended. He formed an alliance with the Mistress and the Soul Glutton to stop Buffy and D'Hoffryn from rewriting the rules of magic (*Buffy* "I Wish"). He later brought his flesh golems while attempting to steal the Asclepian Vial, but Andrew thwarted the plan as a superhero under the vial's spell (*Buffy* "Love Dares You"). Buffy's team went up against the Sculptor and destroyed his army, but he escaped and began putting back together fragments of the Restless Door (*Buffy* "Old Demons"). The Sculptor attempted to bribe Andrew into bringing him the Scythe with a promise to resurrect Jonathan, but Andrew double-crossed him. In the subsequent battle, Willow killed him (*Buffy* "In Pieces on the Ground").

SCYTHE | See M?.

SCYTHIAN DEATH SPEAR | Three-pronged, category-six weapon located on the third shelf of the weapons cabinet in the Hyperion. It can be used to kill small Rodentius Demons or poodles (*AtS* "Fredless").

SEA BREEZE | Lorne's favorite drink, consisting of vodka, cranberry, and fresh grapefruit (*AtS* "Happy Anniversary").

SEAL OF DANZALTHAR | Located directly beneath the principal's office in the basement of the new Sunnydale High School, this large, circular hatch was decorated with runic symbols in the shape of a pentagram surrounding the head of a goat (*BtVS* "Conversations with Dead People"). The seal covered an enormous cavern filled with thousands of frenzied Turok-Han (*BtVS* "Get It Done"). The blood of humans or animals could open it, while tears of repentance could close it again (*BtVS* "Storyteller"). The seal emitted evil energy, which began to affect the students and faculty of the school, before spreading to the rest of Sunnydale as the moment for the final battle drew near.

SEBANCAYA | Mountain god to whom the Incas sacrificed their princess. It is also the name of the region where the Incas performed that sacrifice (*BtVS* "Inca Mummy Girl").

SEBASSIS, ARCHDUKE | LELAND CROOKE | Demon nobility and the end of a pure bloodline. The light-skinned, horned demon drank the blue blood of a slave (Ryan Alvarez) he kept on a chain (*AtS* "Life of the Party"). A member of the Circle of the Black Thorn, Sebassis sat at the head of the Circle's table and had forty thousand demons at his command. The other members of the Circle feared him, making him Angel's target in the assassinations that led to the battle of Los Angeles. He died in his bathtub when Angel poisoned the slave he drank from (*AtS* "Not Fade Away").

SEBASTIAN | Vampire in Nashua, New Hampshire (*Tales* "The Thrill").

SECURITY GUARD | DON TIFFANY | Employee of the Blinnikov World Ballet Corps. Likes bribes (*AtS* "Waiting in the Wings").

SEED OF WONDER | The world—or more accurately, this dimension—came from the Seed. It predated humans, demons, and even the First Evil. The Earth was created from the Seed. Powerful magic that had seeped into the human dimension was prevented from trickling back out because of the Seed, which acted like a cork. When Angel and Buffy evolved and created Twilight, the Master was revealed to have been the protector of the Seed for eight hundred years, but the demons of Twilight were determined to take the Seed into the Twilight dimension. A huge battle ensued, and while it raged, Aluwyn revealed to Willow that the loss and/or destruction of the Seed would result in the loss of all magic in Earth's reality. However, when Angel came under the influence of Twilight and killed Giles, Buffy destroyed the Seed in a rage (*Buffy* "Last Gleaming"). The effects were immediate: witches and other magic users were cut off from magic; demons from other dimensions could not return; and newly sired vampires were feral and violent (*Buffy* "Freefall"). Willow realized that the world was dying because there was no magic in it, and after going on a mystical walkabout, produced a second Seed while in the Deeper Well. Severin provided the energy needed to hatch the Seed and magic was reborn in Earth's dimension (*Buffy* "The Core").

SEERS | RISHI KUMAR, KAREN LU, AND ALEX BUCK | Three children from different parts of the world, who together had the power to see into the heart of things. As they get older, their power will mature. They were rescued from Vanessa Brewer's attack on their safe house and now reside with their mentor (*AtS* "Blind Date").

SEIDEL, OLIVER | RANDY OGLESBY | Professor and Fred's physics advisor who originally sent her—and others—to Pylea. She tried to kill him but couldn't, so Gunn snapped his neck for her and dropped the body into a portal (*AtS* "Supersymmetry").

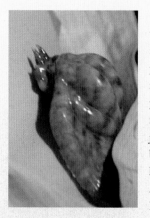

SELMINTH PARASITE | Demon whose teeth inject an anesthetic, making the host oblivious to its presence as it pumps neurotoxins into the body, causing paralysis, hallucinations, and fever dreams. Angel killed the junior one that was giving him bad dreams, and Spike killed the larger one that Eve set free in Angel's bedroom (*AtS* "Soul Purpose").

SELTREX | Highly powerful migraine medication that Cordelia took to counter the pain she experienced when having a vision (*AtS* "Birthday").

SEMKHET | Totem of the Ra-Tet who lived in a cave in Death Valley. The Beast ripped him apart (*AtS* "Long Day's Journey").

SENIH'D DEMON | Spiny demon who manifests in its physical form for one purpose only—to feed. Cordelia's vision of one rising in midcity interrupted her reunion with Groo. When killed, the demon dissolved into an oily puddle (*AtS* "Couplet").

SENIOR PARTNERS | Incredibly powerful demons known as the Wolf, the Ram, and the Hart, who run the interdimensional law firm Wolfram & Hart. The Senior Partners were minor demons during the time of Illyria's reign, but they have amassed considerable power over the millennia (*AtS* "Shells").

SEPHRILIAN | Elite "Tichajt" demon who existed between realities. He revealed to Willow that Buffy was robbing banks to fund the Slayer Organization, showed Willow's future romance with Saga Vasuki, and let the Slayer know that she would be betrayed. When he threatened to reveal these secrets to Buffy's enemies, she and Willow destroyed the demon and his domain (*Buffy* "No Future for You").

SERENA | DAPHNEE DUPLAIX | Friend of Cordelia who liked partying and nightclubs. She was impregnated by Jason on behalf of a procrea-parasitic demon and freed when Cordelia killed it (*AtS* "Expecting").

SEVERIN (THE SIPHON) | Originally a trust-fund baby, Severin discovered that he had the power to drain vampires when his girlfriend, Clare, became a zompire. He then began draining zompires of their magical essence, leaving behind human corpses (*Buffy* "Freefall"). Severin continued to ingest power in the hopes of turning back time to before Clare was sired. He teamed up with Simone Doffler, who wanted to kill Buffy. Together, they tempted Xander with the promise that with time travel, they could make sure Twilight never happened and Dawn would never fade. Severin began to absorb the energy of the Deeper Well just as Willow gave birth to the new Seed. When it became clear that Severin wouldn't be able to survive or accomplish his goal, he transferred his energy to the Seed, causing magic to return to the world (*Buffy* "The Core").

SHADOW MEN | GEOFFREY KASULE, KARARA MUHORO, AND DANIEL WILSON | Three ancient men who chained Sineya (the Primitive) to a rock and forced her to ingest a demon. They attempted to do the same to Buffy (*BtVS* "Get It Done").

SHADY HILL CEMETERY | One of twelve cemeteries in Sunnydale. Lagos unsuccessfully hunted for the Glove of Myhnegon there (*BtVS* "Revelations").

SHADY LADY | KAREN CHARNELL | Riley pulled a gun on her in Willy's Place. She escaped unharmed (*BtVS* "Goodbye Iowa").

SHAMAN | FRANK "SOTONOMA" SALSEDO | Holy man who lived in a remote region of the Yoro Mountains of Honduras. This very powerful, very magic practitioner tried to identify Darla's baby but said it wasn't meant to be known (*AtS* "That Vision Thing").

SHANNON | MARY WILCHER | Potential whom Caleb attacked and used to bait Buffy with a message that Shannon delivered from her hospital bed (*BtVS* "Dirty Girls"). She was activated as a Slayer at the Battle of the Hellmouth (*BtVS* "Chosen").

SHANSHU | Word in the Aberjian scroll that could mean either "life" or "death." The language descended from the ancient Majars but has roots in many different languages. The most ancient source for the word is the proto-Bantu. They considered life and death the same thing, part of a cycle, because a thing that's not alive never dies (*AtS* "To Shanshu in LA").

SHANSHU PROPHECY | As written in *The Prophecies of Aberjian*, the vampire with a soul, once he fulfills his destiny, will *shanshu* (or become human) as a reward for surviving the coming darkness, the apocalyptic battles, a few plagues, and several fiends that would be unleashed. He would both live and die, because he would become human, live a normal life, and then die (*AtS* "To Shanshu in LA"). The prophecy also said that a vampire with a soul would play a pivotal role in the coming apocalypse, but it didn't name the vampire, suggesting it could be either Angel or Spike. To prove his loyalty to the Circle of the Black Thorn, Angel signed away his claim, forgoing his right to be the champion of the prophecy (*AtS* "Not Fade Away"). However, it was later revealed that Angel would be fighting for evil in the apocalypse (*Angel* "After the Fall").

SHARD OF STRONNOS | Magical artifact with the power to transform energy into matter and back again. Edna Giles and her son were charged with its care. Edna gave the shard to her sisters, and they in turn gave it to Angel to use in his efforts to resurrect Rupert Giles (*Angel and Faith* "Daddy Issues").

SHARON | Friend of Dawn whose older brother supposedly knew a girl who died because she choked on her boyfriend's tongue (*BtVS* "The Replacement").

SHARP, FRANCINE | MARIA CHAMBERS | Friend of Virginia Bryce "from the country club," who brought her daughter to Angel Investigations to have a demon removed from her head

(*AtS* "The Thin Dead Line"). Her husband wouldn't let her pay when the job was successfully completed. Skilosh killed her after luring Cordelia to her home (*AtS* "Reprise").

SHARP, STEPHANIE | LEAH PIPES | Angel Investigations client who was bitten by Skilosh on her way home from swim practice. She had a baby Skilosh gestating in her head, but it was banished by the team. Skilosh killed her in retribution (*AtS* "Reprise").

SHAY, MORGAN | RICH WERNER | Sunnydale High student ventriloquist who worked with Sid, the demon hunter masquerading as a dummy. Morgan's brain was removed by the creature Sid was hunting, but Morgan's brain cancer made it useless to the demon (*BtVS* "The Puppet Show").

SHEMPIRE | EVAN ARNOLD | Vampire who had been a child of eternal darkness since 1992. His vampire face hid his skin condition, which inhibited his progress with the ladies when he was human. When Darla was again human, she convinced him to try to turn her as he had never turned anyone before, but Angel staked him before he could (*AtS* "The Trial").

SHEMPY VAMP | PAUL GREENBERG | Vampire who hit the Buffybot over the head (*BtVS* "Bargaining, Part 1"), then tried to ingratiate himself with the Hellions by telling them about the robot. Razor tore off his head (*BtVS* "Bargaining, Part 2").

SHORSHACK BOX | Mystical artifact that looks like an Ethros Box but has about a twenty-dollar price difference and is not available in mahogany. It was pieced together by mute Chinese nuns (*AtS* "I've Got You under My Skin").

SHORSHACK DEMON | A little smaller than the average Ethros Demon (*AtS* "I've Got You under My Skin")

SHROUDED MAN | GARY BULLOCK | Green-skinned man with yellow glowing eyes that owed Rupert Giles a debt because Giles had introduced him to his wife. He alerted Giles that Mayor Wilkins had hired him to steal Angel's soul (*BtVS* "Enemies").

SHROUD OF RAHMON, THE | Mystical artifact acquired by the Natural History Museum from a tomb unearthed by archaeologists from the University of New Mexico. The shroud was woven by the head priest, who was said to have been driven mad by the demon Rahmon himself. Once Rahmon was defeated, the priest dyed the shroud with the blood of seven virgin women sacrificed on the first full moon, then laid it upon Rahmon's body in order to prevent his resurrection. The shroud supposedly absorbed Rahmon's power. It was kept in a case made of consecrated wood with edges sealed in gold. The box was lined with lead and weighed about a ton. In 1803 the shroud was removed from its box and the entire population of El Encanto went insane. The shroud's estimated worth was about two million dollars on the black market. Angel burned it (*AtS* "The Shroud of Rahmon").

SHUR-HOD | Life-sucking demon monks who spew a blue froth (*AtS* "Heartthrob").

SHY | Band that played at the Bronze. Veruca was its lead singer (*BtVS* "Living Conditions").

SHY GIRL | SUJATA DECHOUDHURY | Student at the new Sunnydale High School who began to go invisible. Buffy snapped her out of it (*BtVS* "Storyteller").

SID | TOM WYNER | Demon hunter trapped inside a ventriloquist dummy by his targets, the Brotherhood of Seven. Sid had killed six of the seven and came to Sunnydale to kill the last. Once the seventh was dispatched, Sid's soul was at rest (*BtVS* "The Puppet Show").

SIEGFRIED AND ROY | Former Las Vegas Strip staple magic act with big cats. According to Wolfram & Hart's file, Siegfried is evil, Roy not so much (*AtS* "Home").

SILAS | MICHAEL PHENICIE | Red-robed, red-skinned demon with facial markings of eyes who served as head of the Covenant of Trombli on Pylea. Silas tested Cordelia for the curse of sight and elevated her to princess (*AtS* "Over the Rainbow"). He didn't want her to get too full of her role, so he had Lorne executed to keep her in check (*AtS* "Through the Looking Glass") and killed rebel slaves in the castle. Silas planned to kill Cordelia after the *Comshuk* passed her vision gift to the Groosalugg, but she cut off his head before he could kill all the slaves (*AtS* "There's No Place like Plrtz Glrb").

SILBER, KATRINA | AMELINDA EMBRY | Warren's ex-girlfriend. When she discovered he had made a "sexbot" named April, she broke up with him (*BtVS* "I Was Made to Love You"). Warren sapped her of her will with the Cerebral Dampener then killed her when she tried to escape (*BtVS* "Dead Things").

SIMON | ADAM WEINER | Bronze patron who—along with his friend Ryan—asked Amy Madison and Willow to dance, then dissed them. Willow and Amy turned both of them into go-go dancers (*BtVS* "Smashed").

SIMON, OLIVER | MICHAEL MANTELL | Forthright agent who represented actress Rebecca Lowell (*AtS* "City of"). Simon hired another client—a stuntman—to pretend to stalk the actress for the publicity (*AtS* "Eternity").

SINEYA (THE FIRST SLAYER, THE PRIMITIVE) | SHARON FERGUSON | Ancient African girl whom the Shadow Men chained to a rock and forced to ingest a demon so she would become the first Slayer (*BtVS* "Get It Done"). Because she was part demon, Sineya's village feared her and sent a little girl to ask her to leave. That girl told Sineya that her essence would pass from one Slayer to the next, and so in that way she would live on (*Tales* "Prologue"). She served as Buffy's spirit guide (*BtVS* "Intervention") and attempted to kill Buffy's closest allies after the Enjoining Spell because she felt that the Slayer should walk alone (*BtVS* "Restless"). After the end of magic, Sineya communicated with Buffy to tell her that the Scythe was the key to restoring magic, but that it was for Willow to accomplish (*Buffy* "Freefall"). Sineya also allowed Billy Lane to see visions, signaling her approval of his status as a Vampire Slayer (*Buffy* "New Rules").

SIRK, RUTHERFORD | MICHAEL HALSEY | Former Watchers Council member who served as Wesley's escort when the gang toured the Wolfram & Hart office (*AtS* "Home"). Sirk reviewed the Shanshu Prophecy in its original language and purposely misled Angel and Spike into the desert. When they searched for him afterward, he'd disappeared (*AtS* "Destiny").

SISTERHOOD OF JHE | Fierce female demons with devil-like faces, long pointed ears, and rows of horns on their heads. They were an apocalypse cult defeated by the Scooby Gang (*BtVS* "The Zeppo").

SITCH, THE | Shorthand for "the situation". As in, "What's the sitch?" (*BtVS* "Welcome to the Hellmouth").

SKALE, ROBERT (BOB) | **ROBERT DOLAN** | Security guard at the Natural History Museum who was in on the heist for the shroud. Vyasa decapitated him (*AtS* "The Shroud of Rahmon").

SKANKY VAMP | **ADAM PAUL** | Vampire who couldn't go through with his attack on Buffy because she smelled bad from her Doublemeat Palace job (*BtVS* "As You" Were").

SKENCH DEMON | Creature known to take over a home. It ejects blue phlegm and the best method for killing it is cutting off its head (*AtS* "Double or Nothing").

SKILOSH DEMON | Notoriously violent, asexual, self-replicating species of demon who has the distasteful habit of injecting its demon spawn into the cranium of a human host. One of the key diagnostic symptoms is the telltale third eye that forms on the back of the host's head. If this condition is not arrested in time a newborn Skilosh will erupt, fully grown, from the skull of its human host (*AtS* "The Thin Dead Line"). One killed the Sharp family and blamed Wesley, Cordelia, and Gunn for destroying its spawn. It can be killed by being hacked with a blade, but it emits yellow gore (*AtS* "Epiphany").

SKIP | **DAVID DENMAN** | Jailer in a demon fortress who worked for the Powers That Be. Skip's will kept Billy Blim imprisoned in a cage of fire with the sound muted, and he forced Angel to fight him in order to trade Billy for Cordelia's life (*AtS* "That Vision Thing"). Skip later served as a guide for Cordelia as he showed

her how her life could have been if she had not received the visions, ultimately making her part-demon so she could continue to use that gift (*AtS* "Birthday"). He also revealed that Cordelia getting her visions—along with Lorne leaving Pylea, Gunn's sister dying, Fred going to Pylea, and Wesley sleeping with Lilah—was a manipulation to help bring forth Jasmine. Wesley shot Skip in the head through the hole Angel had left in Skip's armor in an earlier fight (*AtS* "Inside Out").

SKYLER | **MICHAEL MANASERI** | Demon with muttonchop sideburns and short horns who offered to sell Buffy and Faith the *Books of Ascension*. Faith murdered him and stole them instead (*BtVS* "Enemies").

SLAYAGE | Colloquial term for the killing of vampires (*BtVS* "Halloween").

SLAYER | See following pages.

SLAYER EMERGENCY KIT | Robin Wood kept this "Slayer heirloom" after his mother, Nikki, died. Inside the leather satchel were a book written in Sumerian and a set of "shadow casters" (shadow puppets), what looked like a boomerang, and an urn. These objects propelled Buffy through an exchange portal into the realm of the Shadow Men and sent a demon back through to Sunnydale for balance (*BtVS* "Get It Done").

SLAYERETTES | Term that Willow coined to describe Xander, Giles, and herself (*BtVS* "Witch").

SLAYERFEST '98 | Big game hunt for Buffy and Faith organized and conducted by Mr. Trick. Cordelia was mistaken for Faith and, together, she and Buffy defeated the hunters. The event brought Mr. Trick to the attention of the Mayor (*BtVS* "Homecoming").

SLAYER HANDBOOK | Basic guide to slaying. Giles never bothered to give it to Buffy because he figured it would be no use to her (*BtVS* "What's My Line? Part 2").

SLAYER ORGANIZATION | After the New Slayers were activated, Buffy and her team began contacting them and organizing them into squads. Almost five hundred Slayers have joined the organization that was divided into ten different squads in such places as Japan, Scotland, Italy, and Spain (*Buffy* "The Long Way Home").

SLAYER SANCTUARY | Rumored haven near Hanselstadt for Slayers who did not want to follow their calling. In reality, former Watcher Duncan Fillworthe started this lie so that he could feed the Slayers to the local demon, which kept the nearby vampires at bay (*Buffy* "Predators and Prey").

SLAYPIRE | A Slayer turned vampire (or zompire), the result of a project first undertaken by Simone Doffler in her quest to destroy Buffy. Simone turned Tessa Freer into the first known Slaypire (*Buffy* "Welcome to the Team") and had herself bitten by Maloker when he emerged from his sarcophagus in the Deeper Well (*Buffy* "The Core").

SLIME-COVERED DEMON | ANDREW COOPER WASSER | Demon with large, ram-like horns that played kitten poker with Spike (*BtVS* "Life Serial").

SLIME DEMON | Lived behind a waste-treatment plant in Elscando. Angel killed it (*AtS* "To Shanshu in LA").

SLOTH DEMON | Incinerated (*AtS* "Judgment").

SLUGGOTH DEMON | Large, nasty underground natural predator that resembled an enormous toothed worm. These demons died out around the Crusades, but Anyanka manifested one when a young woman wished for revenge on her abusive boyfriend (*BtVS* "Beneath You").

SLUK | Translucent demon who resembles the Glass Eels of the Krag Swamps in UxenBlarg. Sluks have a hive mind and need water to survive. One was killed by the combination of heat and alcohol, which dried it up (*AtS* "The Price"). Connor forced them to go through the portal from Quor'toth and followed the trail they left.

SLURG'S SUPERNATURAL AMERICAN SOCIAL CLUB | Location where Buffy and Spike met Vicki while planning to fight back against D'Hoffryn (*Buffy* "New Rules").

SMALLWOOD, CORKY | Human criminal turned to pixie crime boss by the plague ball. Corky hired the Glass Blower to make containers for the magic his henchmen collected and sold. Angel ultimately imprisoned Corky in one of his own glass bottles (*Angel and Faith* "Where the River Meets the Sea").

SMITH | KEVIN OWERS | One of three Watchers Council Special Operatives sent first to capture and later to assassinate Faith. Angel threw him out of a helicopter (*BtVS* "This Year's Girl"; *AtS* "Sanctuary").

SNOOPY DANCE | Xander's signature dance from *A Charlie Brown Christmas* (*BtVS* "Passion"). He performed the famed move to verify his identity when Toth split him in two (*BtVS* "The Replacement").

Slayer

Into every generation a Slayer is born: one girl in all the world, a chosen one. She alone will wield the strength and skill to fight the vampires, demons, and the forces of darkness; to stop the spread of their evil and the swell of their number. She is the Slayer." The Slayer line has existed for millennia, dating back to the ancient time in which the Shadow Men forced Sineya to swallow a demon (*BtVS* "Get It Done"). Slayers are charged with fighting the evil beings that infect Earth, be they vampires, demons, or even gods. They possess superstrength and healing abilities and are acutely attuned to their surroundings. They also have prophetic dreams (*BtVS* "Welcome to the Hellmouth"). For most of their history, only one young woman bore the mantle of the Slayer at a time. In the moment of her death, the next Slayer was called (*BtVS* "What's My Line? Part 1"). The First Evil attempted to end the Slayer line by killing all the Potentials, a possible future scenario that the Watchers Council had considered (*BtVS* "Sleeper"). Seizing on that idea, Buffy suggested disrupting the line further by sharing her power. Willow performed a magic spell on the Scythe that activated all the Potentials to become full Slayers (*BtVS* "Chosen"). After this occurred, Buffy and company began searching for Slayers. At last count, they had identified 1800 and recruited 500, in ten separate squads, for the new Slayer Organization (*Buffy* "The Long Way Home"). After the end of magic, no more Slayers could be called (*Buffy* "Freefall"). However, magic was restored to the world by the activation of a new Seed of Wonder, and it is assumed that the Slayer line will continue (*Buffy* "The Core").

Known Slayers:

Aiko	Cole, Abigail	**Fray, Melaka**	**Leah**
Alexia	**Colleen**	Freer, Tessa	**Lehane, Faith**
Amanda	**Cori**	Gilbert, Florence	**Mai**
Amirah, Princess	Courtney	Gish, Arabella	**Makimura, Yuki**
Anaheed	**Dana**	Hanover, Lucy	**Malita**
Ayumi	Daphne	**Holly**	Malone, Belle
Caridad	**Doffler, Simone**	**Kennedy**	**Marianne**
Chao-Ahn	Dominique	**Kira**	**Marsh, Tonia**
Claudine	Donna	**Lane, Billy**	**Martina**

"...I'VE GOT MY MUSCLE WITH ME."

Naayéé'neizghani

Nadira

Nell

Nisha

O'Connor, Rachel

Posey

Renee

Rona

Rowena

Saabira

Satsu

Savidge, Lady Genevieve

Shannon

Sineya (The First Slayer, The Primitive)

Soledad

Sonnenblume, Anni

Summers, Buffy

Vanessa

Vi (Violet)

Weston, Elizabeth

Wood, Nikki

Young, Kendra

Unnamed Slayers:

Aztec Slayer

Boston Slayer

Buffy's Rome Decoy

Buffy's Underground Decoy

Chicago Slayer

Chinese Slayer

Flapper Slayer

Gunn's Prisoner Training Slayers

Indian Slayer

Korean Slayer

Maiden, The

Oklahoma Slayer

Pilot Slayer

Slayer of Tom Mitchell

Slayer Quarry of Lady Genevieve Savidge

Softball Slayer

Spanish Slayer

SNYDER, PRINCIPAL R. | ARMIN SHIMERMAN | Principal Flutie's successor at Sunnydale High. Snyder didn't like students and valued order and control above all else (*BtVS* "The Puppet Show"). He colluded with the police and the Mayor to mask supernatural attacks as commonplace events like backed-up sewer lines and gangs on PCP (*BtVS* "School Hard"). He took great delight in expelling Buffy after Kendra was murdered (*BtVS* "Becoming, Part 2"). Despite all his efforts, Buffy was allowed to graduate with her class, an occasion marked by Snyder's death when the Mayor—who had by then ascended as the demon Olvikan—devoured him (*BtVS* "Graduation Day, Part 2").

SOBEKIAN BLOODSTONE | Runic bloodstone used in transmogrification rituals (*BtVS* "Shadow").

SOLEDAD | Former Las Cuchillas gang member who refused to join the Slayer Organization after she was activated. Soledad attacked Harmony during the filming of the vampire's reality TV show, which revealed the existence of Slayers to the world and put them in a negative light (*Buffy* "Predators and Prey").

SONNENBLUME, ANNI | Young German Slayer during the rise of Adolf Hitler. Anni was a member of the League of German Girls, and her Watcher advised her that there were evil things beyond vampires. Anni observed Nazi atrocities, including Kristallnacht, and attacked a Nazi officer in order to protect her Jewish neighbors. Thereafter in her role as the Slayer, she fought both Nazis and vampires (*Tales* "Sonnenblume").

SONNETS FROM THE PORTUGUESE | Book of classic love poems by Elizabeth Barrett Browning to her husband Robert Browning that Angel gave Buffy on her eighteenth birthday (*BtVS* "Helpless").

SOON | JASON KIM | Owner of the Lotus Spa in Koreatown who treated demons on the side (*AtS* "Parting Gifts").

SOPHIE | LAURA ROTH | Buffy's friend from the Doublemeat Palace who came to her birthday party. She had a lot of food allergies (*BtVS* "Older and Far Away").

SORIALUS THE RAVAGER | According to Cordelia's vision, this demon would come in "a month or so" to destroy the humans that killed her mate. As such, her case was filed under "Pending" (*AtS* "Waiting in the Wings").

SORZANO, SANDRA | Journalist with the *Sunnydale Press* who wrote an article about the "van accident" that led to the siring of Andrew Borba and the rising of the Anointed One (*BtVS* "Never Kill a Boy on the First Date").

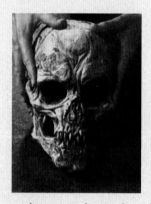

SOUL-EATER | Demon who was buried by the Chumash a couple hundred years ago and was a central figure in Cordelia's vision to restore Angel's soul. Connor and Gunn dug up the body, but it moved too fast for them to catch it. The demon latched on to Connor and began draining his soul. Gunn cut off its arm, then its head. Its remains were used as an ingredient in the spell to restore the soul (*AtS* "Calvary").

SOUL GLUTTON, THE | Massive and Cthulhu-like in appearance, this devourer of human souls swore revenge on the Aztec Slayer who had slain his family, but he arrived in Sunnydale centuries too late to enact his vengeance. Buffy stopped Andrew Wells from attempting to resurrect Tara Maclay, as ingesting a resurrected soul would have made the Soul Glutton invincible (*Buffy* "I Wish"). The Soul Glutton formed an alliance with the Mistress and the Sculptor to stop Buffy and D'Hoffryn from rewriting the rules of magic, but the team ultimately failed. Forcing the starved Soul Glutton down to a tiny size, D'Hoffryn crushed him underfoot (*Buffy* "In Pieces on the Ground").

SOUTHERN CALIFORNIA TRAVEL | Office front for Wolfram & Hart's body farm (*AtS* "Dead End").

SPADER, JAMES | Actor in Cordelia's "Are You Cool" quiz given to Buffy (*BtVS* "Welcome to the Hellmouth").

SPANKY | **MICHAEL SHAMUS WILES** | Freelance mystic who made the mystical container for Corbin Fries. Drinks daiquiris. Doesn't hit men. Was hit by Angel (*AtS* "Conviction").

SPARROW, DR. | **MARC VANN** | Wolfram & Hart employee who gave Gunn the legal implant on behalf of the Senior Partners (*AtS* "Conviction") and later offered to install a permanent upgrade if Gunn approved a shipment of his held up in customs (*AtS* "Smile Time"). He informed Gunn that Fred's soul was gone. Spike tortured him for information about Illyria (*AtS* "Shells"). Senator Brucker wanted Sparrow to hypnotize the population with false information about her opponent and Angel approved the plan (*AtS* "Power Play").

SPELL OF RESTORATION | Jenny Calendar's translation of the original text of the Curse of Elder Woman to return Angelus's soul to his body. Willow made two attempts on the spell before it was a success, though she didn't realize it at the time in spite of feeling something flow through her. The successful spell was translated as "*What is lost, return. Not dead ... nor not of the living.*

Spirits of the interregnum, I call. Return. I implore you, Lord, do not ignore this request. Neither dead, nor of the living ... Let this Orb be the vessel that will carry his soul to him" (*BtVS* "Becoming, Parts 1 & 2").

SPELL TO ACCESS THE NETHER REALM | Tara introduced Willow to this spell in order to find out who was inhabiting Buffy's body when Faith had taken control. Tara explained that access was like astral projection and that she would serve as Willow's anchor to keep her on this plane. The chant was "*The Inward Eye, the Sightless Sea, Ayala flows through the River in Me ...*" (*BtVS* "Who Are You?").

SPELL TO HAVE ONE'S WILL DONE | Magic attempted by Willow after Oz left her. As a result of the spell, Giles went blind, demons found Xander irresistible, and Buffy and Spike got engaged. The counterspell: "*Let the healing power begin. Let my will be safe again. As these words of peace are spoken, let this harmful spell be broken*" (*BtVS* "Something Blue").

SPELL TO REVOKE A VAMPIRE'S INVITATION TO ENTER A DOMAIN | According to Giles, the ritual is a fairly basic recitation of a few rhyming couplets, burning of moss herbs, and sprinkling of holy water (*BtVS* "Passion").

SPENCER | **MOROCCO OMARI** | Head of security at the Tropicana; he beat Lorne when necessary and alerted DeMarco to things going on in his casino, like Angel suddenly winning. He was shot in the fight at the casino (*AtS* "The House Always Wins").

SPHERE OF THE INFINITE AGONIES, THE | Binding spell in which every second lasts a lifetime. Angel threatened Skip with this punishment, conjured by Fred (*AtS* "Inside Out").

SPIDER MONSTER | **JEFF RICKETTS** | Gray multilimbed creature with pincers for hands who made a ritual of a vampire sacrifice. The Spider Monster had an orb he called the key to his world, a place where there is no air for humans. Angel killed him by stabbing him in the head with one of his own pincers (*AtS* "Sacrifice").

SPIKE | Fictional character that is Angel's love interest in the film *Last Angel in Hell*. Differences between her and the actual Spike include the fact that she was recently turned ... and that she's female (*Angel* "After the Fall").

Spike

WILLIAM PRATT, WILLIAM THE BLOODY | JAMES MARSTERS |

Formerly a nineteenth-century human fop who considered himself a poet, though his work was deemed "bloody awful" by some. Sired by Drusilla in 1880 (*BtVS* "Lies My Parents Told Me"), Spike joined her, Angel, and Darla as they wreaked havoc on humanity. He formally met Angelus in the Royal London Hotel the same year he was sired. William was in awe of Angelus's evil. He was also convinced that Drusilla was his destiny, since she showed him all he could be, until he discovered her having sex with Angelus (*AtS* "Destiny"). Though this affected his relationship with Angelus, it only deepened his feelings toward Drusilla and the two began a tortuous relationship that lasted over a century. Spike killed his first Slayer in 1900 during the Boxer Rebellion in China, and his second in New York in 1977 (*BtVS* "Fool for Love"). He arrived in Sunnydale with a weakened Drusilla, offering to rid the town of its Slayer (*BtVS* "School Hard"), which led him to attempt to kill Buffy many times.

After Drusilla left Sunnydale, the Initiative captured Spike and inserted a chip inside his brain that delivered an excruciating jolt whenever he attempted to harm humans (*BtVS* "The Initiative"). While "chipped," Spike presented no threat to Buffy and her friends, and after a time he began to actively help them so he could still beat things up (*BtVS* "Doomed"). He and Buffy began an intense sexual relationship that ended with his attempted assault of her (*BtVS* "Seeing Red"), which led to a quest for him to regain his soul (*BtVS* "Grave"). Spike returned to Sunnydale and was nearly killed by Nikki Wood's son, Robin (*BtVS* "Lies My Parents Told Me"). Buffy's belief in Spike's goodness led to his self-sacrifice at the Battle of the Hellmouth, when he wore an amulet that drew down the power of the sun, killed the Turok-Han, and seemed to destroy him in the process (*BtVS* "Chosen").

Spike later materialized at Wolfram & Hart via the amulet, which had been mailed to Angel. Spike's body was insubstantial, but he was not a ghost. He tried to leave but was drawn back to the law firm and occasionally blinked out of existence as he was pulled into hell (*AtS* "Just Rewards"). Spike was eventually made corporeal by a spell that Lindsey mailed to him anonymously (*AtS* "Destiny"). On what Spike believed to be his last day on Earth, he went to a bar where he recited some of his poetry to great applause. He dedicated the first poem to his former human love, Cecily, and announced the next one would be about his mum, whom he shared an unusually close relationship with in his human life (that did not continue when she was briefly turned vampire). Then he went to kill the Fell Brethren and join Angel at the rendezvous for the final battle (*AtS* "Not Fade Away").

After the Fall of Los Angeles, Spike, Connor, and Illyria took care of some human and demon survivors, and became the Demon Lords of Beverly Hills, occupying the Playboy

Mansion. They eventually reunited with Angel, battling Gunn, the other Demon Lords, and Illyria in her Old One form (*Angel* "After the Fall"). Once time was reset, Spike went to Las Vegas with Betta George and Beck, bringing down the Wolfram & Hart Las Vegas branch and pursuing the Senior Partners in his new alien crew's escape pod after the Senior Partners stole their spaceship (*Spike*). Once magic ended, Spike stayed in San Francisco to support Buffy. While there, he assisted with Eldre Koh, the Siphon, and the zompires, but left on his bug ship because of Buffy's ambivalence toward him (*Buffy* "Apart [of Me]"). His insect-like followers eventually relocated to Easter Island, and he went to London to help Angel and Faith resurrect Giles (*Angel and Faith* "Death and Consequences"). Spike stayed in London with them until Dawn began to fade due to the end of magic, then he rushed to her side (*Buffy* "The Core). Dawn was saved, magic was restored, and Spike and Buffy renewed their commitment to each other; they are currently going strong (*Buffy* "Own It").

SPIKE'S HAREM | Women warriors who were released from Non's thrall when he was killed. Spike retrained them and kept them around partly to keep Illyria from morphing into Fred (because she felt they posed a threat) and partly to project a "Playboy Mansion" vibe as the Lord of Beverly Hills. Spider (Maria) and Ms. Clean were two members of the harem (*Angel* "After the Fall").

SPIRIT GUIDES, THE | Beings who exist out of time, but have knowledge of the future. They appear as a bright roiling cloud (*BtVS* "The Zeppo").

SPIVEY | **KEN ABRAHAM** | Employee of mob boss Tony Papazian. Kate roughed him up during an investigation, which was the impetus for the precinct to undergo sensitivity training (*AtS* "Sense and Sensitivity").

SPIVEY, PHILIP J. | **JOHN SHORT** | Angel Investigations client from Inglewood who approached the team for help finding his dog. A Sluk attacked him and possessed his body until he withered into dust from dehydration (*AtS* "The Price").

SPRING FLING | Sunnydale High School spring formal; Cordelia was its May Queen (*BtVS* "Out of Mind, Out of Sight").

STABBING VAMPIRE | **CHRIS DANIELS** | Vampire tricked out like an '80s rocker who almost killed Buffy, prompting her to ask Spike how he killed his two Slayers. Riley staked the vampire and blew up his nest (*BtVS* "Fool for Love").

STACY | Young gamer who longed for a more exciting life. She was delighted when she was turned into a vampire (*Tales* "Stacy").

STACY | **JON INGRASSIA** | Owner of Stacy's Gym Supplies. Professional muscle who worked for Russell Winters and probably did some time (*AtS* "City of").

STAFF OF DEVOSYNN | Magical artifact with the power to remove one's will and make that person a slave. The word "atistrata" engages the staff, which was kept in Wesley's vault (*AtS* "Lineage").

STAKE | Weapon of choice for a Slayer. The small, cylindrical wooden spear can be hand-carved or created from found material. Once the sharp point of a stake pierces a vampire's heart, that vampire immediately dusts unless under the protection of some mystical power (*BtVS* "Welcome to the Hellmouth").

STANLEY, JAMES | **CHRISTOPHER GORHAM** | Student at Sunnydale High School in 1955 who was having an affair with his teacher, Grace Newman. On the night of the Sadie Hawkins dance, James killed her because she'd broken up with him and then fatally shot himself. Both of their ghosts possessed other people who reenacted the murder scene until the ghost of Grace granted him forgiveness (*BtVS* "I Only Have Eyes for You").

STARNS, MRS. | Wesley's upstairs neighbor (*AtS* "Epiphany").

STAVROS, PRIVATE | Initiative soldier ordered to place Buffy and her team under arrest (*BtVS* "Primeval").

STEELE, ANNE (CHANTERELLE, LILY, SISTER SUNSHINE) | **JULIA LEE** | Former teen in Sunnydale who originally went by the name Chanterelle and was part of a group of vampire-worshipping "true believers" until Buffy saved her from actual vampires (*BtVS* "Lie to Me"). She encountered Buffy again in Los Angeles when Buffy had run away from home. Chanterelle was going by the name Lily while Buffy was using her middle name, Anne. Lily was tricked into entering a demon hell dimension but she helped Buffy free the human prisoners there. After that encounter she started over again, taking the name Anne, along with Buffy's job as a waitress (*BtVS* "Anne"). Anne later met up with Angel in Los Angeles. By then she'd adopted the name Anne Steele and had gotten her life in order. She was running the East Hills Teen Center, which unwittingly brought her into the schemes of Wolfram & Hart (*AtS* "Blood Money"). Anne occasionally sought help from the Angel Investigations team while they found solace with her and the good work she did in the community. Gunn spent his final day before the Battle of Los Angeles helping her at the center (*AtS* "Not Fade Away").

STEIN, DETECTIVE | JAMES G. MACDONALD | Sunnydale homicide detective who investigated several deaths, including Ted's (*BtVS* "Ted"), Kendra's (*BtVS* Becoming, Part 2), and Allan Finch's (*BtVS* "Consequences").

STEINGOTT, HANNAH | German woman in the 1930s who baked the Slayer Anni Sonnenblume's birthday cake because the family would no longer buy goods from the Greens, who were Jewish. Anni's brother Karl said the cake tasted like sour shoes (*Tales* "Sonnenblume").

STEPHAN | Vampire whom Buffy staked with Angel's tag-team help (*BtVS* "Some Assembly Required").

STEVE | Faith's klepto ex-boyfriend (*BtVS* "Revelations").

STEVENS, LAKE | Director of the Department of Defense Unified Supernatural Combatant Command and former girlfriend of Willow. Lake recruited Willow when the Sculptor opened the dimensional portals and she insisted on following orders when the military attempted to bomb D'Hoffryn out of existence. Aware that their methods didn't mesh, Willow broke up with her (*Buffy* "In Pieces on the Ground").

STEVENSON HALL | Dormitory at UC Sunnydale in which Buffy lived during her freshman year (*BtVS* "The Freshman").

STEVENS, PRINCIPAL | ANNE BETANCOURT | Dawn's junior high school principal who warned Buffy that if Dawn didn't come to school more regularly, Buffy might lose custody of her (*BtVS* "Tough Love").

STOLER, JOHN | SAM WITWER | Man who was permanently scarred by Jasmine's touch. Stoler alone was able to see her true nature and tried to kill her. Fred went to see him to learn the truth about Jasmine (*AtS* "Shiny Happy People").

STOKLEY, AL | SEAN MAHON | Driver who hit the corporeal Sahjhan with his borrowed truck (*AtS* "Forgiving").

STRALEY, RICHARD | CARLOS JACOTT | Ano-movic Demon whose family owns Straley's Steakhouse. They still speak Aratuscan. He is nice and polite, but his attempt to eat Doyle's brain in order to bless his marriage to Doyle's former wife Harry led to a broken engagement. His family includes his mom, Rachel (Kristen Lowman); dad; brother, Nick (Chris Tallman); a cousin; Aunt Martha (Lauri Johnson); and Uncle John (Brad Blaisdell) (*AtS* "The Bachelor Party").

STRAUSS, HANS AND GRETA | SHAWN PYFROM AND LINDSAY TAYLOR | Two halves of a German demon who incited people to burn witches at the stake by first appearing as a dead boy and girl bearing a ritualistic occult symbol on their palms. They appeared in news reports every fifty years. The earliest writings about them came from a cleric in a village near the Black Forest in 1649, in which their names and ages were first given. They were believed to be the inspiration for the story of Hansel and Gretel (*BtVS* "Gingerbread").

STREET COP | GEOFF KOCH | Officer who tried to arrest Gunn, George, and Rondell. He shot Wesley and was then shot by Rondell. At that point, his body reanimated and he called for backup (*AtS* "The Thin Dead Line").

STRESSED-OUT BOY | ALAN LOAYZA | Student at the new Sunnydale High School who exploded because his already-intense stress level was magnified by the Seal of Danzalthar (*BtVS* "Storyteller").

STROM DEMON | Creatures that ingest the body organs of their victims. Their bodies have regenerative abilities (*AtS* "Release").

SUE | Property manager where Darla was staying who was sympathetic to Cordelia's fake story about Darla's parents (*AtS* "Darla").

Summers, Buffy Anne

BUFFY THE VAMPIRE SLAYER, THE SLAYER
| SARAH MICHELLE GELLAR |

Slayer born in 1981 (*BtVS* "The Gift") and activated in 1996 at the age of fifteen. She began her life as a Slayer under the tutelage of her Watcher, Merrick, until he died protecting her (*BtVS* "Becoming, Part 1"). During a fight with vampires she burned down the gym at Hemery High School in Los Angeles, which led to her expulsion. Largely as a result of Buffy's actions, she and her recently divorced mother, Joyce, moved to Sunnydale. Buffy was unaware that she was still expected to serve as the Slayer in her new town and didn't initially recognize Rupert Giles, the school librarian, as her Watcher (*BtVS* "Welcome to the Hellmouth"). Angel—a mysterious stranger who turned out to be a vampire—warned her that the Harvest was coming, and to save her new friends, she took up her stake once more (*BtVS* "The Harvest"). In the ensuing months, she and her friends Willow Rosenberg and Xander Harris, plus her Watcher—the "core four" Scoobies—fought many of the vampires and demons drawn to the mystical energy of the Hellmouth, such as a Kleptes-Virgo (*BtVS* "Teacher's Pet"), as well as humans who had gotten too close to the supernatural, including a youth-obsessed witch (*BtVS* "Witch"), and the Sunnydale swim team, which was turned into Gill Monsters (*BtVS* "Go Fish").

The first Big Bad she came up against was the Master, an ancient vampire who succeeded in killing her. She was revived by Xander and destroyed the vampire (*BtVS* "Prophecy Girl"). The Master was succeeded by Spike, who, with his weakened paramour Drusilla, sought to kill the Slayer as well as her now-boyfriend Angel, the vampire with a soul, as he was Drusilla's sire and his blood could make her well. Buffy also became aware that another Slayer, Kendra, had been called because of Buffy's brief death (*BtVS* "What's My Line? Part 1"). After Buffy and Angel consummated their relationship, Angel lost his soul, and Buffy was forced to send him to hell (*BtVS* "Becoming, Part 2"). When the Powers That Be returned him to Earth, he realized that he and Buffy could never be together. After defeating her latest nemesis, Mayor Richard Wilkins, Buffy ended her relationship with Angel as he left for Los Angeles. Buffy was also faced with the existence of another Slayer, Faith, who chose the dark side for a time (*BtVS* "Graduation Day, Part 2"). Buffy and Angel briefly reunited when contact with a demon's blood turned Angel human again and he could be with her without the fear of triggering his curse. When it became necessary for Angel to turn back into a vampire to battle another demon, the Oracles undid the events of the day, so Buffy departed Angel's office the same day she arrived, thinking they'd just met briefly and agreed to not see each other (*AtS* "I Will Remember You").

Buffy matriculated at University of California, Sunnydale, where she met and began dating Riley Finn. She also destroyed Adam, a demon-cyborg-human hybrid (*BtVS* "Primeval"). Next she was sent a mystical Key in the form of a sister created from her blood (*BtVS* "No Place Like Home"). Having this new, younger family member proved a challenge for Buffy in many of the traditional ways of sibling dynamics, but it became particularly challenging after the loss of her mother (*BtVS* "The Body"). Now solely responsible for her sister, Buffy dropped out of school and ultimately sacrificed herself in 2001 to save Dawn along with the world (*BtVS* "The Gift"). Willow resurrected Buffy, pulling the Slayer out of what she believed was heaven. Buffy had a difficult time transitioning to being alive once more and found comfort in the arms of Spike. Their complicated relationship grew even more challenging when he attempted to rape her, which led the vampire on the path toward regaining a soul (*BtVS* "Seeing Red," "Grave"). Buffy and Spike eventually pushed past their darkest period, but she remained torn between two vampires with souls as she prepared for her ultimate battle with the First Evil. With Willow's magical assistance, Buffy was able to share her power with all the Potential Slayers whom Rupert Giles could bring to Sunnydale to do battle. And for the first time since the Slayer line began, Buffy had an army of similarly powered young women to assist her in the fight (*BtVS* "Chosen").

After the Sunnydale Hellmouth was closed, Buffy founded the Slayer Organization, coordinating five hundred Slayers into ten squads around the world. As humanity became aware of the existence of both Slayers and vampires, public opinion favored the vampires, and the military decried Slayers as terrorists (*Buffy* "The Long Way Home"). An unusual entity called Twilight joined with the military to fight the Slayer Organization, inflicting many casualties (*Buffy* "Retreat"); it was later revealed that Angel was Twilight, and this was part of a prophecy to force Buffy to grow stronger and to evolve to a point where she and Angel together could give birth to a new dimension of harmony and balance called Twilight. This was to be done at the expense of humanity, which would fall prey to hordes of demons (*Buffy* "Twilight"). During the fray, Buffy discovered the existence of the Seed of Wonder and destroyed it after Angel, under the influence of Twilight, killed Rupert Giles (*Buffy* "Last Gleaming").

Existing in a world without magic, Buffy attempted to live a mundane existence, reviled by many Slayers and resented by Willow (*Buffy* "Freefall"), who eventually realized that the world was dying because there was no magic in it. Buffy traveled with a team to the Deeper Well to successfully restore magic (*Buffy* "The Core"), but this was a new magical reality requiring new rules and the formation of a Magic Council (*Buffy* "New Rules"). Attempts to go about this in various ways yielded new enemies including D'Hoffryn, who murdered the other members of the Magic Council (*Buffy* "In Pieces on the Ground"). After they defeated D'Hoffryn, a new Council was formed, and Buffy and the newly-resurrected Rupert Giles are currently serving on it, while she and Spike continue to enjoy a strong committed relationship (*Buffy* "Own It").

Summers, Dawn

THE KEY | MICHELLE TRACHTENBERG |

Human girl created by the Monks of Dagon to house a mystical Key. Dawn was given the memories of an entire life history from birth to her teen years that she, her family, and friends all believed to be true. In fact, she did not realize that she wasn't real until she read Rupert Giles's diary (*BtVS* "Blood Ties"). Up to that time she was treated as the baby of the family, which she resented and rebelled against both before and after the death of her mother. Despite considerable danger to herself and others, Dawn snuck out of the house and was nearly killed on more than one occasion, and she struggled with petty theft, which was largely seen as a cry for attention. She felt that no one loved her and desperately attempted to raise her mother from the dead (*BtVS* "Forever"). The Hellgod Glory, searching for her Key, closed in on Dawn and kidnapped her (*BtVS* "Spiral"). Glory then attempted to open the portal to her home dimension in a ritual that would kill Dawn. When Buffy and company came to her rescue, and Buffy sacrificed her own life to save her, it finally became clear to Dawn that she was loved and valued as a sister and friend (*BtVS* "The Gift"). In Buffy's brief absence, Dawn became the unofficial

ward of her sister's friends as she continued to grow and make a place for herself in the world. Even without powers, she contributed to the final battle against the First Evil, fighting on the side of her returned sister (*BtVS* "Chosen").

As Dawn grew into adulthood, she and Xander confessed strong feelings for each other and became a couple during the Twilight crisis (*Buffy* "Retreat"). The realization that she is still a supernatural entity has been both a boon and a problem for Dawn. When magic ended, she began to fade away, but when she was restored, she no longer felt as close to Xander as she once had (*Buffy* "The Core"). When the Soul Glutton and the Mistress opened a hell portal with the Restless Door, Dawn volunteered to close it, which she could do since that was her original function (*Buffy* "In Pieces on the Ground"). After the successful mission, she and Xander, who had volunteered to accompany her, traveled through many dimensions in their attempt to return home. The intimacy of this adventure has since rekindled their relationship, albeit slowly (*Buffy* "Own It").

SUMMERS, HANK | DEAN BUTLER | Father to Buffy and (later) Dawn; ex-husband of Joyce. Hank was attentive to his daughter when Buffy and her mom first moved to Sunnydale, and he invited Buffy to his home in LA for the summer (*BtVS* "When She Was Bad"). But he eventually dropped out of her life altogether by not attending Joyce's funeral (*BtVS* "The Body") or helping his children with the bills (*BtVS* "Flooded"). He later met up with Buffy and Dawn in San Francisco to ask Buffy not to attend his upcoming wedding because of the danger the Slayer's presence would pose (*Buffy* "Old Demons").

SUMMERS, JOYCE (MOM) | KRISTINE SUTHERLAND | See following page.

SUMMERS, PAIGE | Buffy and Dawn's stepmother (*Buffy* "Old Demons").

SUN CINEMA | Local movie theater in downtown Sunnydale (*BtVS* "The Wish").

SUNDAY | KATHARINE TOWNE | Leader of a group of UC Sunnydale vampires who, along with her followers, had taken over an abandoned frat house. They developed a pattern of leaving a note indicating that the student who wrote it had given up on school and left. Then they would either kill or sire their victim. In either case, they would steal the victim's belongings, often mocking the student's youthful taste in posters and fashions. Buffy staked her after Sunday tried to make it look like Buffy dropped out (*BtVS* "The Freshman").

SUN-LOVING VAMPIRE | Being who underwent a procedure to have his heart removed and replaced with silver so that he could endure the sunlight. He would die in twenty-four hours as a result, but he was tired of feeling cold. However, once the surgery was complete, he disliked feeling so warm (*Tales* "Some Like It Hot").

SUNNY | ERIKA THORMAHLEN | Connor's first friend on Earth. She was so grateful to Connor for saving her from a drug-dealing pimp that she took Connor back to her crash pad at an abandoned motel and offered him clothes to wear. She introduced Connor to junk food and gave him his first kiss before she died from a drug overdose (*AtS* "A New World").

SUNNYDALE ARMS | Abandoned boardinghouse on Prescott Lane, fortified under the direction of Quentin Travers to serve as the location for Buffy's Cruciamentum (*BtVS* "Helpless").

SUNNYDALE, CALIFORNIA | Town founded in 1899 by Richard Wilkins in an area Spanish settlers had named *Boca del Inferno*, referencing the fact that the town was built atop a Hellmouth. Located on the Pacific Ocean in central California, about two hours north of Los Angeles, Sunnydale had a population of over thirty thousand people before residents abandoned the town in the lead-up to the battle against the First Evil. That fight ended with the entire town swallowed by the Hellmouth, leaving nothing but a giant crater behind (*BtVS* "Chosen").

SUNNYDALE FUNERAL HOME, THE | Location Buffy frequented—including on her first (and last) date with Owen Thurman (*BtVS* "Never Kill a Boy on the First Date").

SUNNYDALE HIGH SCHOOL | See following pages.

SUNNYDALE MEMORIAL HOSPITAL (SUNNYDALE GENERAL HOSPITAL) | See following pages.

Summers, Joyce

MOM | KRISTINE SUTHERLAND |

other to Buffy Summers, her biological daughter, and Dawn Summers, a child mystically created by the foes of Glory the Hellgod (*BtVS* "Listening to Fear"). Joyce and her husband Hank fought over Buffy's erratic behavior in Los Angeles (*BtVS* "Becoming, Part 1"), eventually divorcing. Joyce moved Buffy to Sunnydale because it was so hard to find a school that would have her daughter after she burned down the Hemery High School gym (*BtVS* "Witch"). Joyce operated an art gallery and raised Buffy as a single mom as her ex-husband became progressively less involved in their daughter's life (*BtVS* "Helpless"). Joyce was concerned when her daughter's problems at school followed her to Sunnydale, but the protective mother was ultimately proud to discover she'd raised a strong daughter who looked out for others. Upon learning that Buffy was a Vampire Slayer, Joyce rashly threw Buffy out of the house, but accepted Buffy's unique status when she returned from running away to Los Angeles (*BtVS* "When She Was Bad").

Joyce served as a surrogate mother to all the Scoobies including Spike (*BtVS* "Fool for Love") and had a fling with Giles while under the spell of enchanted band candy (*BtVS*

"Band Candy"). She also accepted her new daughter, Dawn, without question as memories of the child were implanted into her mind by powerful forces in the battle between good and evil. After surgery to remove a brain tumor, Joyce suffered a brain aneurism and died (*BtVS* "The Body"). The loss was felt deeply by her family and all of her daughters' friends. Dawn performed a spell to bring her back from the dead but broke it when she realized her mom would come back wrong (*BtVS* "Forever"). The First took advantage of Dawn's longing for her by appearing as Joyce to plant seeds of doubt about Buffy (*BtVS* "Conversations with Dead People").

SUNNYDALE MISSION | Holy site formerly presumed lost. While digging the foundation for the UC Sunnydale Cultural Partnership Center, Xander crashed through its roof and rediscovered it. The mission had been buried in an earthquake in 1812 (*BtVS* "Pangs").

SUNNYDALE NATURAL HISTORY MUSEUM | Location where Doug Perren examined Acathla's sarcophagus (*BtVS* "Becoming, Part 1").

SUNNYDALE ZOO | Location where Buffy's class went on a field trip, resulting in four students becoming possessed by hyena spirits (*BtVS* "The Pack").

SUNSET CLUB | Space rented by Diego (Marvin) as a place for Sunnydale's vampire wannabees to await "the blessing"—being sired (*BtVS* "Lie to Me").

SUNSET RIDGE | Section of Sunnydale in which two people went missing when Mr. Trick and Kakistos arrived in town (*BtVS* "Faith Hope and Trick").

SUPERBIA | Demon image consultant on Harmony's PR team (*Angel and Faith* "Live through This").

SUPERSTAR DEMON | **ZACH HUDSON** | Monster that Jonathan accidentally created while casting an augmentation spell to make himself the most popular celebrity on the planet. Jonathan killed the demon by pushing it into a pit to save Buffy (*BtVS* "Superstar").

SUREKILL EXTERMINATORS | Company hired by Wolfram & Hart to fumigate the Hyperion Hotel (*AtS* "That Vision Thing").

SUVARTA, MR. | Senior Partner who advised Lilah on how to deal with Linwood (*AtS* "Deep Down").

SUVOLTE DEMON | Massive demons the approximate size and bulk of a bear. They are fast breeders with leathery eggs that are prized on the black market. The eggs must be kept frozen or they will hatch at an unpredictable rate. The demons are untrainable and are useful only when dropped in a populated area during wartime to "cleanse" it of living things (*BtVS* "As You Were").

SVEA PRIESTESSES (SVEAR) | Mystical order of descendants of the powerful Nordic priestess Svea. They were very powerful and big into banishing. They hunted and banished the Beast in Prussia in 1789. The current priestesses live in Pacoima, with office hours Monday through Friday from 10 a.m. to 4 p.m. The Beast slaughtered them, but Wesley found the banishment incantation they'd been working on (*AtS* "Soulless").

SVEN | **HENDRICK ROSVALL** | Swedish exchange student who spoke perfect English, even though Cordelia never realized it (*BtVS* "Inca Mummy Girl").

SVF | Acronym for "Sexy Vampire Forehead," a term Harmony invented (*Buffy* "Predators and Prey").

SWEET | **HINTON BATTLE** | Demon Lord of the underworld who compels people to sing true statements and dance until they burst into flames. Xander summoned the demon to find out what his future with Anya held (*BtVS* "Once More, with Feeling").

SWELL, THE | Vampy Cats clustered together to make one monster under the command of Twilight (*Buffy* "Predators and Prey").

SWORD DEMON | After Buffy stabbed this demon with its own sword, it melted into the blade and reemerged inside her house. When she broke the blade, the demon was vanquished (*BtVS* "Older and Far Away").

Sunnydale High School

Public educational institution in the town of Sunnydale, California, built directly above the Hellmouth. There were two high schools: the first one was blown up when the Mayor ascended and the graduating class fought his vampire army and the Mayor himself (*BtVS* "Graduation Day, Part 2"). The second was built on top of the ruins of the first high school and was destroyed—along with Sunnydale itself—during the Battle of the Hellmouth (*BtVS* "Chosen").

Faculty & Staff (Original School)

Baird, Mr. (History)

Barton, Ms.

Beach, Mr.

Beakman, Miss (American Literature)

Calendar, Jenny (Computer Science)

Chomsky, Mr. (History)

Cox, Mr.

DeJean, Mr. (French)

Flutie, Principal Doug

Foster, Coach (P.E.)

Frank, Mrs.

Franklin, Mrs.

French, Miss (Biology - Substitute)

George (Janitor)

Giles, Rupert (Librarian)

Greenliegh, Ruth (Nurse)

Gregory, Dr. Stephen (Science)

Herbert (Mascot)

Herrold, Coach (P.E.)

Jackson, Mrs. (History/ Algebra II)

Litto, Miss (Self-Defense)

Lunch Lady (Name unknown)

Marin, Coach Carl (Swim Team)

Miller, Mr.

Miller, Mrs.

Moran, Ms. (Contemporary American Heroes)

Murray, Ms.

Platt, Stephen (Guidance Counselor)

Pole, Mr. (Driver's Ed)

Snyder, Principal R.

Taggert, Mrs. (Chemistry)

Tishler, Mrs.

Whitmore, Mr. (Teen Health)

Faculty & Staff (New School)

Corrigan, Mr. (Trigonometry)

Davis, Mr.

Hildebrand, Mr. (Trigonometry)

Lonegrin, Mr.

Matthew

Miller, Mr.

Summers, Buffy (Counselor)

Wood, Principal Robin

Students (Original School)

Adam

Albert, Paul*

Aphrodesia

Aura

Ben

Big Bob

Blaisdell, Larry

Blake, Michelle

Blue

Boal, Chris

Braeburn, Holly

Brooks, Lance

Bud

Bulac, Dorothy*

Bushy, Tim

Calton, Lynette*

Charleston, Holly

Chase, Cordelia

Cheryl

Chervin, Ted (Wishverse)

Clarner, Pete

Crandle, Billy

Czajak, Michael

Dale

Diaz, Selena*

Dickie

Dino

Donaldson, Mandy

Doug

Doyle, Nancy

Dutton, Lisa*

Dwyer, Sean

Eastman, Eva

Elliot

Emily

Epps, Chris

Epps, Daryl

Eric

Fargo, Mitch

Foley, Debbie

Frank

Fritz

Garrity

Ginger (Wishverse)

Gittleson, Eric

Grove, Amber

Guy

Gwen

Hamm, Lisa

Harris, Xander

Helf, Mark*

Hoelich, Andrew

Hope, Scott

Hyde, Alan

Iverson, Freddy

Jeffries, Doug

Jesse

John Lee

Jo-Jo

Joy

Justin

Keidler, Siriporn

Kendall, Harmony

Kevin

Klein, Mimi

Lance

Laura

Levinson, Jonathan

Lisa (Tuba player)

Lisa (Cheerleader)

Lishanne

Lysette

MacLeish, Devon

Madison, Amy

Martin, Hogan

Martini, Sheila

Mayhew, Jack

McAlvy, Dodd

Mears, Warren

Metz, David

Michelle

Mitch

Moll, Blayne
Munson, Rodney
Niemi, Pries*
Orkin, Jeff
Osbourne, Daniel (Oz)
O'Toole, Jack
Parker
Ramsay, Heather*
Ray, Donnie
Rosenberg, Willow
Ross, Marcie
Roy
Ruskin, Victoria
Sancton, Daryl*
Sean
Shanice
Shay, Morgan
Shepherd, Tyke*
Siener, Tara*
Silverman, Nancy*
Sinclair, Megan*

Sing, Eric*
Smith, Jonathan*
Stadeal, Owen
Steve
Steve
Summers, Buffy
Thurman, Owen
Vega, Annie
Walden, Tricia
Walken, Jeffrey
Walker, Cameron
Webster, Holden
Wells, Andrew
Wells, Tucker
Wendell
West, Percy
Wheeler, Jason

Considered a potential vote for Buffy in the Homecoming Queen election.

Students (New School)

Amanda
Brooks, R.J.
Grimes
Helgenberg, Mike
Hoffman
Holburn, Kit
Josh
Margot
Newton, Cassie

Nicols, Peter
O'Donnell
O'Keefe
Roger
Summers, Dawn
Tomas
Trejo, Carlos
Wilder, Martin

Past Faculty/Alumni

David (Student–1955)
French, Natalie (Biology Teacher–Retired 1972)
Hall, Mrs. (Teacher–1955)

Newman, Grace (Teacher–1955)
Stanley, James (Student–1955)

Sunnydale Memorial Hospital

SUNNYDALE GENERAL HOSPITAL

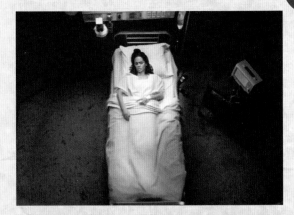

*L*ocal community hospital in Sunnydale where almost every member of Buffy's inner circle were patients at some point before the hospital was sucked into the Hellmouth.

Medical Attention Received at Sunnydale Memorial Hospital:

Anya: broken arm (*BtVS* "Real Me")

Buffy: flu, blood loss, gunshot wound (*BtVS* "Killed by Death,""Graduation Day, Part 2,""Villains")

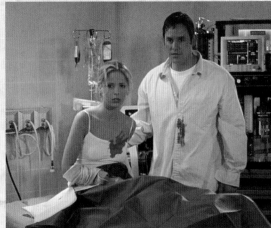

Cordelia: flesh wound from impaling (*BtVS* "Lovers Walk")

Dawn: broken arm (*BtVS* "Wrecked")

Faith: blood loss, coma (*BtVS* "Graduation Day, Part 2,""This Year's Girl")

Joyce: brain tumor (*BtVS* "Shadow")

Tara: mental trauma (*BtVS* "Tough Love")

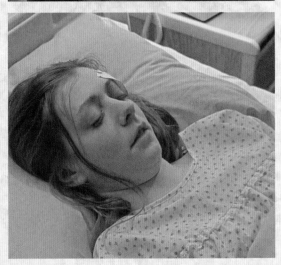

Willow: head trauma (*BtVS* "Becoming, Part 2")

Xander: broken arm, loss of eye (*BtVS* "Becoming, Part 2," "Dirty Girls")

Potentials: Various battle wounds (*BtVS* "Dirty Girls")

SWORD IN ACATHLA'S HEART | Weapon used by a virtuous knight to slay Acathla. When Acathla turned to stone, the sword was stuck fast in his body and only the worthy could remove it (*BtVS* "Becoming, Part 1").

SWORD OF MOSKVA | Russian weapon named after the Moskva River (*BtVS* "End of Days").

SYMBOL OF ANYANKA | Jeweled necklace originally worn by Anyanka the Vengeance Demon when she came to Sunnydale to fulfill Cordelia's wish after Xander kissed Willow. Anyanka created an alternate dimension in which Buffy had never come to Sunnydale, and the Giles of that reality destroyed the pendant to extinguish the demon's powers (*BtVS* "The Wish"). Anya cajoled Willow into attempting a spell to reclaim it but was unsuccessful (*BtVS* "Doppelgangland").

TABOR, LOU | Antiquities expert at the Washington Institute who told Sunnydale Natural History Museum curator Doug Perren to contact Giles regarding the stone sarcophagus containing Acathla (*BtVS* "Becoming, Part 1").

TAE | COLBY FRENCH | Vigory of Oden-Tal who arrived via portal, sent by his people to stop Jhiera. Angel sent him back home (*AtS* "She").

TAGGIS ROOT | Required ingredient for general reversal spells. The magic shop had run out of it when Giles went blind as a result of Willow's spell to have one's will done (*BtVS* "Something Blue").

TAGORAK | Human in Kennedy's employ at Deepscan charged with training Slayers to be bodyguards (*Buffy* "Guarded").

TAHVAL DEMON | Creature whose spawn are formidable fighters that age at an accelerated rate (*AtS* "Expecting").

TAK HORN | Body part that projects from the forehead of Kungai Demons. It is the source of their power that allows them to drain a person's life force (*AtS* "Parting Gifts").

TALAMOUR | A burrower; a wormlike demon who preyed on young singles and gave them hope that the loneliness would end. It eviscerated its victims as it moved from body to body after some kind of a sex act. Amazingly strong, it fought Angel to a draw while it possessed a human body. Angel set it on fire and Kate shot its host (*AtS* "Lonely Hearts").

"TALES OF BRAVE ULYSSES" | Rock song performed by Cream that Giles listened to while mourning Joyce Summers's death (*BtVS* "Forever").

TAMIKA | DANIELLE NICOLET | Vampire who worked in the Wolfram & Hart stenographer pool for five years. She typed eighty words a minute and had an exceptionally pleasant phone voice. Jealous of Harmony's promotion to the best desk in the building, Tamika spiked Harmony's drink at the bar and killed Toby to make it look like Harmony did it. Harmony ultimately staked her in return (*AtS* "Harm's Way").

TAMMY | HEATHER WEEKS | Seventeenth-century woman whom Skip used as an example to show Cordelia the effects of the power of visions on a human. Tammy was to be burned at the stake as a witch, but her last vision blew out the back of her head first (*AtS* "Birthday").

TAPPARICH | ROGER MORRISSEY | Mok'tagar Demon whom was searching for his errant daughter, Buffy's first college roommate, Kathy. He wore a cloak and had glowing green eyes, and his skin was orange and fissured. He created a portal to return to his home dimension (*BtVS* "Living Conditions").

TARA | TAMARA BRAUN | Vampire Buffy tortured with her cross necklace to learn where Absalom had taken his intended sacrifices: Cordelia, Ms. Calendar, Willow, and Giles (*BtVS* "When She Was Bad").

TARANTULA | REBECCA JACKSON | Spike's goth date at Anya and Xander's wedding (*BtVS* "Hell's Bells").

TARELLIAN PLAGUE | Andrew said that Dawn was suffering from this disease when he and Xander masqueraded as a doctors to transfer Dawn from one part of the hospital to another (*Buffy*

"Welcome to the Team"). The disease was named for an illness affecting an alien species in an episode of *Star Trek: The Next Generation*.

TARNIS | Twelfth-century monk and one of the founders of the Order of Dagon; author of *The Book of Tarnis* (*BtVS* "Blood Ties").

TECHNOPAGAN | Individual who practices occult rituals and magic via the Internet; Jenny Calendar was one (*BtVS* "I Robot . . . You Jane").

TED | PATRICK FISCHLER | Bookstore owner who fell under Jasmine's spell but remained a conspiracy theorist. He helped Fred research mass hypnosis but thought she just wanted to spread Jasmine's word. Under Jasmine's thrall, he remained in his shop as it burned down (*AtS* "Magic Bullet").

TEETH (BRO'OS) | RAYMOND O'CONNOR | Known in Sunnydale by his nickname, this loan shark—with a shark-shaped head—came after Spike to reclaim a debt of forty Siamese kittens. After Spike and Buffy dusted most of Teeth's vampire henchmen, he told Spike to forget about repaying him (*BtVS* "Tabula Rasa"). When Wolfram & Hart sent Los Angeles to hell, Teeth worked his way up to Demon Lord of Santa Monica and pretended to go along with the plot to assassinate Angel. However, with Angel's collusion, he tricked the other Lords into killing themselves, stepped down as Demon Lord, and received a block of waterside property. When Wolfram & Hart turned back time, the Demon Lords hunted him down and killed him for betraying them (*Angel* "After the Fall").

TEMPLE, LUCIUS | Acolyte of Acathla and an expert on demons. Giles and Buffy consulted Temple's diary in their search for an explanation regarding why Angel was seeing apparitions of his victims during Christmas (*BtVS* "Amends").

TEMPLE OF SOBEK (SOBEKITES) | Ancient Egyptian cult that worshiped Sobek, a reptilian demon. Led by their high priest, Kuhl, the cult hoped to create a reptile race through the use of transmogrifying stones (*BtVS* "Shadow").

TEMPORAL DISTORTION | Chip device invented by Warren to speed up time around Buffy (*BtVS* "Life Serial").

TEMPORAL FLUX | A shift in time signaled by objects appearing and disappearing. It can sometimes be caused by a summoning spell (*BtVS* "Fear Itself").

TENNANT, DAVID | Scottish *Doctor Who* actor who is friends with Harmony Kendall (*Angel and Faith* "Live through This").

TEZCATCATL | Powerful Aztec demon warrior. Tezcatcatl tried to harness the sun in a talisman and was sentenced to die. He was cursed by a shaman to return every fifty years to search for the talisman. In his latest incarnation, *Numero Cinco* lured him to the cemetery where Angel stabbed him in the heart (*AtS* "The Cautionary Tale of Numero Cinco").

THAUMOGENESIS | Process by which demons are created as an unintended side effect of a spell. They include Skaggmore Demons, Tellbane Demons, Skitterers, Large and Small Bone-Eaters (*BtVS* "After Life"), as well as the demon Jonathan Levinson created when he became a celebrity (*BtVS* "Superstar") and the creatures that invaded the Hyperion after Angel used dark magic to give Sahjhan corporeal form (*AtS* "The Price").

THELMA | One of two Sirens who lured Xander and Spike to the Mistress's lair. Spike killed them both (*Buffy* "I Wish").

THELONIUS | Monk who helped trap Moloch in a book that was later scanned at the Sunnydale High library (*BtVS* "I Robot . . . You Jane").

THESULAC DEMON | TONY AMENDOLA | Paranoia demon who whispered to its victims, feeding on their innate insecurities. One haunted the Hyperion Hotel for decades, keeping Judy Kovacs prisoner to her guilt. This gray-faced demon with tentacles had to be made corporeal through a Raising ritual before it could be killed by electrocution (*AtS* "Are You Now or Have You Ever Been").

THOMAS | Vampire boy who invited Willow out for ice cream in order to feed her to the Master (*BtVS* "Welcome to the Hellmouth").

THOMAS, DR. | JANET SONG | Emergency-room doctor (*AtS* "First Impressions").

THOMAS, RICKIE | CHAD TODHUNTER AND HARRISON YOUNG | Homeless young man on the streets of LA who was lured into the Family Home's demon dimension. After spending decades in that dimension, he committed suicide as an old man who was recognizable as Rickie only by the tattoo on his arm (*BtVS* "Anne").

THORPE, LYDIA | BELINDA WAYMOUTH | Headmistress at Thorpe's Academy when Gwen Raiden was brought there as a child (*AtS* "Ground State").

THORPE'S ACADEMY | School for "special" students; located in Gills Rock, Wisconsin (*AtS* "Ground State").

THRAXIS DEMON | A creature with blood that kind of burns when one is covered in it (*AtS* "Life of the Party").

THREE, THE | Members of the Order of Aurelius sent by the Master to kill Buffy. After failing, they were executed by Darla at the Master's request (*BtVS* "Angel").

THREE SISTERS, THE | MARITA SCHAUB, LESLEE JEAN MATTA, AND JENNIFER SLIMKO | Dracula's female companions in Sunnydale, who imprisoned Giles in a pleasurable manner while in the castle (*BtVS* "Buffy vs. Dracula").

THURMAN, OWEN | CHRISTOPHER WIEHL | Sunnydale High student who loved the poetry of Emily Dickinson. Buffy began to date him after winning out over Cordelia for his affections. He was nearly killed when he accompanied Buffy to the Sunnydale Funeral Home while she was searching for the Anointed One. Buffy broke up with him to keep him safe (*BtVS* "Never Kill a Boy on the First Date").

TIBERIUS MANIFESTO | Lost book about the Slayer prophecy (*BtVS* "Out of Mind, Out of Sight").

TICHAJT | Demon elite who can walk in the human reality and that of the Old Ones. Sephrilian was a Tichajt (*Buffy* "No Future for You").

TIEN SHENIN | Demon species local to Kazakhstan (*AtS* "Judgment").

TIERNAN, COMMANDER | LEE ARENBERG | Demon who led the Scourge in LA (*AtS* "Hero").

TILSON, GARY | T. FERGUSON | Doublemeat Palace employee killed and eaten by the Wig Lady. Upon discovering his finger in the grinder, Buffy incorrectly assumed that the Doublemeat secret ingredient was human flesh (*BtVS* "Doublemeat Palace").

TIMOTHY | Purple demon able to spy on people through the creation of viewports. After Los Angeles was sent to hell, he lived in Silverlake and assisted Angel during his battle with the champions of the Demon Lords (*Angel* "After the Fall").

TINA | Little girl murdered by Der Kindestod at Sunnydale Memorial Hospital (*BtVS* "Killed by Death").

TINA | TRACY MIDDENDORF | Waitress at the Coffee Spot who became Angel's first assignment from the Powers That Be. Tracy came to LA to be a movie star, but after constant rejection she just wanted to go back to Missoula, Montana. Angel rescued her from Russell Winters's henchmen at Margo's party. She started to trust Angel, but when she saw the piece of paper with her name on it from Doyle, she suspected Angel of working for Russell. When she discovered Angel was a vampire, she hid from him, allowing Russell to find and kill her (*AtS* "City of").

TINK | Nickname of the fairy who was with the underground decoy Buffy when she died (*Buffy* "The Long Way Home"). The fairy later invaded the dream Buffy had in which Sineya told her to give the Scythe to Willow for repair—and hinted to Buffy that she was currently the Buffybot (*Buffy* "Freefall").

T'ISH MAGEV | Powerful swami who lived in Ojai and was a friend of Lorne. Magev practiced psychiatry through magic, specializing in instant cures for phobias, compulsions, and identity crises. He was killed and replaced by a soulful thug (Art LaFleur) whose mission was to keep Angel out of the way during a ritual to raise the goddess Yeska. The truth was revealed when Angel caught him (literally, with a fishhook) (*AtS* "Guise Will Be Guise").

TITO | Party-throwing friend of Gunn (*AtS* "First Impressions").

TITO | JOHN JABALEY | Xander's plumber friend who gave Buffy an estimate to repair her house (*BtVS* "Flooded").

TÓ BÁJÍSHCHÍNÍ | Tormented vampire whose mother was Diné (Navajo), while her human father—whom she killed—was Caucasian. She also killed Naayééʼneizghání's Watcher and mortally wounded the Slayer herself before Naayééʼneizghání staked her (*Tales* "The Glittering World").

TODD | RYAN RADDATZ | Doublemeat Palace employee who gave Buffy the lowdown on company politics (*BtVS* "As You Were").

TODD, MEREDITH | Member of the Fondren High pep squad who died in a car accident. Her corpse was stolen from her grave to create a Frankenstein monster-style mate for Chris Epps (*BtVS* "Some Assembly Required").

TODD, PHILLIP | DOUGLAS BENNETT | Doublemeat Palace employee who showed Buffy how to work the grill and told her about how the grease buildup in his ears was a job hazard (*BtVS* "Doublemeat Palace").

TOM | MACE LOMBARD | Originally a member of Sunday's vampire gang (*BtVS* "The Freshman"). He was captured by the Initiative and warned Spike not to drink the blood (*BtVS* "The Initiative").

TOMMY | Corky Smallwood's husky demonic enforcer. He was

sent to kill Angel but failed (*Angel and Faith* "Where the River Meets the Sea").

TONY | Construction worker who was first dismissive of Buffy's work on his crew but later came to respect her (*BtVS* "Life Serial").

TOOTH OF AMMUT (DEVOURER OF ANCIENT EGYPTIAN SOULS) | Mystical object that acts as a magnet for fragments of the soul. Angel imbedded it into his chest so he could absorb pieces of Giles's soul (*Angel and Faith* "Daddy Issues").

TOOTH OF LIGHT, THE (THE SWORD OF THE BOSH M'AD) | Weapon with the power to destroy the Beast, though it is possibly imaginary (*AtS* "Awakening").

TOPKNOT | Vampire who followed Doyle back to the office from his nest and attacked Cordelia and Pierce. Doyle dusted him (*AtS* "The Bachelor Party").

TORG | JOSH BRAATEN | Demonic gatekeeper for the Beljoxa's Eye who also worked at a restaurant in Sunnydale. Torg once had a fling with Anyanka, who rejected him. After a threat from Giles, he spilled his blood and performed an incantation that allowed Anya and Giles access to the Eye (*BtVS* "Showtime").

TORTO DEMON | BOB JESSER | Horned demon with a parasite growing out of his side (*AtS* "Happy Anniversary")

TORU | Leader of the Japanese vampires who beat Dracula at cards to obtain his powers. Toru killed Renee the Vampire Slayer with the Scythe. After Willow took away Toru's ill-gotten extraordinary powers, Dracula hacked off his limbs and Xander decapitated him (*Buffy* "Wolves at the Gate").

TOTH | MICHAEL BAILEY SMITH | Last member of the Tothric Demon clan, intent on splitting Buffy into two halves with a Ferula Gemini, but he split Xander instead. Toth had fissured skin and a skull-like face with milky, glowing eyes. Buffy killed him with a sword (*BtVS* "The Replacement").

TRAFALGAR | British gnome who unsuccessfully attempted to break through the wards Roden had set up to protect Lady Genevieve Savidge's estate (*Buffy* "No Future for You").

TRANSCENDING FURIES (MUSES) | HEIDI MARNHOUT, AN LE, AND MADISON GRAY | Three spirits who cast the nonviolence spell on Caritas monthly and had fond memories of Angel (*AtS* "That Old Gang of Mine"). Also known as Muses, they restored the nonviolence spell on Caritas with the chant "*Violence abounds, violence restrain, this space a sanctuary was and shall be again*" (*AtS* "Offspring"). They also put a protective spell around the Hyperion, with an emergency exit in the basement, protected by a Pylean word (*AtS* "Dad").

TRAVELER DEMON (THE WHITE WOMAN) | LISA HOYLE | Demon who traveled with Buffy when Willow brought her friend back from the dead. The demon was out of phase with the human dimension, requiring Willow and Tara to perform the following spell to make the demon solid: "*Child of words, hear thy makers. Child of words, we entreat. With our actions did we make thee. To our voices wilt thou bend. With our potions thou took motive. With our motions came to pass. We rescind no past devotions. Give thee substance, give thee mass*" (*BtVS* "After Life").

TRAVERS, QUENTIN | HARRIS YULIN | Head of the Watchers Council who orchestrated Buffy's Cruciamentum, then fired Rupert Giles for having a father's love for his Slayer (*BtVS* "Helpless"). Smug and unyielding, Travers tried to test Buffy to determine her suitability to receive information about Glory, but Buffy called his bluff and had Giles reinstated (retroactively) as her Watcher (*BtVS* "Checkpoint"). He died in the explosion Caleb set at Watcher headquarters in London (*BtVS* "Never Leave Me").

TRAVIS | EDWARD EDWARDS | The First Evil appeared as this victim of Angelus to emotionally torture Angel with his evil past deeds (*BtVS* "Amends").

TREE DEMON | Being that used a DSL connection to attract lonely people online and lure them to Plummer Park where it could pull them underground and drain them of energy. When it tried to suck Angel's heart, the cold, lifeless thing paralyzed it. Gunn was then able to free himself from the demon's grip and stab it to death (*AtS* "Couplet").

TREE SELLER GUY | TOM MICHAEL BAILEY | Sunnydale Christmas-tree lot employee who pointed out a ring of dead trees to Buffy, which turned out to be above the hideout of the Harbingers (*BtVS* "Amends").

TREJO, CARLOS | DAVID ZEPEDA | Dawn and Kit's new friend on their adventure with the restless dead in the basement of the new Sunnydale High (*BtVS* "Lessons").

TRENSIDUF OF THE GATHWOK CLAN | WILLIAM NEWMAN | Old Pylean man who captured Cordelia and traded her for a pig and a pint of flip liquor (*AtS* "Over the Rainbow").

TREPKOS, VAL | JUAN A. RIOJAS | Demon with twenty kills at the XXI fight club before he fought Angel (*AtS* "The Ring").

TRICIA | Plague ball human who wound up with green hair, pointed ears, and yellow skin. She sought shelter at Nadira's sanctuary (*Angel and Faith* "Where the River Meets the Sea"), where she met Parker, and together they fought at the battle against Archaeus. Parker died in her arms (*Angel and Faith* "A Tale of Two Families").

TRICK, MR. | K. TODD FREEMAN | Vampire who accompanied Kakistos to Sunnydale but abandoned him to Buffy and Faith (*BtVS* "Faith, Hope & Trick"). He came to the attention of the Mayor after organizing SlayerFest '98 (*BtVS* "Homecoming"). He hired Ethan Rayne to make enchanted band candy (*BtVS* "Band Candy") and sent a "welcoming committee" to get rid of Spike (*BtVS* "Bad Girls"). Both efforts ultimately failed to achieve their desired results. Faith staked him and later replaced him as the Mayor's confidant (*BtVS* "Consequences").

TRIONIC | Process of writing one book over three volumes, where passages in one book continue in another and then a third, before returning to the first. All three books must be read together (*AtS* "Through the Looking Glass").

TRIO, THE | Composed of Jonathan Levinson, Warren Mears, and Andrew Wells, three nerds who decided to become super-villains and take over Sunnydale (*BtVS* "Flooded"). Their first forays into a life of crime were rather comedic but took a darker turn as Buffy continued to thwart them. Their actions moved to pure evil when Warren killed Katrina, his ex-girlfriend, after attempting to rape her by means of a Cerebral Dampener, and then tried to pin her murder on Buffy (*BtVS* "Dead Things"). After a botched theme park robbery showed Warren's true alliance to only himself, Warren's humiliation was so acute that he decided to shoot Buffy with a gun, but he accidentally killed Tara Maclay in the process (*BtVS* "Seeing Red"). At this point, the Trio split up, with Dark Willow flaying Warren alive and Jonathan and Andrew fleeing to Mexico (*BtVS* "Villains"). They were metaphorically reunited when the First appeared as Warren to Andrew and convinced him to kill Jonathan on top of the Seal of Danzalthar (*BtVS* "Conversations with Dead People").

TRISH | NICHOLL HIREN | Fictional perfect wife of Lindsey—and later Gunn—in the Senior Partners' Holding Dimension (*AtS* "Underneath").

TRO-CLON | The person or being who brings about the ruination of mankind, as predicted in the Nyazian Scrolls. Due to various translations, there was confusion as to whether the Tro-Clon was going to be born or to simply arrive. First the team believed it was Angel's baby, but then they realized it might refer to Holtz (*AtS* "Offspring"). Eventually they determined it was not a person, but a confluence of events referring to Connor's birth and the incidents that followed (*AtS* "Quickening").

TRUTH SPELL | Willow and Giles planned to use one on Spike to obtain the location of the Initiative lab, but Willow did not complete preparations for it. Motherwort is one of the ingredients, and fragments of the incantation include these words: "*Enemy, enemy, be now quiet . . . Let your deceitful tongue be broken. Let no untruths be spoken*" (*BtVS* "Something Blue").

TUMBLE | One of Buffy's roommates in San Francisco (*Buffy* "Freefall").

TURFOG | Thrall Demon whose hypnotic powers can be used to force its worshippers to kill each other (*AtS* "Dear Boy").

TURLOCK, DETECTIVE | R. EMERY BRIGHT | Investigator who questioned Wesley about the heist at the Natural History Museum (*AtS* "The Shroud of Rahmon").

TURNER, DYLAN | Human friend of Spike who became a successful painter and had a showing at Verde, which Spike and Buffy attended as a couple (*Buffy* "I Wish"). Later, Dylan and Spike discussed the dynamics of the vampire's relationships with women (*Buffy* "In Pieces on the Ground").

TUROK-HAN (UBERVAMP) | CAMDEN TOY | The purest form of vampire in this dimension (other than Archaeus himself). Their white faces are batlike and they are all bald. They wear crude clothing made of skins and are extremely strong and feral (*BtVS* "Bring On the Night"). Giles had assumed that these monstrous, primordial vampires were a myth (*BtVS* "Never Leave Me"). They were so powerful that Buffy had trouble killing even one (*BtVS*

"Showtime"), but the Turok-Han were defeated after Buffy shared her power with the Potentials and Spike's amulet drew down the power of the sun (*BtVS* "Chosen").

TWILIGHT | Being that influenced Angel to challenge Buffy so that she could gain enough power to evolve and mate with him to create the dimension of Twilight. His followers had a scar that symbolized the sun setting over a mountain. Angel wore a mask and chest armor that effectively disguised him from everyone except Spike (*Buffy* "Twilight"). Allies of Twilight included the US military, Whistler, Pearl, and Nash. Once revealed, Angel and Buffy created the Twilight dimension, but realized that its existence would doom the Earth to being overrun by demons, and abandoned it. This event had been foretold in the Slayer prophecies, and was so terrifying that in 1680, thirty Watchers took their own lives when they thought it was beginning to form (*Buffy* "Last Gleaming").

TWILIGHT COMPENDIUM, THE | Written by Sir Robert Kane, this book was one that Giles could inform Gwendolyn Post he had in his library (*BtVS* "Revelations").

TYKE | **ANTHONY STARKE** | Drug-dealing pimp who took Connor's necklace and ordered him killed. Connor cut off his ear. Tyke was presumed dead after a shoot-out with police (*AtS* "A New World").

TYLER | Buffy's boyfriend back in Los Angeles when she went to Hemery High School. (*BtVS* "Becoming, Part 1").

U

UGLY MAN | Manifestation of Billy Palmers's Kiddie League coach in Billy's astrally projected nightmares. He was bald with burned facial features and one hand was made of a club (*BtVS* "Nightmares").

UNCLE BOB'S MAGIC CABINET | Magic shop located on Main Street in Sunnydale that became the Magic Box (*BtVS* "The Zeppo").

UNCLE FRANK | Anderson family friend believed to have died in a fire in Akron, Ohio, though the police never found the body. Probable cause of death: Ryan Anderson (*AtS* "I've Got You under My Skin").

UNDER-COMMUNITY | Location where decoy Buffy was sent to help the alliance of fairy, Slimefolk, Ravenclan, and the Great Ronok fight Yamanh of Hoht (*Buffy* "The Long Way Home").

UNIVERSITY OF CALIFORNIA, SUNNYDALE | See following page.

URKONN | Big scarlet demon sent by the Old Ones Vrill and Boluz to train Melaka Fray to be a Slayer (*Fray* "Big City Girl"). He staged a vampire attack and killed Melaka's friend Loo to force the reluctant Slayer into the fight (*Fray* "All Hell").

URN OF OSIRIS | Required object for the Resurrection Spell favored by Willow for raising the dead. It is no longer in existence (*BtVS* "Bargaining, Part 1").

UURTHU | Entity Jack O'Toole called upon to revivify his dead friends (*BtVS* "The Zeppo").

University of California, Sunnydale

Campus of the University of California system located in Sunnydale, California. Buffy, Oz, and Willow matriculated together (*BtVS* "Choices"); Riley Finn was a teacher's assistant there (*BtVS* "The Freshman"); and Willow met Tara there (*BtVS* "Hush"). The school was also secretly a headquarters of a government antidemon taskforce known as the Initiative (*BtVS* "The Initiative").

Faculty & Staff

Blackmaster, Surrinda (Assistant to the Dean)
Gerhardt, Professor (Anthropology)
Hawkins, Professor
Mike (Sociology Professor)
Riegert, Professor
Roberts, Professor (History)
Walsh, Professor Maggie (Psychology)

Students

Abrams, Parker
Cheryl*
Dav
Doug
Eddie
Edward
Evan
Finn, Riley**
Gates, Forrest**
Jamie
Kip
Maclay, Tara
Melody
Miller, Graham**
Nicole*
Osbourne, Daniel (Oz)
Parker, Eric
Paul
Paula
Peralta, J.D.
Pruitt, Jeff
Rachel
Rachel
Robinson, Judy
Rosenberg, Lisa
Rosenberg, Willow
Roy
Ruskin, Victoria
Solis, Leo
Solomon, David
Speed, Tim
Starkey, Mike
Steve
Summers, Buffy
Suta, Brian
Therlault, Paul
Thomson, Kelly
Tomb, Brooks
Vaughne*
Veruca

*Member of the Daughters of Gaia
**Member of the Initiative

Campus Buildings

Dunwirth Hall
Fischer Hall
Grotto, the
Judd
Kresge Hall
Lowell House
Porter Hall
Rocket Café
Stevenson Hall
Student Center
Wiesman Hall
Wolf House

Fraternities, Sororities, and Social Clubs

Alpha Delta
Beta Delta Gamma
Daughters of Gaia
Psi Theta (lost its charter in 1982)

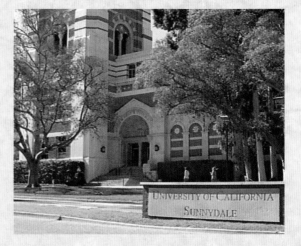

V

VAHLA HA'NESH | Name for the Los Angeles area when it was under Illyria's rule (*Buffy* "Welcome to the Team"), and specifically Illyria's temple, where her army of doom was entombed with her idol. The temple is out of phase with the time stream so that only Illyria can open it. In modern day, she entered through a bank and found the temple destroyed (*AtS* "Shells").

VAHRALL DEMON | According to a research book belonging to Rupert Giles, these demons are "slick like gold and gird in moonlight, father of portents and brother to blight. Limbs with talons, eyes like knives; bane to the blameless, thief of lives." Three Vahrall Demons arrived in Sunnydale planning to enact the Sacrifice of Three, in which they would take the blood of a man, the bones of a child, and the Word of Valios (an amulet) with them as they jumped into the Hellmouth. At the very last moment, Buffy jumped in and retrieved the third demon, preventing the apocalypse (*BtVS* "Doomed").

VAIL, CYVUS | DENNIS CHRISTOPHER | Red-skinned demon with long thinning white hair who oversaw a large empire in LA as one of Wolfram & Hart's go-to warlocks when it came to the magical mojo. He specialized in memory restructuring, mind control, and temporal shifts and "rebuilt" Connor by giving him the false memories of a different life. For this Wolfram & Hart paid him a large amount of money on the day Angel and the

gang accepted the deal to work for them. Vail later threatened to return Connor's real memories if Angel didn't get Connor to defeat Sahjhan (*AtS* "Origin"). He later tried to lure Wesley into betraying Angel and finally turned Wesley's spells on him and stabbed him. Illyria put her fist through his head (*AtS* "Not Fade Away").

VAKMA | SUSAN BLOMMAERT | Pylean woman who bought Cordelia and collared her as a slave (*AtS* "Over the Rainbow").

VAL | VICTORIA L. KELLEHER | Assistant in Gene Rainey's physics lab (*AtS* "Happy Anniversary").

VALET, THE | JIM PIDDOCK | Being who oversaw the trials Angel underwent to save Darla. The Valet had never seen anyone get past the first trial before. When Angel refused to spare himself, the Valet confessed he was beginning to like the vampire (*AtS* "The Trial").

VAMPIRE | Hybrid being in which the soul of a dead person vacates the body and is replaced by a demon. The body subsequently resurrects (*BtVS* "Lie to Me"). Thus in the demonic world, vampires are considered halfbreeds (*AtS* "The Scourge"). The sire of the first vampire was an Old One named Malokor (*Buffy* "The Core"). Archaeus was the demon responsible for the vampiric line that contained members of the Order of Aurelius: the Master, Darla, Angel/Angelus, Drusilla, and Spike (*Buffy* "Love Dares You"). Vampires can be killed by decapitation or being staked (*BtVS* "Welcome to the Hellmouth"). They can also be forced to drink holy water (*BtVS* "Helpless"), exposed to sunlight (*BtVS* "Amends"), or set on fire (*BtVS* "Becoming, Part 1").

Types of vampires:

ENSOULED VAMPIRE

NEW VAMPIRE

SLAYPIRE

TUROK-HAN (UBERVAMP)   **ZOMPIRE**

VAMPIRE WILLOW | ALYSON HANNIGAN | In the Wishverse, Willow was a sexy, feared vampire (*BtVS* "The Wish"). This manifestation crossed over into the human Willow's dimension and wreaked havoc until the vampire was sent back, ostensibly to die (*BtVS* "Doppelgangland").

VAMPIRE XANDER | NICHOLAS BRENDON | This version of Xander was Vampire Willow's dark lover in the Wishverse that Anyanka brought into being as a result of Cordelia's heartbroken wish that Buffy had never come to Sunnydale (*BtVS* "The Wish").

VAMPIRICUS CONQUESTUS | Book on vampires written by Larson McMillan that documents some of the encounters Holtz had with Angelus and Darla. According to the text, Holtz killed 378 vampires in pursuit of the couple (*AtS* "Dad").

VAMPY CAT | Cute but very evil white feline stuffed animals that allied with Twilight and killed and/or brainwashed their victims. Vampy Cats clumped together to create a creature called the Swell. Buffy and the Slayer Organization torpedoed the Swell, along with the freighter that was carrying it to Scotland (*Buffy* "Predators and Prey").

VAMPYR | Ancient text that was effectively a slayer handbook and largely ignored by Buffy when Giles tried to give it to her upon her arrival in Sunnydale (*BtVS* "Welcome to the Hellmouth"). Giles left the book to Buffy in his will, but the pages turned blank following the creation of a new Seed of Wonder. Slowly, the pages filled on their own as the rules of magic were restored, but it was also true that anything written on the blank pages would come true (*Buffy* "I Wish," "The Core").

VAN ELTON CRYPT | The one with the cute little gargoyle (*BtVS* "Bargaining, Part 1").

VANESSA | New Slayer who was part of Faith's London squad. Eyghon the Sleepwalker inhabited her body after she was knocked out in battle (*Angel and Faith* "Death and Consequences").

VARTITE MONSTER | Demon who took Angel two days to kill (*AtS* "Judgment").

VAUGHNE | MEGALYN ECHIKUNWOKE | UC Sunnydale student member of the Daughters of Gaia and an actual witch (*BtVS* "The Killer in Me").

VENGEANCE DEMON | Type of lower being who can grant the wishes of humans who have been hurt or betrayed by others. D'Hoffryn, the Lord of Arashmaharr, was their leader, operating from the offices of Vengeance LLC (*Buffy* "Own It"). Each demon has a mission: Anyanka specialized in betrayed women (*BtVS* "Selfless") and Halfrek focused on abused and neglected children (*BtVS* "Older and Far Away"). Jonathan Levinson briefly became a Vengeance Demon but quit (*Buffy* "Own It").

VENOBIA, ARCHDUCHESS | Demonic member of the Circle of the Black Thorn who withheld information about D'Hoffryn from Buffy. She later joined the newly re-formed Magic Council. (*Buffy* "Own It")

VERNON | MICHAEL KRAWIC | Psychic friend of Lorne who does celebrity readings. He was able to take the team through a crime that happened in the home of a rogue Slayer named Dana (*AtS* "Damage").

VERONICA | ANGEL PARKER | Gunn's friend who was injured—but not critically—during a vampire attack at a party (*AtS* "First Impressions").

VERUCA | PAIGE MOSS | UC Sunnydale student, lead singer of Shy, and a werewolf (*BtVS* "Living Conditions") who tried to steal Oz away from Willow (*BtVS* "Beer Bad"). Oz killed her when she attacked Willow (*BtVS* "Wild at Heart").

VIC | Vampire minion of Charles Gunn (*Angel* "After the Fall").

VICKI | First Evolved (New) Vampire who was sired during the Battle of Santa Rosita just as the new Seed of Wonder released magic back into the world (*Buffy* "The Core"). She can shape-shift, fly, and withstand sunlight.

VIDEO HUT | Store in which Anya might have wound up working if Giles had decided not to make her his partner in the magic shop (*Buffy* "Bargaining, Part 1").

VIGEOUS, ST. | Medieval vampire who led a crusade sweeping through Edessa, Harran, and points east. His feast night is when all vampires' powers are at their peak, making it a propitious time to attack the Slayer (*BtVS* "School Hard").

VIGORIES OF ODEN-TAL | Fierce warriors from a dimension in which the women are enslaved. They are herbivores that eat a thick stew made from rotting plants and flowers, and they need to consume half their body weight in food a day. They "restore" a woman by removing the ridges protruding from her back as a punishment that makes her less than she was before. The Vigories believe they must stop the women from escaping their dimension or their whole society will crumble. Angel sent them home with a warning (*AtS* "She").

VILLAGERS | TAYLOR SUTHERLAND, MARYBETH SCHERR, AND ALESSANDRO MASTROBUONO | Neighbors of Aud and Olaf who chased Olaf after Aud (Anyanka) turned him into a troll (*BtVS* "Selfless").

VINCE | NOEL ALBERT GUGLIELMI | Worker on Xander and Buffy's construction team (*BtVS* "Life Serial").

VINCENT | ALEX SKUBY | Vampire leader of the El Eliminati. He attempted to assassinate the Mayor but was apprehended by Mr. Trick. Later, the Mayor encouraged Vincent to attack him with a sword, and when he failed, Mr. Trick dusted the vampire (*BtVS* "Bad Girls").

VINJI DEMON | Clan of gray-skinned creatures with ridges around the eyes that have been battling the Sahrvin clan for five generations. Both clans believe poodles are bad luck and consider camel meat a delicacy. Upset by the murder of their negotiator, Toby Dupree, the Vinji demanded the killer be found or a sacrifice be made (*AtS* "Harm's Way").

VISHNU | Hindu god. Giles kept a statue of Vishnu in his personal collection in the Sunnydale High School library (*BtVS* "Teacher's Pet").

VISIGOTH PYRE SPELL | Purification spell (with attached apparel enchantment): "*Nyekta zon. Kiren aron. Mastel wens*" (*Willow: Wonderland*).

VIVIAN | BRITTANY ISHIBASHI | Audience member and chef who attended Lorne's Vegas show as part of a going-away party. Lorne's reading revealed she would have three five-star restaurants in the future (*AtS* "The House Always Wins").

VOCAH | TODD STASHWICK | Demon summoned by a pair of chanting monks on the grounds of Wolfram & Hart who was brought forth to conduct the Raising of Darla. Vocah killed the Oracles to cut off Angel's path to the Powers That Be, flooded Cordelia with painful visions, stole back the Aberjian scroll, and blew up the office (with Wesley inside) to render Angel powerless. Vocah conducted the Raising but was beaten and killed by Angel afterward (*AtS* "To Shanshu in LA").

VOLL, GENERAL | US military officer in charge of the operation to wipe out all Slayers, who were assumed to be demonic threats (*Buffy* "The Long Way Home"). He was allied with Twilight (*Buffy* "Last Gleaming"). Voll shot and killed Ethan Rayne (*Angel and Faith* "Death and Consequences").

VOLTAR WITCH | Member of a coven that wore Brahenian battle shrouds woven from the skin of dead children, which resembled a Laura Mina original shawl valued at $1,000 (*AtS* "Belonging").

VON HAUPTMAN FAMILY CRYPT | Burial site that was the location of the Glove of Myhnegon (*BtVS* "Revelations").

VORPAL BLADE | Sword used to decapitate Eyghon while the demon was in his true form (*Angel and Faith* "Death and Consequences").

VOYNOK DEMON | A creature with nine lives summoned by Professor Seidel to attack Angel. Their species is hard to kill, but Angel managed to do so (*AtS* "Supersymmetry").

VRILL | Old One with red skin, a bulbous head, and an extended jaw. Vrill allied himself with Boluz to unleash an apocalypse during the time of Melaka Fray (*Fray* "Out of the Past").

VYASA | TONY TODD | Spiny, unpredictable demon who took part in the heist at the Natural History Museum. He was related to Rahmon's tribe (*AtS* "The Shroud of Rahmon").

WAINAKAY DEMON | Creatures known to harass families, usually taking the eldest son. Foxglove and hellebore keep them contained (*AtS* "Happy Anniversary").

WALKEN, JEFFREY (JEFF) | Sunnydale High jazz band member who was one of Pete Clarner's murder victims (*BtVS* "Beauty and the Beasts").

WALKER, CAMERON (CAM) | JEREMY GARRETT | One of the two best swimmers on the original Sunnydale High's swim team. Cameron attempted to rape Buffy in her car before he transformed into a Gill Monster (*BtVS* "Go Fish").

WALSH, MAGGIE | LINDSAY CROUSE | Professor and civilian scientist who led the Initiative; her specialty was operant conditioning, and she had written a respected treatise on Dietrich's work (*BtVS* "The Freshman"). She was secretly creating a demon-human-cyborg named Adam in Lab 314 with her assistant, Dr. Angelman. When she grew afraid that Buffy would find out about the secret project, Walsh tried to kill the Slayer. Walsh was secretly drugging Riley and other Initiative team members, a fact that came to light when Adam killed her (*BtVS* "The I in Team") and Riley went into withdrawal (*BtVS* "Goodbye Iowa"). Her final plan was to turn Riley into a cyborg as well. Ironically, Adam turned her into a robotic drone to fulfill that mission, but Riley destroyed her (*BtVS* "Primeval").

WALT | Member of the Order of Aurelius. Buffy staked him during the ritual to revivify the Master (*BtVS* "When She Was Bad").

WARD, MR. | BOB FIMIANI | Official in the Department of Defense (*BtVS* "The Yoko Factor") who recommended that the Initiative program be terminated and the secret laboratory be filled with concrete (*BtVS* "Primeval").

WARNER, TOM | TODD BABCOCK | Crestwood College student and head of the Delta Zeta Kappa fraternity, which sacrificed young girls to the demon Machida as tribute. He invited Buffy to a frat party in hopes of feeding her and Cordelia to Machida. He was arrested after Machida's death (*BtVS* "Reptile Boy").

WASSERMAN, DR. | DOUG TOMPOS | Hospital obstetrician who performed a prenatal exam on Cordelia. Unnerved by what the ultrasound showed, he fled when the amniotic fluid proved acidic (*AtS* "Expecting").

WATCHER | Men and women assigned to train Slayers (and Potentials, if they were identified) in combat, strategy, and tactics to fight the demons, vampires, and forces of darkness. They served as members of the Watchers Council, which was based in England. Rupert Giles was Buffy's Watcher (*BtVS* "Welcome to the Hellmouth") as was, for a time, Wesley Wyndam-Pryce (*BtVS* "Bad Girls"). After Caleb blew up the Watchers Council headquarters, there were few of the traditional Watchers left aside from Duncan Fillworthe (*Buffy* "Predators and Prey"). New Watchers are now allied with the Slayer Organization, including Rupert Giles, Xander Harris, and Andrew Wells (*Buffy* "The Long Way Home").

WATCHERS ACADEMY | Institution in which Watchers honed their craft. In 1972, Rupert was head boy at the Academy (*Angel and Faith* "Daddy Issues").

WATCHERS COUNCIL | Governing body of the Watchers. It was destroyed when Caleb blew up the headquarters in London (*BtVS* "Never Leave Me").

WATCHERS FILES, THE | Text that incorporated all of Giles's compiled knowledge and experience as a Watcher. Angel and Faith consulted the files for many of their missions, including Angel's personal obsession with raising Giles from the dead (*Angel and Faith* "Live through This").

WEATHERBY | JEFF RICKETTS | Super-hostile Watchers Council Special Operative sent with Collins and Smith to apprehend and/or assassinate Faith (*BtVS* "This Year's Girl"), but she escaped (*BtVS* "Who Are You?"). Weatherby considered the Council's board of directors to be miserly bastards. Wesley shot him in the neck with a powerful drug when he came hunting for Faith in LA (*AtS* "Sanctuary").

WEBSTER, HOLDEN | JONATHAN M. WOODWARD | Vampire whom Buffy used to know in high school before he was sired by Spike. Buffy and Holden fought during a cemetery confrontation and she killed him (*BtVS* "Conversations with Dead People").

WEINBERG, CODY | Guy who owned a 350 SL and told Harmony she was number three on his list of girls to ask to the pledge dance (*BtVS* "Bewitched, Bothered, and Bewildered").

WELLS, TUCKER | BRAD KANE | Sunnydale High student and brother of Andrew Wells. Tucker trained Hellhounds to go after people in formalwear and he set them loose at the prom (*BtVS* "The Prom").

Wells, Andrew

| TOM LENK |

Inspired by his hellhound-raising brother Tucker, Andrew sent flying monkeys to interrupt the Sunnydale High production of *Romeo and Juliet*. He later joined Jonathan Levinson and Warren Mears to become supervillains, occasionally referred to as "the Trio" (*BtVS* "Flooded"). Andrew's "evil" specialty was summoning demons (*BtVS* "Life Serial"). At first, the Trio pulled off cartoonish capers, but the situation turned much darker for Andrew when he summoned Rwasundi Demons who convinced Buffy she had killed Katrina Silber (*BtVS* "Dead Things"). He also summoned a demon whose sting rendered the Slayer insane (*BtVS* "Normal Again"). After fleeing to Mexico with Jonathan Levinson to escape the wrath of Dark Willow, Andrew returned in order to kill Jonathan on top of the Seal of Danzalthar while under the thrall of the First Evil (*BtVS* "Conversations with Dead People"). When Buffy and company caught Andrew, his moral compass swung back toward the light and he fought bravely at the Battle of the Hellmouth even though he fully expected he would die in the fight (*BtVS* "Chosen").

After the founding of the Slayer Organization, Andrew became a Watcher based in Italy (*Buffy* "Damage"). Giles sent him to LA to retrieve the rogue Slayer, Dana. Andrew was thrilled to find Spike alive and have the opportunity to school Wesley in the way of things now that Giles was training him. Backed up by several Slayers, Andrew took custody of Dana away from Angel on the authority of Buffy (*AtS* "Damage"). Andrew had another run-in with Angel in Italy (*AtS* "The Girl in Question") and later fought at the Battle of Twilight (*Buffy* "Twilight"). When magic ended, he went to San Francisco and transferred Buffy's consciousness into a robot body without her knowledge to keep the Slayer safe from harm (*Buffy* "On Your Own"). When magic was restored, Andrew stole the *Vampyr* book in hopes of resurrecting Tara (*Buffy* "I Wish") and was tempted by the Sculptor, who promised to resurrect Jonathan if Andrew stole the Scythe for him. Andrew did not yield (*Buffy* "In Pieces on the Ground"). Drinking from the Asclepian Vial helped Andrew discover that he is gay and he started a relationship with Clive, a warlock (*Buffy* "Love Dares You").

WENDELL | JUSTIN URICH | Sunnydale High student whose guilt over the death of his arachnid collection manifested in a waking nightmare of spiders crawling out of his book at school, courtesy of the comatose Billy Palmer (*BtVS* "Nightmares").

WEREWOLF | Human suffering from lycanthropy as a result of a bite from a wolf-human hybrid. Once bitten, the victim will regularly transform into a lupine creature on the nights before, during, and after a full moon, losing all sense of humanity and becoming a violent, aggressive predator (*BtVS* "Phases").

WESTBURY HIGH SCHOOL | Daryl Epps scored big against this Sunnydale rival in a football game. His mom watched the footage of his victory over and over (*BtVS* "Some Assembly Required").

WEST, PERCY | ETHAN ERICKSON | Basketball player whom Principal Snyder assigned Willow to tutor. After Vampire Willow from the Wishverse frightened him, Percy became a more diligent pupil (*BtVS* "Doppelgangland") and participated in the battle with the Mayor on Graduation Day (*BtVS* "Graduation Day Parts 1 and 2"). However, after graduation he assured his jealous girlfriend that Willow was "captain of the nerd squad"—a slight she overheard (*BtVS* "Doomed").

WHEELER, JASON | Sunnydale High School graduate whose nickname was Crazy Jay. He really did turn out to be insane and was committed to the chronic ward of Sunnydale Mental Hospital (*BtVS* "Conversations with Dead People").

WHEETABIX | British breakfast cereal Spike uses to thicken the blood he drinks (*BtVS* "Hush").

WHIP | EMMANUEL XUEREB | Head of the vampire suck den Riley frequented. He was angry at Riley for the Slayer's intrusion. Buffy set the place on fire and killed Whip and his toadies (*BtVS* "Into the Woods").

WHISTLER | MAX PERLICH | Half demon whose father was an agent for the Powers That Be and whose mother was a full-blooded demon. The two were executed for this relationship. Whistler was given the sight by the Powers That Be, serving as an agent to maintain balance between good and evil (*Angel and Faith* "Family Reunion"). He was sent to Angel in 1996 to keep the balance, not realizing that Angel would turn to the side of evil by sleeping with the Slayer (*BtVS* "Becoming, Part 1"). After Angel's return from hell, Whistler watched Angel and Buffy, eventually realizing that if Angel assumed the persona of Twilight, he and Buffy would birth a world of perfect balance. When Buffy destroyed the Seed of Wonder, the act destroyed Whistler's gift of the sight and cut him off from the Powers That Be (*Angel and Faith* "Family Reunion"). He then colluded with Pearl and Nash to find another way for the world to evolve (*Angel and Faith* "Live through This"). As they deployed the plague ball, Whistler realized how much suffering it would cause. He absorbed the energy into his body and died to stop them (*Angel and Faith* "What You Want, Not What You Need").

MAY I ASK WHAT YOU'RE PLANNING TO DO WITH THEM?

SAME THING I'VE ALWAYS DONE. KEEP THE *BALANCE.* GOOD AND EVIL...MAGIC AND SCIENCE.

I'M GONNA TAKE HUMANITY-- THE WHOLE PLANET-- TO A HIGHER STATE OF BEING. THE NEXT STEP IN OUR EVOLUTION.

WHITE HART PUB | Location where Slayers hang out in England (*Angel and Faith* "Daddy Issues").

WHITE ROOM, THE | Located in Wolfram & Hart, the White Room is the location where the Conduit to the Senior Partners may be contacted. After pushing the elevator buttons in a specific order—18-23-20-28-27—a white button appears at the top of the panel that, when pressed, takes riders to their destination. There is no exit from the room without the Conduit's help. Lilah worked at the firm for three years before she heard about the place. She'd never been there before she accompanied Angel to meet the little girl (Mesektet) who told him how to find Sahjhan (*AtS* "Forgiving"). Gunn's tour of the law firm included the White Room, where he learned the new Conduit was in the form of a black panther (*AtS* "Home"). When Angel and Spike upended their destinies, both the White Room and the Conduit disappeared into an abyss (*AtS* "Destiny"). Gunn went to the White Room and found a new Conduit had taken form in his body (*AtS* "A Hole in the World").

WHITMORE, MR. | RICK ZIEFF | Teen-health teacher at the original Sunnydale High School who handed out "egg babies" to Buffy's class to teach them the consequences of sex. The eggs were laid by a Bezoar, and Mr. Whitmore and other humans fell under its influence, distributing more eggs in order to put additional humans in its thrall (*BtVS* "Bad Eggs").

WICCA-SLAYERS | Magic-wielding Slayers (*Buffy* "Retreat").

WIERICK, DR. | JAMES STEPHENS | Primal worshipper who enacted a ritual to absorb the spirit of the hyenas in the zoo. After he attacked Giles, Willow, and Xander, the Slayer threw Wierick into the hyena pit, where he was devoured (*BtVS* "The Pack").

WIGGINS | Slang for a freaky, scary sensation (*BtVS* "Nightmares").

WILDER, MARTIN | JARRETT LENNON | Sunnydale High student who worshipped Avilas (*BtVS* "Help").

WILKERS, PETER | P. J. MARINO | Private security guard who was burned to death in an ice factory when a young woman from Oden Tal reacted to his presence (*AtS* "She").

WILKINS, EDNA MAE | Human wife of Mayor Wilkins, who died cursing him for his health and youth. They were married in 1908 (*BtVS* "Choices").

WILKINS, RICHARD (THE MAYOR) | HARRY GROENER | Richard Wilkins (I, II, and III) arrived in California after the Diné (Navajo) Slayer leveled the vampire-demon town of *Boca del Infierno* ("the Mouth of Hell"). He then founded the town of Sunnydale on the same land, making deals with the demons drawn to the mystical energy of the Hellmouth. Upon Buffy's arrival in Sunnydale over a century later, the Slayer began to thwart his evil plans, such as the time she killed the demon Lurconis, to whom the Mayor had planned to give babies as tribute (*BtVS* "Band Candy"). The Mayor's motives for placating the demons became clear when the countdown of One Hundred Days to Ascension began; at his Ascension he would transform into the Old One Olvikan (*BtVS* "Graduation Day, Part 1"). By turns jovial and threatening, he proved to be a doting father figure to the rogue Slayer Faith, providing for her even after his death (*BtVS* "This Year's Girl"). He married his wife, Edna Mae, in 1903 and offered his opinion that it was selfish of Angel— both a vampire and immortal—to try to have a relationship with Buffy (*BtVS* "Choices"). After ascending, the Mayor chased

Buffy through the halls of Sunnydale High School in his new demonic form after she taunted him with the knife she had used to severely wound Faith. She lured him into the library, which was rigged with explosives, and he was blown up and destroyed (*BtVS* "Graduation Day, Part 2").

WILKINSON, BEN | CHARLIE WEBER | Created specifically as a mortal body to house the Hellgod Glorficus, Ben attempted to forge a life of his own. He was an intern at Sunnydale Memorial Hospital, which was how he came to the attention of Buffy (*BtVS* "Out of My Mind"). Not realizing she was the Slayer, Ben attempted to date Buffy, but she decided to focus on her family (*BtVS* "I Was Made to Love You"). He summoned a Queller Demon to kill the people who had gone insane from Glory feeding on their brains (*BtVS* "Listening to Fear"). Ben eventually learned that Dawn was the Key and did his best to hide the information from Glory (*BtVS* "Blood Ties"). However, he let slip that the Key was "an innocent" (*BtVS* "Forever"), which led the Hellgod to eventually discover Dawn's true identity (*BtVS* "Tough Love"). Dawn was prepared for sacrifice, and though Ben attempted to withstand Glory's dominance, eventually he succumbed to her stronger personality. After Buffy beat him, Ben promised that he and Glory would never bother her family again. However, Giles realized Glory would reemerge and he suffocated Ben to stop her (*BtVS* "The Gift").

WILKINSON, DR. | JUANITA JENNINGS | Buffy's physician when the Slayer was admitted to the hospital for a flu virus. Wilkinson fought Dr. Backer's protocol of raising the temperatures of a ward full of sick children who were dying one by one (*BtVS* "Killed by Death").

WILLIAM | Fictional vampire caught in a love triangle with the werewolf Jared in Maria Harley's *Twinkle* book series (*Spike* "Alone Together Now").

WILLIAMS, CARTER | Forger who created false IDs for Angel at Lilah's request (*AtS* "Carpe Noctem").

WILLIS | Initiative soldier killed by a demon who resembled a werewolf at the same time that Oz returned to Sunnydale. This led Riley Finn to assume that Oz had killed the soldier (*BtVS* "New Moon Rising").

WILLY THE SNITCH | SAVERIO GUERRA | Bartender and owner of a demon bar in Sunnydale, which was first called Willy's Bar and later Willy's Place (*BtVS* "Goodbye Iowa"). Willy played both sides, delivering Angel to Spike and Drusilla (*BtVS* "What's My Line? Part 1") but delivering information to both demon and Slayer alike through the years. He was formerly the owner of Whiskey Willy's, a demon bar in the town of *Boca del Infierno*, which would later become Sunnydale (*Tales* "The Glittering World").

WILSON, DR. | Doctor at Sunnydale Memorial Hospital (*BtVS* "Bargaining, Part 1").

WIMPS | Acronym for Weakly Interactive Massive Particles (*AtS* "Supersymmetry").

WINGED DRONE BOMB | Weapon that Warren deployed against Dark Willow. The small box equipped with tiny wings exploded when it reached Willow (*BtVS* "Villains").

WINSLOW, DETECTIVE | CARLEASE BURKE | Investigator who questioned Giles about the death of Philip Henry and requested that he identify Henry's body (*BtVS* "The Dark Age").

WINSLOW, MATTHEW | CHRIS FLANDERS | Owner of Winslow Media and friend of Police Chief Tyler, who attended demon fights at XXI with his wife (*AtS* "The Ring").

WINTERS, RUSSELL | VYTO RUGINIS | Vampire investment banker who helped people get started in their careers, paid his taxes, kept his name out of the paper, didn't make waves, and in return expected to be able to do whatever he pleased, like eating pretty young women. The Wolfram & Hart client (represented by

Lindsey McDonald) sent for Cordelia after spotting her in one of Margo's videos. Cordelia realized he was a vampire and escaped his home with Angel. When Russell met with his lawyers to discuss the incident, Angel showed up and pushed him out the window, where he burned up in the sunlight (*AtS* "City of").

WITCH | Magic practitioner skilled in the natural arts of witchcraft. Other magical beings including warlocks, sorcerers, and mystics.

WITCHCRAFT | Title of the spell book Willow used to create a De-Lusting Spell for Xander and herself (*BtVS* "Lovers Walk").

WITTEN, ED | California Physics Institute student considered to be the Nomar Garciaparra of physics (*AtS* "Supersymmetry").

WOLFRAM & HART (THE HOME OFFICE) | See following page.

WOMAN CUSTOMER | WINSOME BROWN | Shopper at the Magic Box who came to buy a mummy hand and became caught in Jonathan Levinson's time loop, which continued to play until she finally left as a satisfied customer (*BtVS* "Life Serial").

WOOD, NIKKI | K. D. AUBERT AND APRIL WEEDEN | Seventies-era Slayer who was mother to Robin. It has been strongly implied that Nikki's lover, the NYPD cop Li, may have been Robin's father (*Tales* "Nikki Goes Down!"). Nikki was pregnant with Robin when she underwent her Cruciamentum, and her Watcher, Bernard Crowley, tried to get her out of the slaying game with a passport and tickets to South America. However, she couldn't stay away from slaying, much to young Robin's chagrin (*Buffy* "On Your Own"). Spike killed her in 1977 on a New York City subway and took her leather coat for himself (*BtVS* "Fool for Love").

Wood, Robin

| DB WOODSIDE |

Freelance vampire hunter and the son of the slain Slayer Nikki Wood (*BtVS* "First Date"). Robin was the first and only principal of the new Sunnydale High and sought revenge on Spike for killing his mother (*BtVS* "Lies My Parents Told Me"). However, he fought alongside Spike at the Battle of the Hellmouth. He shared a brief, intense relationship with Faith, promising to surprise her—and succeeding—by refusing to die in the battle (*BtVS* "Chosen").

Robin later moved to Cleveland to fight the demons attracted to the Hellmouth there (*Buffy* "No Future for You"). When Buffy thought she was pregnant, she asked Robin for his perspective on having a mother as a Slayer, discovering in the process that Nikki Wood had actually quit being a Slayer for a time, living with Robin in South America. They returned to New York when his mother couldn't stay away from the fight. Spike killed Nikki when Robin was four (*Buffy* "On Your Own").

Wolfram & Hart

THE HOME OFFICE

Law firm specializing in the supernatural, with offices in Los Angeles, Las Vegas, and other domestic and international locations as well as other dimensions. The Senior Partners of the firm are rarely seen, but they are incredibly powerful demons known as the Wolf, the Ram, and the Hart. As the deceased Holland Manners explained "For us, there is no fight. Which is why winning doesn't enter into it. We go on no matter what. Our firm has always been here in one form or another: the Inquisition, the Khmer Rouge. We were there when the very first caveman clubbed his neighbor. See, we're in the hearts and minds of every single living being. And that, friend, is what's making things so difficult for you. See, the world doesn't work in spite of evil, Angel. It works with us. It works because of us. . . . If there wasn't evil in every single one of them out there, why, they wouldn't be people. They'd all be angels" (*AtS* "Reprise"). The firm has the finest library of mystical, occult, and supernatural reference material in the world, and it offers full medical, dental, and a 401(k) package (*AtS* "A New World"). When the Beast came to this dimension, it took out everyone in the Los Angeles office, including field operatives, liaisons, and even people out sick that day. Lilah Morgan was the only one to survive the attack, though Cordelia—acting under Jasmine's influence—ultimately killed the lawyer (*AtS* "Calvary").

Employees signed a standard perpetuity clause that extended beyond death, and Lilah returned to offer Angel and the team the keys to Wolfram & Hart's rebuilt and restocked LA office because they actually helped Wolfram & Hart's cause by defeating world peace. Angel accepted their offer on the condition that the Senior Partners helped Connor and Cordelia (*AtS* "Home"). Eve served as the team's connection to the firm and the Senior Partners (*AtS* "Conviction"), but when Eve became too distracted by her love for Lindsey McDonald, the Senior Partners sent another liaison in Marcus Hamilton, and Eve had to sign away her immortality and other privileges (*AtS* "Underneath"). The Senior Partners ultimately sent Hamilton to dispatch Angel when the vampire and his team made a move to sever the Wolf, the Ram, and the Hart's ties with Earth through the destruction of the Circle of the Black Thorn. After Hamilton

was killed, the Senior Partners attacked with a demon army (*AtS* "Not Fade Away") and sent Los Angeles to hell, primarily to punish Angel.

When it became clear that Angel would allow himself to be killed so that he couldn't fulfill their anticipated outcome of Angel overrunning humanity, the Senior Partners reset time so that he would continue to exist in this dimension (*Angel* "After the Fall"). Abandoning Los Angeles, the firm concentrated resources on the Las Vegas office, but when it became apparent that Spike and his team were going to destroy it, the Senior Partners made plans to seize an alien spaceship. Spike pursued them, though it is unclear if he found them (*Spike* "Stranger Things"). Wolfram & Hart employee Lilah Morgan was last seen placing a homing beacon on Dawn and Xander as they moved through various dimensions in order to return to Earth (*Buffy* "Own It").

Staff (Mostly Former Staff)

Senior Partners	Charlie
Acrey, Hunt	Chuck
Allen	Chu, Madeline
Angel	Cyril
Bianchi, Ilona Costa (Rome	Danny
Office)	Eli
Bill	**Eve**
Burke	Forsch, Worm
Burkle, Winifred (Fred)	**Gunn, Charles**
Carlo	**Hamilton, Marcus**

Harvey

Hauser

Hayes

Howard

Hunt

Keel, Desmond

Kendall, Harmony

Knox

Leon

Lopez

Lorne

Manners, Holland

McDonald, Lindsey

Mercer, Lee

Morgan, Lilah

Murrow, Linwood

Novac

Numero Cinco

Park, Gavin

Preston

Price, Robert

Rabinnovitch, Brad

Rabinowitz, Cindy

Radion, Erica

Reed, Nathan

Ronnie

Royce, Dr.

Rudy

Scott, Bradley

Shepherd, Lacey

Shriva, Mistress

Sirk, Rutherford

Sparrow, Dr.

Spike

Tafall, Master (Underlord of Pain)

Tamika

Vail, Cyvus (Freelance)

Wyndham-Pryce, Wesley

Departments

Ancient Symbols and Icons

Ancient Languages

Ancient Relics

Curses

Demon Resources

Entertainment

Fairfield Clinic

Files and Records

Human Resources

Internment Acquisitions

Division

Nonhuman Resources

Operations

Practical Science

Psyche Component Storage

Facility

Real Estate

Research and Intelligence

Ritual Sacrifice

Special Projects

Security

Voodoo

White Room, The

WO-PANG | ROGER YUAN | Shaman from the Order of the Kun-Sun-Dai who likes Orange Zinger tea. As a dark mystic, Wo-Pang claimed that he could extract souls and restore them, and he was called on to awaken Angelus for information on the Beast (*AtS* "Awakening"). Wo-Pang had no backup plan when Angel's soul was stolen, but he could tell it was still in the Muo Ping (*AtS* "Calvary").

WORTH, LESTER | HAL ROBINSON | Professor and vulcanologist who wrote about an expedition he led to Kauai, where he found what he assumed were the remains of a giant, unknown species of dinosaur. The Mayor realized that what Worth had actually found were the remains of Olvikan, the same demon he planned on becoming after his Ascension. Faith killed Worth for the Mayor to conceal the fact that Olvikan could be killed (*BtVS* "Graduation Day, Part 1"). Worth's daughter brought flowers to his grave once a year until Sunnydale was destroyed; now she drops them into the crater. Faith explored trying to resurrect Worth or traveling back in time to keep from killing him, but Giles told her that it was not possible (*Angel and Faith* "Live through This").

WRAITHER DEMON | Being who infects human hosts and turns them into members of its species, adding a finger, a spiny projection or some other demonic attribute. The mystical antibiotic for the infection is twenty milligrams of Cylenthium powder, taken twice a day for a month (*AtS* "Sleep Tight").

WRATHFUL TIBETAN GODDESSES | Beings who absorbed the magic that Buffy, the Slayers, and Willow allowed to drain into the earth in Tibet (*Buffy* "Retreat").

WRITINGS OF DRAMIUS, THE | Text in which the Order of Taraka is described in volume 6 (*BtVS* "What's My Line? Part 1").

WYNDAM-PRYCE, ROGER | ROY DOTRICE | Wesley's distant and disapproving father, who was also a member of the Watchers Council (*AtS* "Destiny"). Roger arrived at Wolfram & Hart to evaluate Wesley's fitness for helping to restore the Watchers Council. He reprimanded, corrected, and eventually knocked out Wesley to steal the Staff of Devosynn. He also tried to kidnap Angel, but Wesley shot him when he threatened Fred. He was then revealed to be a cyborg ninja under a glamour. The real Roger was alive and well in England (*AtS* "Lineage").

Wyndam-Pryce, Wesley

| ALEXIS DENISOF |

Young Englishman sent to replace Rupert Giles as Buffy and Faith's Watcher (*BtVS* "Bad Girls"). Wesley appeared to be ineffectual, but upon learning that Faith had taken a human life (actually two), he attempted to arrest her and have her taken back to England to face the judgment of the Council. However, she escaped and offered her services to the Mayor (*BtVS* "Consequences"). He remained in Sunnydale to fight at graduation, suffering minor injuries, and also discovered upon kissing Cordelia that they had no chemistry (*BtVS* "Graduation Day, Part 2"). He later arrived in LA as a rogue demon hunter and crossed paths with Angel and Cordelia just after Doyle was killed. He was invited to stay on and join their team (*AtS* "Parting Gifts").

Wesley's klutzy behavior fooled many into assuming he was harmless, but his intelligence, research methods, and dexterity with weapons served Angel well over the years. The Watchers Council tried to get Wesley to betray Angel in pursuit of Faith, but he turned on them, siding with Angel and seeing Faith brought to justice (*AtS* "Sanctuary"). Initially attracted to Fred, he was disappointed that she chose Gunn over him and threw himself into his work (*AtS* "Waiting in the Wings"). When he discovered the prophecy that Angel would kill Connor, Wesley injured Lorne and

tried to disappear with the baby, but Justine betrayed him and slit his throat (*AtS* "Sleep Tight"). Wesley survived, but Angel and the others—except Fred—believed he was the one who betrayed them and shut him out. Ruthless and colder, Wesley formed his own demon-hunting team but was constantly being sought by one member of the gang or another to help them. When Angel disappeared, Wesley began his own search, keeping Justine chained in his closet so he could get her help (*AtS* "Deep Down"). He began a physical relationship with Lilah, and they both used each other to get information, but eventually he developed feelings for her. He returned to the gang when they summoned Angelus. He was heartbroken when Cordelia—acting under Jasmine's influence—killed Lilah, but he also remembered that Faith was still in town and could help capture Angelus (*AtS* "Salvage"). Once freed from Jasmine's spell, Wesley was willing to sacrifice himself so Angel could save the world (*AtS* "Sacrifice").

Wesley accepted a position at Wolfram & Hart where he had access to all of the necessary texts he would ever need, including some from the Watchers Council. A robot assassin designed to impersonate his father revealed much to his friends about his strained relationship with the man who never thought he was good enough. But when forced to choose between shooting his "father" and saving Fred's life, he shot his father. He felt guilty for not even hesitating, but it changed his relationship with Fred (*AtS* "Lineage"). She finally made a move on him, and they were briefly happy before she was infected by Illyria and died in his arms (*AtS* "A Hole in the World"). Wesley joined Angel's fight against the Circle of the Black Thorn, but he was mortally wounded by Cyvus Vail. Illyria arrived in time to hold Wesley and he agreed to let her look like Fred while he died in her arms (*AtS* "Not Fade Away").

When the Senior Partners sent Los Angeles to hell, Wesley was forced to haunt the Wolfram & Hart building, serving as a Conduit between Team Angel and the Senior Partners. It was he who realized that if Angel allowed the sired Charles Gunn to kill him, the Senior Partners would have to reset time. Though it would mean that Wesley would no longer exist, he communicated this notion to Angel. Wesley's plan worked, and in gratitude and honor, Angel had a wing of the Los Angles Public Library renamed the Burkle Wyndam-Pryce Wing (*Angel* "After the Fall").

— X/Y/Z —

XIOCHIMAYAN CODEX | Pre-Hispanic text—specifically Mesoamerican—that Wesley summoned into one of his template books for research (*AtS* "The Cautionary Tale of Numero Cinco").

XXI | Demon fight club owned by the MacNamara brothers. Demon prisoners were kept in check by wrist cuffs forged by ancient sorcerers. If the prisoners crossed beyond the marked area, the wristband would disintegrate them. The club disbanded when Angel led the demon prisoners to revolt (*AtS* "The Ring").

YAMANH OF HOHT | Horned demon with deep-set yellow eyes and a batlike face with large teeth who commanded a demon horde at war with the Under-Community. Satsu the Slayer reported that she and her squad defeated the demon, although they were too late to save the Buffy decoy that had been sent in first (*Buffy* "The Long Way Home").

YARBNIE DEMON | STEVEN NIEL | Nonviolent, balancing entities that tend to nest in urban areas under roadways. Gio and crew murdered a member of this species in a sewer near Century City when they started attacking demons without bothering to confirm that they were evil (*AtS* "That Old Gang of Mine").

YATARO | Series of trials initiated by the Overseer to create an elite class of Nitobe warriors (*Angel and Faith* "United").

YESKA | DANICA SHERIDAN | Not a goddess but a Davric Demon. She appears with a flicker of lightning and eats live sacrifices, generally virgin girls. Davric Demons grant huge power to people who offer a sacrifice on their fiftieth birthday. Her raising incantation is "*Yeska of the razor eyes and stone heart, take this offering. I cast my most precious emerald into the ocean on the moment of my birth plus fifty years. Take this gift, let her death return tenfold onto me my power. The hour approaches, Yeska. Do not be blind to my plea. Yeska, I beseech thee.*" Yeska departed when it was determined that her sacrifice wasn't pure (*AtS* "Guise Will Be Guise").

YORK, CYNTHIA | AIMEE GARCIA | In the alternate reality Skip created for Cordelia, Cynthia lived in Reseda and tried casting a spell to get her father to move back in with her family. She failed, raising a demon instead. She was a big fan of TV star Cordy and wanted her own design firm like the character (*AtS* "Birthday").

YOUNG, KENDRA | BIANCA LAWSON | Slayer from Jamaica who was called after Buffy died at the hands of the Master. She tried to kill Angel (*BtVS* "What's My Line? Part 1") but later rescued him and tried to stop the ritual to heal Drusilla (*BtVS* "What's My Line? Part 2"). Kendra returned to Sunnydale and gave Buffy the sword she used to kill Angelus. Kendra also gave Buffy her favorite stake, which she had named Mr. Pointy. Drusilla killed Kendra, but Buffy kept the stake in remembrance of her (*BtVS* "Becoming, Part 1").

YU BA YA SA NA | Primal incantation that allows people to become possessed by magical hyenas (*BtVS* "The Pack").

ZABUTO, SAM | Kendra's Watcher. He raised Kendra himself and was very strict about her upbringing (*BtVS* "What's My Line? Part 1").

ZACH | CHRISTIAN BOEWE | Lindsey's adorable school-age son in the Holding Dimension (*AtS* "Underneath").

ZACHARY | Vampire acolyte of the Master, presumed to have been slain by Buffy (*BtVS* "Angel").

ZACK | DAVE POWER | Vampire friend of Justin, Dawn's first date. Rupert Giles dusted him by throwing him onto a tree branch (*BtVS* "All the Way").

ZANE PHARMACEUTICALS | British pharmaceutical company currently doing research and development on combined magical and scientific advancements and cures. CEO Reese Zane has also focused her attention on Illyria/Fred, the hybrid god-human who resides in Magic Town (*Angel and Faith* "United").

ZANE, REESE | Daughter of Walt Zane, who was the founder of Zane Pharmaceuticals. She hired Deepscan to augment a military search for her father in South America. Discovering that he had been sired, Reese refused to become a vampire and staked him (*Angel and Faith* "Lost and Found"). When she returned to London, she ramped up Zane Pharmaceuticals to research and hopefully cure the adverse effects of magic on the population, as well as to study Fred/Illyria (*Angel and Faith* "United").

ZANE, WALT | Head of Zane Pharmaceuticals who was sired in South America. He became the titular king of a tribe and intended to sire his daughter, Reese, to make her their princess. She staked him (*Angel and Faith* "Lost and Found").

ZEN CATERPILLAR | Guardian of the Spring of Memories that Willow drank from while searching for the source of magic (*Willow: Wonderland*).

ZEPPO, THE | Term used to describe someone who is considered unknown and unnecessary. The name is inspired by the fourth Marx brother (*BtVS* "The Zeppo").

ZOMBIE | Revivified human body. The flesh eating is a myth. Zombies merely mangle, mutilate, and occasionally wear human flesh (*AtS* "Provider"). They are slow-moving, dimwitted things that crave human flesh. Not like Angel (*AtS* "Habeas Corpses").

ZOMPIRE | Term coined by Xander. When the Seed of Wonder was destroyed, demons were no longer able to cross into this dimension to inhabit the soulless dead bodies, so the beings that rose were mindless feral creatures. When they died, they did not dust, but remained in human form (*Buffy* "Freefall"). These creatures were eventually eradicated and when the new Seed of Wonder was created, were no longer made.

X/Y/Z

ZOMPIRE

Buffy the Vampire Slayer (BtVS)

Season One

Buffy Summers reluctantly resumes her slaying duties when she moves to Sunnydale, a town located directly above a Hellmouth. New friends Xander Harris and Willow Rosenberg, hottie vampire Angel, and new Watcher Rupert Giles, aid in closing that Hellmouth and dusting the Master. Plus shopping!

"Welcome to the Hellmouth"

"The Harvest"

"Witch"

"Teacher's Pet"

"Never Kill a Boy on the First Date"

"The Pack"

"Angel"

"I Robot . . . You Jane"

"The Puppet Show"

"Nightmares"

"Out of Mind, Out of Sight"

"Prophecy Girl"

Season Two

Demons, vampires, and a horrific curse ensnarl the Scooby gang as they welcome Oz and Cordelia into their ranks. Spike and Drusilla come to town, leaving destruction in their wake as they ally with the reawakened Angelus, who is determined to make the Slayer regret ever loving his ensouled better half. Giles finds and loses love before Angel regains his soul and Buffy must send her vampire lover to hell.

"When She Was Bad"

"Some Assembly Required"

"School Hard"

"Inca Mummy Girl"

"Reptile Boy"

"Halloween"

"Lie to Me"

"The Dark Age"

"What's My Line? (Part 1)"

"What's My Line? (Part 2)"

"Ted"

"Bad Eggs"

"Surprise"

"Innocence"

"Phases"

"Bewitched, Bothered and Bewildered"

"Passion"

"Killed by Death"

"I Only Have Eyes for You"

"Go Fish"

"Becoming Part 1"

"Becoming Part 2"

Season Three

After running away, Buffy returns to Sunnydale to find that Angel is back as well. Couples shuffle and Faith, the new (extra) Slayer in town, embraces her bad side, believing that's all there is to her. Graduation day ushers in new beginnings as the students destroy an ancient demon, along with the high school. And Angel moves on to Los Angeles so that Buffy can have some semblance of a normal life.

"Anne"	"Helpless"
"Dead Man's Party"	"The Zeppo"
"Faith, Hope & Trick"	"Bad Girls"
"Beauty and the Beasts"	"Consequences"
"Homecoming"	"Doppelgangland"
"Band Candy"	"Enemies"
"Revelations"	"Earshot"
"Lovers Walk"	"Choices"
"The Wish"	"The Prom"
"Amends"	"Graduation Day Part 1"
"Gingerbread"	"Graduation Day Part 2"

Season Four

Freshman year at UC Sunnydale finds Buffy falling for a guy who is not a vampire, demon, or monster of any kind. He just fights them, along with other members of a covert military operation called the Initiative. Willow bids farewell to Oz and begins a relationship with Tara, a fellow magic practitioner while Xander dates the demon Anyanka. The Initiative implodes when cyborg-demon-humanoid Adam wages war, forcing Buffy to unite with her estranged friends to save the day.

"The Freshman"	"A New Man"
"Living Conditions"	"The I in Team"
"The Harsh Light of Day"	"Goodbye Iowa"
"Fear Itself"	"This Year's Girl"
"Beer Bad"	"Who Are You?"
"Wild at Heart"	"Superstar"
"The Initiative"	"Where the Wild Things Are"
"Pangs"	"New Moon Rising"
"Something Blue"	"The Yoko Factor"
"Hush"	"Primeval"
"Doomed"	"Restless"

Season Five

Buffy's magical sister, Dawn, appears, and no one seems surprised to see her until the team discovers the young girl is a mystical key sent for the Slayer to protect. Buffy's beloved mother, Joyce Summers, manages to survive the horrors of Sunnydale only to succumb to a brain tumor, leaving her daughters and their friends devastated. Buffy then sacrifices her own life to protect her new sister and close the portal opened by the hellgod, Glorificus, saving the world one more time.

"Buffy vs. Dracula"	"Checkpoint"
"Real Me"	"Blood Ties"
"The Replacement"	"Crush"
"Out of My Mind"	"I Was Made to Love You"
"No Place like Home"	"The Body"
"Family"	"Forever"
"Fool for Love"	"Intervention"
"Shadow"	"Tough Love"
"Listening to Fear"	"Spiral"
"Into the Woods"	"The Weight of the World"
"Triangle"	"The Gift"

Season Six

Buffy is expelled from a heavenly dimension when her friends
think they are rescuing her from hell. Willow becomes addicted
to magic, while Buffy develops an addiction to Spike. The trio—
Jonathan, Warren, and Andrew—fail as super villains, but when
Warren kills Willow's beloved Tara, Willow goes to the dark
side. Plus singing.

"Bargaining (Part 1)"
"Bargaining (Part 2)"
"After Life"
"Flooded"
"Life Serial"
"All the Way"
"Once More, with Feeling"
"Tabula Rasa"
"Smashed"
"Wrecked"
"Gone"
"Doublemeat Palace"

"Dead Things"
"Older and Far Away"
"As You Were"
"Hell's Bells"
"Normal Again"
"Entropy"
"Seeing Red"
"Villains"
"Two to Go"
"Grave"

Season Seven

Aided by evil preacher, Caleb, the First Evil throws down,
targeting the Slayer line for extinction by killing off all the
Potential Slayers. In Buffy's quest to regain control, she loses her
friends—while Xander loses an eye—but they reunite to rebuild
their army and save the day by sharing her Slayer power with all
the Potentials in the world. Spike sacrifices himself (temporar-
ily), and Sunnydale is swallowed up by the Hellmouth (perma-
nently). Shopping resumes elsewhere.

"Lessons"
"Beneath You"
"Same Time, Same Place"
"Help"
"Selfless"
"Him"
"Conversations with Dead
People"
"Sleeper"
"Never Leave Me"
"Bring On the Night"
"Showtime"

"Potential"
"The Killer in Me"
"First Date"
Get It Done"
"Storyteller"
"Lies My Parents Told Me"
"Dirty Girls"
"Empty Places"
"Touched"
"End of Days"
"Chosen"

Angel (AtS: Angel, the Series)

Season One

Angel's lost in LA, trying to help people without getting too attached to them. A half demon named Doyle arrives to be Angel's conduit to the Powers That Be and provide the vampire with specific cases of people who need help. Angel loses his first client, but rescues Cordelia instead. The loss of Doyle and the arrival of Wesley Wyndham-Pryce, as well as encounters with Buffy and Faith, confirm for Angel that Los Angeles is his city to protect, and he'll assemble his own team to do so. A prophecy promises him redemption in the form of a natural life, followed by a mortal death.

"City Of"   "Expecting"
"Lonely Hearts"   "She"
"In the Dark"   "I've Got You under My Skin"
"I Fall to Pieces"   "The Prodigal"
"Rm w/a Vu"   "The Ring"
"Sense and Sensitivity"   "Eternity"
"The Bachelor Party"   "Five by Five"
"I Will Remember You"   "Sanctuary"
"Hero"   "War Zone"
"Parting Gifts"   "Blind Date"
"Somnambulist"   "To Shanshu in LA"

Season Two

Gunn's tragic loss of his sister highlights the risk family members pose to Angel's resolve. As the vampire private eye builds a network of like-minded fighters and helpers—adding first Gunn, then Lorne—his mission to earn redemption becomes clearer. Wolfram & Hart throw a revived, human Darla in Angel's path. Though he is tempted by the ease of falling back into his old patterns, a trip to Pylea allows Fred and the team to see his true nature. Their acceptance of Angel for all that he is allows him to realize that he is not alone.

"Judgment"   "Blood Money"
"Are You Now or Have You   "Happy Anniversary"
   Ever Been"   "The Thin Dead Line"
"First Impressions"   "Reprise"
"Untouched"   "Epiphany"
"Dear Boy"   "Disharmony"
"Guise Will Be Guise"   "Dead End"
"Darla"   "Belonging"
"The Shroud of Rahmon"   "Over the Rainbow"
"The Trial"   "Through the Looking Glass"
"Reunion"   "There's No Place like Plrtz
"Redefinition"   Glrb"

Season Three

Surprised to find he can survive the loss of Buffy, Angel throws himself into helping Fred adjust to Earth again. Angel is shocked to learn he's become a father when Darla kills herself to save their child. Suddenly Angel has someone to protect and provide for. He throws himself into parenting baby Connor with something he hasn't had in a long time: hope. Once again fate—and Wolfram & Hart—snatch it away from him when Holtz escapes with Connor to a demon dimension. Grieving, Angel turns on Wesley as Connor returns as a teen with enormous father issues. Angel tries to establish a new relationship with Connor just as he's beginning to establish one with Cordelia. Her sudden disappearance and Connor's betrayal leave Angel sunk.

"Heartthrob"
"That Vision Thing"
"That Old Gang of Mine"
"Carpe Noctem"
"Fredless"
"Billy"
"Offspring"
"Quickening"
"Lullaby"
"Dad"
"Birthday"

"Provider"
"Waiting in the Wings"
"Couplet"
"Loyalty"
"Sleep Tight"
"Forgiving"
"Double or Nothing"
"The Price"
"A New World"
"Benediction"
"Tomorrow"

Season Four

Angel continues to dream of the comfort of family, even as he retreats from the betrayal of Wesley and Connor. Cordelia's return only heightens the fractures in the team, but the arrival of the Beast overshadows all of their personal problems. They are forced to call upon Angelus, and Angel has to trust his team can handle things without him. With the help of old friends Faith and Willow, the Beast is banished, and Angel is able to return and try to set things right. The appearance of Jasmine makes everything good and easy, but at too high a price. Angel is forced to make a deal with the devil—in the form of Wolfram & Hart—to take care of his family.

"Deep Down"
"Ground State"
"The House Always Wins"
"Slouching toward Bethlehem"
"Supersymmetry"
"Spin the Bottle"
"Apocalypse, Nowish"
"Habeas Corpses"
"Long Day's Journey"
"Awakening"
"Soulless"

"Calvary"
"Salvage"
"Release"
"Orpheus"
"Players"
"Inside Out"
"Shiny Happy People"
"The Magic Bullet"
"Sacrifice"
"Peace Out"
"Home"

Season Five

Convinced he can change things from the inside, Angel settles into his role as head of Wolfram & Hart's LA office, though members of his team have difficulty adjusting and frequently question their new mission. Stripped of his son and his love, Angel is able to focus on the work, but as layers of evil are revealed all around him, his resolve wavers. Even the arrival of his old companion—and more recent enemy—Spike doesn't make the transition of power smooth. Having Cordelia at his side again, even briefly, shows him the path, and Angel sets about to destroy Wolfram & Hart, and disrupt the Senior Partners from within. As the losses pile up, Angel goes all in with his plan to bring the law firm down: he signs away his claim to the Shanshu Prophecy and the potential for a normal life. At the final battle, a very different family stands beside him than the one he gathered just a few years earlier, but they stand together.

"Conviction"
"Just Rewards"
"Unleashed"
"Hell Bound"
"Life of the Party"
"The Cautionary Tale of Numero Cinco"
"Lineage"
"Destiny"
"Harm's Way"

"Soul Purpose"
"Damage"
"You're Welcome"
"Why We Fight"
"Smile Time"
"A Hole in the World"
"Shells"
"Underneath"

"Origin"
"Time Bomb"
"The Girl in Question"
"Power Play"
"Not Fade Away"

Comic Books

ANGEL: AFTER THE FALL

SPIKE: AFTER THE FALL

"LAST ANGEL IN HELL"

SPIKE: THE COMPLETE SERIES

BUFFY THE VAMPIRE SLAYER (BUFFY) SEASON EIGHT

Volume 1: "The Long Way Home"

Volume 2: "No Future for You"

Volume 3: "Wolves at the Gate"

Volume 4: "Time of Your Life"

Volume 5: "Predators and Prey"

Volume 6: "Retreat"

Volume 7: "Twilight"

Volume 8: "Last Gleaming"

BUFFY SEASON NINE

Volume 1: "Freefall"

Volume 2: "On Your Own"

Volume 3 "Guarded"

Volume 4 "Welcome to the Team"

Volume 5: "The Core"

BUFFY SEASON TEN

Volume 1: "New Rules"

Volume 2: "I Wish"

Volume 3: "Love Dares You"

Volume 4: "Old Demons"

Volume 5: "In Pieces on the Ground"

Volume 6: "Own It"

WILLOW: WONDERLAND

ANGEL & FAITH SEASON NINE

Volume 1: "Live through This"

Volume 2: "Daddy Issues"

Volume 3: "Family Reunion"

Volume 4: "Death and Consequences"

Volume 5: "What You Want, Not What You Need"

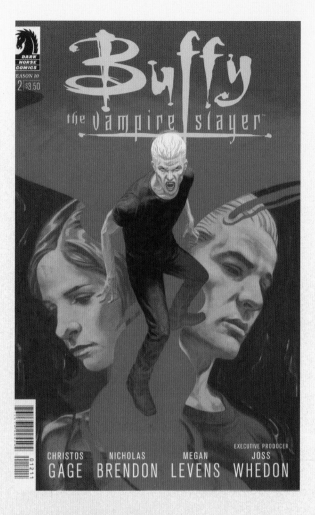

ANGEL & FAITH SEASON TEN

Volume 1: "Where the River Meets the Sea"

Volume 2: "Lost and Found"

Volume 3: "United"

Volume 4: "A Little More than Kin"

Volume 5: "A Tale of Two Families"

FRAY

TALES

Acknowledgments

NANCY HOLDER

Thanks so much to my agent, Howard Morrhaim, and his assistant, Kim-mei Kirkland; to our editor, Paul Ruditis; our designer, Rosebud Eustace; photo researcher Farley Bookout; our production manager Cindy Curren; Nicole Spiegel at Fox; Rebecca Hunt, Lynne Yeamans, and Marta Schooler at HarperCollins; and to friends and fellow superfans Gene Popa of SlayerLit and my dear Mariann Palmer, as well as the casts, crews, artists, and writers across the Buffyverse. Thanks to Lisa and all the editors she mentioned in her acknowledgments; to the late Scott Ciencin, who first told me that Alicia Condon was looking for Buffy writers, and to Alicia Condon for pointing me toward my own dear Termineditor, Lisa Clancy. Last but certainly not least to Mark Mandell, for taking such good care of me. You are the Slayer.

LISA A. CLANCY

In the beginning (circa 1992), there was my boss who handed me a screenplay with an improbable title. Working with an author, I spent weeks deciphering Buffy-speak and I've never looked back. But if I did, I'd remember a phone call in March 1997 where an agent told me two authors would do "anything" to write a Buffy book. From that day on Nancy Holder and Christopher Golden propelled the book line to new heights and along the way introduced me to more great people who also happened to be talented authors. With the incomparable Elizabeth Shiflett Encarnacion and Micol Ostow Harlan, a terrific series of books expanded what "based on" could mean, and I am grateful for the experience of having them at my side. Paul Ruditis came into my life through a different portal, and I'm honored he asked me to be involved with this project, with as funny and inspiring an author as Nancy. A special thanks goes out to the staff of the William Jeanes Memorial Library, for the summer of dragons. All writing was done with Lacey unimpressed at my side, ghosts in the room, and my family nearby, so thanks to Sarah, Ryan, Emma, Christine, Scott, Erica, Robert, Michael, Robin, Dad and Mom.

About the Authors

NANCY HOLDER is a *New York Times* best-selling author who has written over four dozen solo and collaborative Buffy and Angel projects, including the very first Buffy original novel, the *Los Angeles Times* best-selling *Buffy the Vampire Slayer: The Watcher's Guide*, and *Angel: The Casefiles*. She has participated in Buffy, Angel, and Firefly celebrations across the country. She has received five Bram Stoker Awards for her supernatural work, as well as a nomination for *The Angel Chronicles: Volume 1*. She is a member of the Board of Trustees for the Horror Writers Association, and is a devoted Sherlockian. Her latest work includes the novelization for *Wonder Woman*, based on the film by the same title. Socialize with her at @nancyholder and on Facebook at nancyholder/fans.

LISA A. CLANCY received her B.A. from Haverford College, a certificate in publishing from New York University, and an MLS from Clarion University. After twenty years of connecting authors with readers as an editor, she moved to the other side of the equation and now connects readers to authors as a librarian. When she isn't reading, editing, writing, watching TV, mocking TV, and/or pursuing the perfect tomato-mozzarella sandwich (the secret is avocado), she is the director of a library in suburban Philadelphia. Her cat is slowly starting to accept her existence. Catch up on her *Angel* rewatch tweets @Termineditor.

Buffy the Vampire Slayer Encyclopedia
Copyright © 2017
Twentieth Century Fox Film Corporation.
All Rights Reserved.

No part of this book may be used or reproduced in any manner whatsoever
without written permission except in the case of brief quotations embodied in critical articles and
reviews. For information address Harper Design, 195 Broadway, New York, NY 10007.

HarperCollins books may be purchased for educational, business, or sales promotional use. For
information please e-mail the Special Markets Department at SPsales@harpercollins.com.

Published in 2017 by
Harper Design
An Imprint of HarperCollins *Publishers*
195 Broadway
New York, NY 10007
Tel: (212) 207-7000
Fax: (855) 746-6023
harperdesign@harpercollins.com
www.hc.com

Distributed throughout the world by
HarperCollins Publishers
195 Broadway
New York, NY 10007

Produced by becker&mayer! an imprint of The Quarto Group

Authors: Nancy Holder and Lisa A. Clancy
Designer: Rosebud Eustace
Editor: Paul Ruditis
Image Researcher: Farley Bookout
Production Coordinator: Cindy Curren

ISBN 978-0-06-265966-8

Library of Congress Control Number: 2017932172

First Printing, 2017
Printed and bound in China

Unless otherwise credited below, all images: *Buffy the Vampire Slayer* ™ & © Twentieth Century Fox Film Corporation.
All Rights Reserved.

Courtesy Todd McIntosh: p. 18, top left; p. 24, left; p. 25, right; p. 45, right; p. 46, bottom left; p. 61; p. 68, left; p. 70, left; p. 78, top left; p. 87, left; p. 89, right; p. 96, right; p. 103; p. 104, right; p. 132, left; p. 147, bottom right; p. 177, left; p. 186, top left.